iftwares

TOYS and
HOUSEWARES
MAGAZINE

1946

ROBERTSON POTTE

Robert Simmons
Ceramics
Original
animal
creations
for
1953

HAND DECORATED

California Pottery

SCRAPBOOK

Identification
and
Value Guide

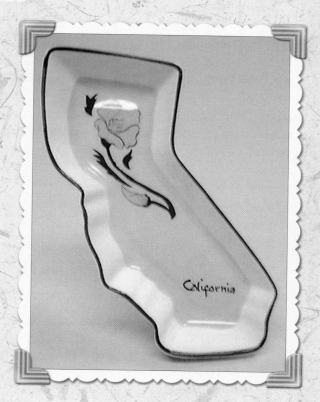

Jack Chipman

COLLECTOR BOOKS

A Division of Schroeder Publishing Co., Inc.

The current values in this book should be used only as a guide. They are not intended to set prices, which vary from one section of the country to another. Auction prices as well as dealer prices vary greatly and are affected by condition as well as demand. Neither the author nor the publisher assumes responsibility for any losses that might be incurred as a result of consulting this guide.

Front Cover: Eugene White 16" chop plate, $250.00; William Maddux 11$\frac{1}{4}$" cockatoos on branch, $225.00; Robert Maxwell 5$\frac{1}{4}$" vase, $80.00.

Title page: 5$\frac{1}{2}$" California state-shaped ashtray produced by Ed and Annie Laura Schell at their Pico, California, pottery, c. 1950s. These ashtrays featured the state flower, bird, or capital. $30.00.

Cover design by Beth Summers
Book design by Terri Hunter

Searching For A Publisher?

We are always looking for people knowledgeable within their fields. If you feel that there is a real need for a book on your collectible subject and have a large comprehensive collection, contact Collector Books.

COLLECTOR BOOKS
P.O. Box 3009
Paducah, Kentucky 42002-3009

www.collectorbooks.com

Copyright © 2005 Jack Chipman

Contents

Kay Finch modeling
Smiley Pig,
c. 1940s.

Dedication

I would like to dedicate this book to the following industry-related people who gave of their time and knowledge: To Barbara Willis for her friendship and the many insights she has provided. She is one of the few surviving industry producers (as well as a living legend) and is always willing to share information. To Robert Maxwell, for the same reasons. He has given me a better understanding of the industry's later years when he was a key participant. To Helen, Dan, and Lois Woodburn Ball for their generous assistance and loans pertaining to Ball Brothers and Ball Artware. To Robert "Bill" Fields for illuminating the histories of the Roselane and Hallfield companies, both of which he founded, and for bringing examples of both to my studio all the way from La Verne. To Craig Lockwood for providing documents and insight into the pottery of his mother, Jane Callender. To Jerry and Evelyn Ackerman, who kindly brought documents and items over to my studio for two separate photo sessions. To Paul White for supplying photos and other documents pertaining to the pottery of his father, Eugene White. To Connie Knutson for bringing Robyn Sikking's daughter, Audrey Turner, and several Robyn pieces to my studio all the way from Fallbrook. To Susan Wind Simpson for her memoirs and photos of Fred Wind Ceramics, a business owned by her father and grandfather. To Luanne Schoup, who is Betty Lou Nichols's daughter, for generously sharing information on several occasions about her mother's business. To Edward, Richard, and Stanley Lerner for the detailed history of their parents' business, the Claire Lerner Studio. Finally, to Chris Crain for his histories of Lee Wollard Ceramics, West Coast Pottery, and Knowles, Taylor & Knowles. His grandmother's sister Bonnie and her husband Lee Wollard were key participants in the industry for many years. Without these first-hand accounts, my overall understanding of a complicated subject would be far cloudier.

Tepco business card.

Technical Porcelain and China Ware Co.

HOME OF "TEPCO" AND "PAMCO" VITRIFIED HOTEL CHINAWARE

ANTONE A. PAGLIERO

MAIN OFFICE & FACTORY
6416 MANILA STREET
EL CERRITO, CALIF.
CONTRA COSTA COUNTY

WAREHOUSE & OFFICE
223 S. LOS ANGELES ST.
LOS ANGELES 12, CALIF.

WAREHOUSE & OFFICE
1706 CONGRESS AVENUE
HOUSTON, TEXAS

Acknowledgments

Many people contributed in a variety of ways to make this book possible. An attempt to name each one who helped me would inevitably lead to someone's name being omitted. The solution is to simply thank them all as a group. Please understand that all your efforts, no matter how small, were appreciated.

Because of their exceptional input, I would like to mention a few names. First and probably foremost, I want to thank Don and Dovie Hein for tirelessly schlepping box after box of pottery from their Los Angeles home to my studio so that I could photograph items from their extensive collection. They were also helpful in identifying unmarked pieces. To Jimm Edgar and Bettie Dakotah, my sincere thanks for bringing numerous items from their amazing collection all the way from Oakland to my studio so that I could include them in the book. Thanks also to Walter Schirra for bringing some key pieces all the way from San Francisco. Kudos to Helen Hierta for her meticulous proofreading of the introduction and photo captions. Many thanks to the staff of Collector Books for allowing me to initiate this new concept and for their diligent production work. I especially want to thank designers Beth Summers and Terri Hunter. You got it right! Finally, I must express my appreciation to the late Harvey Duke, who encouraged and assisted in every aspect of this book's development. His pioneering and passionate dedication to the field of American ceramics will be greatly missed.

These supportive people loaned items from their private collections for me to photograph or provided photographs of their own taking. Without their efforts, this book would be far less comprehensive. Thank you one and all: Evelyn and Jerry Ackerman, Helen Ball, Dan Ball, Lois Woodburn Ball, Carole Borzym, Martin Brodsky, Kirby W. Brown, Ronald Cox, Chris Crain, Bettie Dakota and Jimm Edgar, Harvey Duke, Lansing Duncan, Helen and Jerry Franklin, Clare Graham and Bob Breen, Dovie and Don Hein, Jim Hershoff, Helen Hierta, K.C. Heylin, George Higby, Gary Kent, Connie Knutson and Audrey Turner, Cathy Leow, Craig Lockwood, Pamela and Andre Marchenko, Cathlyn Marshal, Robert Maxwell, Angie and Tim Meikle, Pat Moore of Zeisel-Mostly, Bryan Moss, Jean Oberkirsch, Esther Phillips of Lucky Find Antiques, June Sakata and Tom Boor, Alana Scott, Walter Schirra, Luanne Shoup, Joseph Smith and John Carlotti of Coburg Antique Market, Elaine & George Stecker, Bill Stern, Marilyn Webb, and Barbara Willis.

Hangtag from Darth Vader
tankard designed by
Jim Rumph for California Originals.

You Are Now The Proud Owner Of A California Originals "Collectable Tankard." These Handsome Items Are Finely Hand Detailed By Our California Artists. This Series Will Be Added To Frequently In The Years To Come. The Result Will Be A Beautiful Collection Of Which You Can Be Proud!

Introduction

Following publication of my first book on the subject, Collector's Encyclopedia of California Pottery (Collector Books, 1992), I have watched the collecting of this captivating ware grow at an amazing rate. Evidently, there was a real need for a basic book to help guide collectors and dealers through the maze that "made in California" pottery presents.

That first book (still in print) included what was generally considered at the time to be the best and brightest names in the once-thriving Southern California ceramic industry. I knew at the time of its release that this selection was just the tip of a humongous iceberg. Since then, I have been inundated with requests for information about the many undocumented California companies. It became obvious to me that another book, with a broader scope, was needed. California Pottery Scrapbook was undertaken in response to that need. This time, potteries from throughout the state are included.

I had other goals in mind, too. Because I have witnessed the development of the collectibles phenomenon from its early beginnings, I've seen many reference books on pottery come and go. The best are still around in updated editions. However, a certain formulaic repetitiveness seems to plague these volumes (and I must include my own among them). With this in mind, I decided it was time to do things a little differently; hence the "scrapbook" format. I also wanted to make a change in the way the material would be presented, but more about that later.

More than 800 individual California potteries have been documented, and estimates range as high as 1,200 for the actual number of businesses of various size and ability that operated throughout the state in the heyday of the industry. This peak period was during and just after World War II. With imports from overseas cut off, the nation's home furnishing stores and gift shops were largely dependent on domestic sources for new dinnerware, artware, and giftware stock. California took on the challenge to fill this void like no other state. Before long, the rest of the country was looking westward for the latest trends in tableware and accessories for the home. Innovative objects of all kinds emerged from the kilns of the myriad companies in a steady stream. Today, if one spends just a single week checking the listings under "California Pottery" on online auction giant eBay, they will see an astounding variety in both style and quality.

The quality issue is fundamental to understanding and appreciating California pottery. Not all of it was brilliant or innovative. Some of it was aesthetically weak and much was technically inferior. As in most endeavors, the cream rose to the top and the best producers became the leaders. A few of the inevitable followers were rather blatant in their copying of the leaders. Others didn't quite measure up in terms of creative spirit or technical know-how. Naturally there's unevenness in all productivity. Even the best potters had their bad days and the worst had an occasional burst of genius. In this book, as in my first, I have underscored creativity and know-how in the choice of what to include. I have to admit to a certain bias in my choices, however. Many of the pieces come from my own collection, and I tend to like things that are contemporary, out of the ordinary, and even a bit bizarre, so an open mind and sense of humor may be required to appreciate some of the objects pictured. The balance of the items was purchased or borrowed from other collectors. Many of those choices were also dictated by my personal preference. I'm hopeful that my choices will please the reader as much as they do me.

It was mentioned earlier that the material in this book would be presented a little differently. This time industry styles and themes are the organizing principles, with the material arranged in a natural progression beginning in the late 1920s and ending with a sampling of current work. For instance, figurines of animals were made by many of the potteries, as were figurines of children. During World War II, Americans began to see beyond their borders like never before, and a fascination with foreign countries and cultures ensued. Hollywood exploited this allure. Witness the "Road" series of pictures starring Bob Hope, Bing Crosby, and Dorothy Lamour. Singles and sets of figures representative of many of these exotic faraway places were produced and this theme proved popular with the public well into the 1950s. Design styles evolved over time. From the all-pervasive Art Deco and Moderne modes of the 1930s to the progressive new Modernism following World War II, the wares produced in California tended to reflect and sometimes forecast these developments.

Although this book was conceived as a showcase for the undocumented and under-documented California companies, I didn't want to shirk the well-established names. I also wanted to show how the majors and minors, so to speak, tackled the same styles and themes. Because the focus here is the ware produced by less-familiar potteries, I have intentionally omitted things that are already well known and documented like colored pottery dinnerware and Walt Disney character figurines. I believe that most of the unfamiliar material included is worthy of serious consideration. What information was available about these "esoteric" companies can be found in the photo captions, like notations added under pictures in a real scrapbook. Supporting archival material has been interspersed. I have included a few interesting but unidentified items in the hope that someone will recognize them and share their information. My sincere hope is that readers, no matter how they approach the book, will gain a new appreciation for the marvelous scope and infinite variety of California's industrial ceramics heritage.

Shipping label
used by
William Manker Ceramics.

How to Get the Most Out of this Book

This book's index has been thoroughly considered and is probably the best tool for locating specific items, companies, or individuals, simply because many of them can be found in more than one section. Not the typical arrangement, where all the information about a company is found in one place, this book contains tidbits of information about a particular business under the various photos throughout the book. However, I have tended to record the most basic information related to each company under the initial photo of examples, so that may be the best place to begin to learn about them. NM denotes no mark.

Current values are provided for pottery with an established record of collecting. Many companies and their ware will be new to the reader and therefore no price yet established (NP). When an item is considered rare, a plus sign (+) will follow what I consider to be the bottom line. All prices are for first quality ware in like-new condition. Also, prices reflect what one may expect to encounter at a quality antique show or shop. Please note: Prices are only suggested values and are based largely on my personal experience as a dealer and collector.

Interior view of the San Marcos factory of Freeman-McFarlin.

The 1920s had been the golden age of tile production in California, and the vivid colored glazes of the Hispanic and Moorish styles were the precursors of the brightly colored pottery dinnerware that flourished in the state during the 1930s. In Southern California, J.A. Bauer and Catalina Clay led the way with Pacific, Metlox, Gladding-McBean, and other local companies following suit. These companies and others also produced a bounty of artware - vases, flower arranging bowls, candleholders, etc. - to complement the dishes. In Northern California, the action centered around the erstwhile California Faience factory, a former tile business that invited local artists to take advantage of its facilities. This open-door policy gave rise to a figurine boom in the state, which would have its full explosion in the 1940s.

Panama vase, 18". This massive two color satin-matte glazed vase is believed to have been hand thrown by Victor Axelson, a Swedish immigrant, who was the president of Panama Pottery until his retirement in 1928. NM, $750.00.

Panama vase, 12½". The Panama Pottery of Sacramento was founded in 1914, making it one of the oldest manufacturers of clay products in the state and one of the longest in continuous operation. Early items like this were either hand thrown or jiggered and are often confused with similar ware by Bauer. This cobalt blue glazed vase was jiggered, c. 1935. The pottery remains in operation today. NM, $450.00.

Bauer vase, 16". Matt Carlton's hand thrown work is now familiar and highly prized among collectors. This substantial and well-proportioned example of his signature "twist-handled" vase in black glaze was produced in the early 1930s. NM, $1,500.00+.

Bauer vase, 22⅛". This massive yet elegant turquoise glazed vase was hand thrown by Fred Johnson c. 1936. Johnson was Matt Carlton's nephew, and preceding his work at Bauer he was employed at the Niloak Pottery in Arkansas. NM, $750.00+.

Mark on bottom of Pacific 7⅞" vase. The number may indicate an experimental glaze.

Pacific vase, 7⅞". This early (c. 1930) hand-thrown Pacific vase may have been the work of Fred Johnson (no relation to Bauer's Fred Johnson) and is glazed a mottled green inside. The semi-gloss red finish on the outside is unusual. How was this color achieved at such an early date? It may have been a baked-on automotive paint rather than a true glaze. Pacific was located in the same section of Los Angeles as Bauer. $250.00.

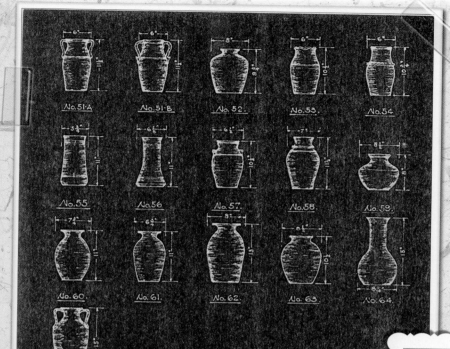

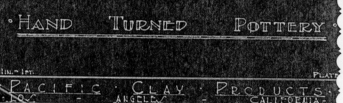

A page from an undated
(early 1930s) Pacific Clay
Products catalog of
blueprints picturing vase
shapes that were labeled
Hand Turned.

Brayton Laguna vase, 5½". A molded and hand-
crimped vase by Durlin Brayton, who officially
established the business in Laguna Beach in 1927
but had begun experimenting as early as 1925.
The earliest ware was incised simply
"Laguna Pottery." This vase (c. 1932) blends
three of Brayton's glazes to superb effect.
Incised: "Brayton Laguna Pottery." $750.00.

Bauer vases, 6". Two hand-thrown fan-shaped
vases by Matt Carlton in orange red glaze, c. 1935.
The orange glaze was achieved by using uranium
oxide imported from Africa. NM, $175.00 each.

Rembrant vase, 5". The Rembrant Pottery of Laguna Beach may have been founded by a former Brayton employee or was at least inspired by its early success because the ware was similar. This vase with uranium orange and yellow glaze dates from about 1933. Incised "Rembrant Laguna Beach." $50.00.

Catalina vase, 5⅛", and Haldeman vase, 5". On the left is the original version of a stepped design vase by Catalina in Toyon red. This vase is marked in-mold: "Catalina" and dates from the mid-1930s. $500.00. Virgil Haldeman, who was the company's ceramic engineer, left the island in 1933 to establish the Haldeman Pottery in Burbank. The orange glazed Caliente Pottery version of the vase probably predates this particular Catalina example, although the shape had been made on the island since about 1933. NM, $150.00.

Tudor vase, 5⅛". This unmarked version of the stepped vase in gunmetal glaze can be attributed to the Tudor Potteries of Los Angeles and dates from about 1934. Possibly under protest, the shape of this vase was modified somewhat in later years. Tudor began business as a tile manufacturer and was reorganized for pottery production in the early 1930s. NM, $200.00.

Tudor vases: 9½" (left) and 5¾" (right). On the right is an example of the stepped vase after Tudor made some alterations to the original Catalina shape. It has a bright yellow glaze on a white clay body. In-mold: "Tudor." $150.00. On the left is an exceptional Tudor vase in orange-red with dark-green veining. In-mold: "Tudor 117." $200.00.

Haldeman vases, 6". These two early (c. 1934) Haldeman Caliente Pottery vases show the pervasive influence of the Art Deco style on California ceramics of the 1930s. The vase on the left in orange glaze is unmarked but retains its foil paper label. The matte blue vase has a raised in-mold mark "© Made in California." $150.00 each.

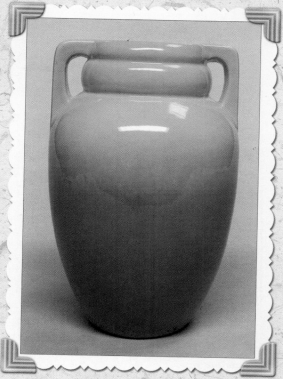

Haldeman vase, 9". The glaze wizardry of Virgil Haldeman is well evident on this striking early Caliente Pottery handled vase that delicately merges pale yellow into turquoise blue. NM, $200.00.

Pacific vases, 12" and 8". Harold Johnson is credited with the blended glazes seen on these vases made by Pacific Clay Products about 1930. The Rose vase on the left is the largest of several sizes. Early ink-stamped "Pacific" in a diamond-shaped logo. $500.00+. The Sawtelle vase came in two sizes and this is the smaller and more common size. NM, $400.00+. (Victoria Damrel photo)

Catalina vase, 7". Harold Johnson, who previously worked his glaze magic at Pacific, worked briefly at Bauer and later owned his own business, enhanced this early shape with a blended polychrome glaze. In-mold: "Catalina." $750.00+.

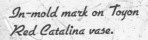

In-mold mark on Toyon
Red Catalina vase.

Catalina vase, 7⅝". A classic urn-shaped
vase, with exceptional Toyon red glaze on the
brown-burning clay indigenous to the island, is
pictured. $650.00.

Winfield Pasadena porcelain vases, 5¼". Three entirely different
outcomes using the same shape are shown here. There were many variations
as this was a favored form by original owner Winfield Leslie Sample.
His forte was glazing and each example demonstrates an aspect of his
skill. The vase at left is probably the earliest and is incised "Winfield"
along with glaze numbers. The vase in the center is incised "Winfield 35"
(the number 35 may be a date). The vase on the right with added slip
decoration is impressed "Winfield." $250.00 – 300.00 each.

Casting ware at the Winfield Pottery
of Pasadena. On the left is
Winfield Leslie Sample.

Winfield Pasadena porcelain vase, 5½". This vase with
a matte exterior and contrasting gloss interior dates from
the late 1930s and shows the influence of Margaret M.
Gabriel, the second owner of the business. Incised
"Winfield Pasadena #93." $100.00.

Marks on bottom of
William Manker lobed vase.

William Manker lobed vase, 14", and fluted vase, 6". The large lobed vase on the left with burgundy and citron green blended glaze was also produced as a lamp base. This early shape was not produced in large numbers and is very hard to find today. $1,250.00+. The smaller fluted vase combines powder blue with rose. Same ink-stamped mark as seen on lobed vase. $200.00.

Shipping label used by William Manker Ceramics.

California Faience covered jars: 3½" (left) and 4¾" (right). The origins of California Faience date back to the early twentieth century when William Bragdon and Chauncy Thomas founded a company in Berkeley known as Thomas & Bragdon. It officially became California Faience in the 1920s. By then, they were known for their exceptional ceramic tiles and artware. These two covered jars date from the late 1920s or early 1930s. At left is a ribbed organic form in the company's signature turquoise. It's incised "California Faience." $500.00. The straight-sided jar in a less common pink glaze is also incised "California Faience." $350.00. (Photo by Kirby W. Brown)

Metlox vases. These three glazed vases date from the mid-to-late 1930s. On the left is 7½" vase #47 in turquoise with ink-stamped mark "Poppytrail by Metlox, 47." $75.00. In the center is 8" vase #43 in orange and not marked. $60.00. On the right is 7¾" vase #137 with in-mold mark "Poppytrail 137 Made in USA." $65.00.

Vernon Kilns vases, 5³/₄" and 6", showing the Art Deco influence. At left is Moon #2 in satin azure glaze by Jane Bennison, the daughter of owner Faye Bennison. $150.00. The orange glazed vase at right is by May and Vieve Hamilton, who were well-known studio ceramists of the 1930s. $1750.00. Both vases have individualized ink-stamped Vernon logos along with vase name and size.

Metlox bottles, 12½". These Art Deco wine bottles of the mid-thirties may have been special ordered by a local winery, although an example with wine label has not been seen. White, yellow, and lime green glazes. All marked in-mold "Metlox." $100.00 each.

La Mirada vase, 6⁵/₈". La Mirada is not known for its Art Deco influenced ware so this vase would be an anomaly and a good-looking one. Paper label. $75.00.

Vernon Kilns bowl, 10" x 4". This angular Art Deco centerpiece bowl in satin rose was designed by Jane Bennison c. 1937. It is the smaller of two sizes produced. Jane Bennison studied art the University of Southern California. Ink-stamped mark. $200.00.

Padre vase, 8½". This half-moon shaped vase is glazed satin pink. In-mold: "Padre 516." $100.00.

Padre vase, 11½". The sunburst was a common Art Deco motif and is used to good effect in this sunny yellow Padre vase with three separate openings for flowers. In-mold: "Padre 243." $225.00.

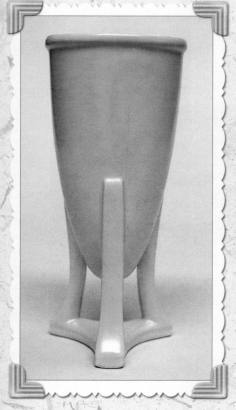

Padre, 9½". The Padre Pottery produced this unusual vase with its conical shape and three buttress-like supports. Padre remains somewhat of a mystery company. Located at 1812 Griffin Ave. in Los Angeles, it was established sometime in the mid-1930s. Charles W. Fourl was the owner, but little else is currently known about the business. A fire completely destroyed the factory in 1943. In-mold: "972." $150.00.

Padre wall pocket, 9½". Padre produced some attractive wall vases and this is one of them. This design utilizing oak leaves is glazed a satiny light green. In-mold: "Padre U.S.A." $100.00.

Bauer vase, 8". Padre was not alone in its use of matte glazes as this matte green Bauer Cal-Art vase proves. Designed by Ray Murray about 1938, it is a typical example of this attractive artware line. NM, $120.00.

Bauer vase, 8". Cal-Art vases were also produced in gloss colors, like this Art Deco design in turquoise. Ray Murray design, c. 1937. In-mold: "Bauer." $135.00.

Garden City vase, 4³/₈" x 7³/₄". The stepped design in relief on this vase or planter (c. 1936) is another typical Deco motif. The Garden City Pottery was located in San Jose, at 506 N. Sixth St., and much of the ware was distributed locally. In his first employment as a ceramic designer, Royal Hickman designed most of the company's early output. NM, $125.00.

Garden City bowl, 3¹/₂" x 6¹/₂", and vase, 5". Besides designing the early cast and jiggered ware, Royal Hickman is credited with hand-thrown artware like this wide-ribbed bowl and bud vase of the mid-1930s. Garden City used colored glazes closely related to Bauer's in the 1930s. NM, bowl, $80.00; vase, $60.00.

California Ra-Art vase, 4½" x 10½", and Garden City vase, 6½" x 10". Concurrent with his employment at the Garden City Pottery, Royal Hickman created a line called California Ra-Art (RA for his first and middle names, Royal Arden). Ra-Art pieces, like this oblong white glazed vase, were produced at the California Art Tile Co. in nearby Richmond. Incised "Cal Ra Art," "Hick" (Hickman's nickname), and "203." $150.00. The orange vase by Garden City is unmarked. $250.00.

Ink-stamped mark on Pacific vase reads: "Pacific Made in Calif, U.S.A."

Pacific vase, 6⅛" x 8". This vase appears to be an example of the Catalina Pottery that Gladding-McBean produced using a mold acquired in the Catalina Island Co. purchase in 1937, but appearances can be deceiving. It's actually a Pacific vase. The satin ivory exterior and turquoise interior adds to the ruse. It was not uncommon for one company to emulate the successful designs of its competitors. Some companies occasionally patented designs, but this was not a widespread practice in California. $150.00.

Catalina vase, 5¾" and Gladding-McBean vase, 8⅜". The influence of classic Chinese vessels can be seen here. The Catalina vase at left in Mandarin yellow was produced c. 1936. In-mold: "Catalina 612." $175.00. The GMB vase in turquoise lined with white is from the Cielito Art Ware line of 1934 – 1937. NM, $200.00+. (Wood bases used for display.)

Gladding-McBean vase, 9½". This ball-shaped vase is from the Ox Blood Art Ware line of 1938 – 1942. The re-creation of the ancient Chinese oxblood was a great achievement by the GMB chemists that worked on it. However, it was an unpredictable glaze and difficult to control, and many interesting (to us today) variations occurred. Most of the shapes were derived from Chinese models of old. The inside was usually glazed in a contrasting white with a hint of pale green. Ink-stamped "Made in U.S.A." $500.00+. (Victoria Damrel photo)

Gladding-McBean vases, 8¾". Even before the celebrated oxblood line was perfected, a short-lived line called Ruby Art Ware (1935 – 1936) became the first successful red glaze in commercial use in California. It was a limited line consisting mainly of Chinese-inspired vases like these. The vase on the left, with hand-written notations on the bottom and anomalies in the glaze, may have been one of many tests conducted before the true ruby red on the right was achieved. $350.00+. The vase on the right is the real ruby. Ink-stamped "GMB" in oval. $250.00+.

Incised mark on bottom of Robertson Hollywood slanted pillow vase. Base has a similar impressed mark.

Robertson Hollywood vase, 7", and base, 1¼". The Robertson Pottery was a partnership between George B. Robertson and his father Fred H. Robertson and was the final chapter in the celebrated history of the Robertson family of potters that had its beginnings in nineteenth-century England. From 1934 to 1952, the small Robertson Pottery produced exceptional ware, much of it with Chinese-inspired crackle glazes like the deep turquoise on this unusual slanted pillow vase. Bases were common accoutrements. Vase, $200.00; base, $100.00.

Page from an undated Robertson Pottery price list that included line drawings of shapes available and their sizes. Note miniature vases.

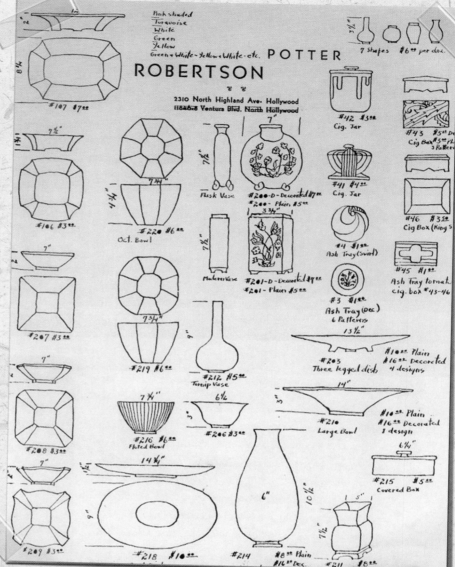

Robertson mini vases usually have only an incised "R" on the bottom.

Robertson Hollywood vases, from 1³/₄" to 3". These miniature vases hint at the array of crackle glazes achieved at the Robertson Pottery. The address of the pottery changed a few times and it was not always located in Hollywood proper but the Hollywood trademark remained, and was the first use of this oft-repeated signage. Note that these small vases are usually incised with only an "R" as shown. $100.00 each.

La Mirada vase, 7". The La Mirada Potteries began operations in Los Angeles in 1935, just a year after the establishment of the Robertson Pottery and at the same location. This pillow vase has a turquoise crackle glaze that was developed by owner Cecil Jones with the help of George B. Robertson. After a fire destroyed the plant in 1940, the business was purchased by Thomas F. Hamilton and merged with his other American Ceramic Products lines at its LA location. In-mold: "La Mirada 123." $45.00.

In-mold mark on GMB vase that includes its shape number obscured by paper label. Added ink-stamp mark, "Made in U.S.A."

Gladding-McBean vase, 7¼" x 8¼". This rarely seen satin ivory vase with raised tropical plant forms has a circular paper label on the bottom indicating it was made for a special display at the Golden Gate International Expo in San Francisco in 1939. The display was a collaborative venture with the Barker Bros. department stores. Other unusual items have been observed in the same glaze with the same label. NP.

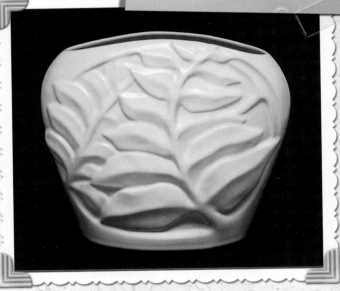

Gladding-McBean vase, 8". From the Encanto Art Ware of 1937 — 1940, this coral vase lined with gray with its embossed bird of paradise bloom and leaves presaged the vogue for all things Hawaiian that would follow in the late 1940s. $200.00.

Ink-stamped mark on GMB Encanto vase.

Cemar vase, 4⅛". This cast vase with hand-crimped opening was an early shape produced by the Cemar Clay Products Co. of Los Angeles. Begun by two former Bauer employees — Cliff Malone and Paul Cauldwell — in the mid-1930s, the company prospered until the mid-1950s. Monochrome glazed vases like this one, along with low bowls and small animal figurines, were the stock-in-trade in the early years. In-mold: "Cemar." $75.00.

Haldeman bowl, 4⅛" x 12⅝". Virgil K. Haldeman established the Haldeman Pottery of Burbank in 1934, after he left his post as plant superintendent at the Catalina Pottery on Catalina Island. He had also been their ceramic engineer and his own company's early glazes were not unlike those he had formulated on the island. Virgil's wife Anna assisted in many aspects of the business located at 41 N. San Jose Ave. The turquoise seen on this mouth-shaped flower bowl is identical to the turquoise found on Catalina pottery of the same period. Incised "49." $45.00.

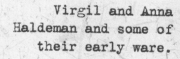

Virgil and Anna Haldeman and some of their early ware.

Haldeman bowls, 3½" x 4½". These Caliente Pottery bowls (c. 1935) were probably designed for serving candy or nuts. There is a larger size as well. The glazes show the range of colors that Haldeman developed for the ware in the early years. Raised in-mold: "40" or unmarked. $30.00 each.

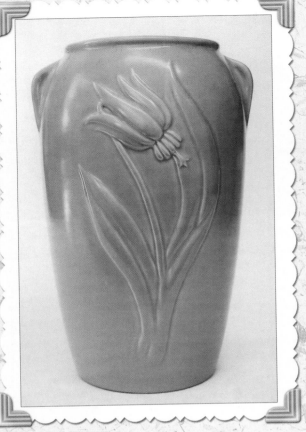

Cemar vase, 12". This striking vase with echoes of Art Nouveau has a pale chartreuse satin glaze inside and out. A larger Cemar vase from the 1930s has not been noted. In-mold: "Cemar." $200.00.

Haldeman vases, 8". These matching tree trunk vases of the mid-1930s exhibit vestiges of the Arts and Crafts look. They could also function as candleholders. The Haldeman's Caliente line was sold to Claire Lerner in 1948. Lerner continued and expanded the line until her business closed in 1958. In-mold: "27." $45.00 each.

La Cañada bowl, 3" x 9½". This flower or fruit bowl with its autumn colored glaze started out as a plain molded bowl. The rim was crimped and overlapped and the leaves delineated by hand prior to firing and before the clay was completely dry. J.M. Roberts established the La Cañada Pottery in the early 1930s. It was originally located in Newhall, on the northern edge of the San Fernando Valley. Probably an operation that remained relatively small, it shared space (and supplies) with the Haldeman Pottery of Burbank during WWII, and managed to carry on until the early 1950s, when it was relocated to Apple Valley in the high desert. Incised "19." $40.00.

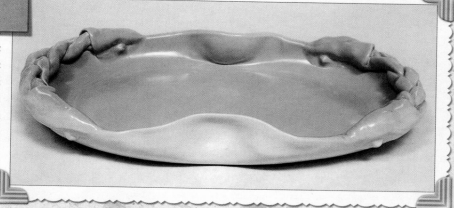

↑ Incised mark on La Cañada
low flower bowl.

La Cañada bowl, 2¼" x 16½". The La Cañada Pottery of Newhall produced this
partly handmade bowl about 1935. A low flower bowl or centerpiece, it includes
braided sections added at either end. Haldeman and KTK developed equivalent
systems of clay manipulation. $45.00.

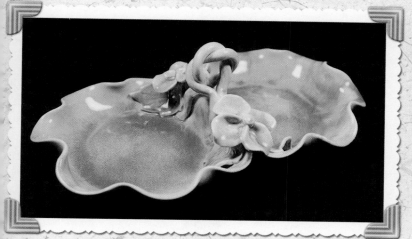

Knowles, Taylor & Knowles bowl, 10"L. This bowl is an
excellent example of the outcome of manipulating a
molded bowl while it's still pliable. Its undulating
edges, decorative rope-like handle, and handmade flowers were added in a similar fashion as the ware produced by Haldeman and La Cañada. It's unclear which
company originated this technique, but both Haldeman
and La Cañada were in business prior to the founding
of KTK. In-mold mark. $60.00. (Chris Crain photo)

Poxon bowl, 2¼" x 11¼". The Poxon China Co. was
located in the Vernon district of Los Angeles and
was the predecessor of Vernon Kilns. George Poxon
founded the business, one of the earliest in the state,
about 1912. Fine china dinnerware in the European
tradition was the company's mainstay, but some artware, like this low bowl, was produced in the 1920s
and early 1930s. The business was sold to Faye G.
Bennison, Vernon Kilns' founder, in 1931. In-mold:
"Poxon Los Angeles 100." $200.00+.

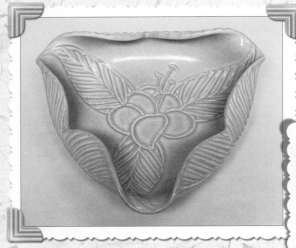

Incised mark on bottom of Chase Originals dragon bowl.

California Ra-Art bowl, 4¼" x 13". Royal Hickman produced this tri-corner low bowl with sloping sides and carved floral design about 1937. It's an elegant item that foreshadows the stylish ware that would make Hickman the most famous designer at the Haeger Pottery of Illinois in the 1940s. In-mold: "California Ra-Art by Hick" and incised "24." $200.00+.

Chase Originals bowl, 2¾"H x 7"W x 17"L. Adele Chase, who had most of her distinctive Art Deco designs produced at California Faience in the 1940s and 1950s, created this marvelous oblong bowl encircled by a dragon. The contrast between the black bowl and the turquoise dragon is dramatic and eye-catching. $175.00. (Kirby W. Brown photo)

Brayton Laguna plate, 6½". Durlin Brayton, who established the business on a modest scale at his Laguna Beach home in 1927, produced this plate with hand-painted underglaze design about 1930. This item is typical of the hand-decorated plates and tiles that were made and sold mainly to local stores and tourists at the time. Incised "Brayton Laguna Pottery." $350.00+.

Brayton Laguna plate, 11½". This hand-painted plate is probably not the work of Durlin Brayton. Brayton hired local artists to help him as the demand for his unique ware increased. The plates used were from the hand-molded dinnerware the pottery produced in the late 1920s and early 1930s in an assortment of luscious glaze colors. Incised "Brayton Laguna Pottery." $500.00+.

Winfield Pasadena plates, 7½". These two charming hand-decorated plates are from a series produced for children in the early 1930s. All designs feature animals and birds. Pictured here are a stork and ostrich. Impressed "Winfield Pasadena 227." $45.00 each.

Pacific flower holder, 6" x 14". Designed as a decorative accent, this vase in the shape of a cockatoo dates from the mid-1930s. Pacific's designers remain shrouded in mystery. Based on patent records for Pacific's dinnerware designs of 1940 and 1941, it's possible that the designer credited was also the person responsible for Pacific's early dinnerware and at least some of its artware. Her name was Isobel Darrow. Another designer who added distinction to the dinnerware and artware lines was Helen M. Crouch. Raised in-mold "Pacific Made In U.S.A. 3802" in a circle. $225.00.

Cemar bird, 6". This highly stylized satin-glazed crane was designed by Fred Kaye. Mid-1930s. NM, $50.00.

Haldeman birds, 5¼", and ostrich, 5⅝". Flower arranging was a popular activity in the 1930s and 1940s and low bowls with matching flower frogs were common items produced in California. Small animal and bird figurines, like these, were made to accent these arrangements. The two Caliente Pottery birds on branch are glazed satin white shading to pink. Impressed "Made in California" and incised "320." $45.00. The pink ostrich is impressed "Made in California" and incised "306 USA." $45.00.

Cemar and Bauer bird-shaped flower frogs, 13¼" and 14". The crane on the left is clearly marked Cemar (in-mold "Cemar 518") while the one on the left is unmarked. The similarities are striking, although the latter is believed to be a copy by Bauer of the Cemar original designed by Fred Kaye. Because two former Bauer employees owned Cemar, a bitter Bauer management may have produced this item and possibly others to get even. The satin pink crane was found with a matching low bowl in the identical glaze marked "Bauer," making it a highly probable attribution. Cemar, $150.00. Bauer, $500.00+.

Pacific birds, 12¾". This item was listed as Futuristic Bird Figure in an undated Pacific Artware catalog of the late 1930s. The solid colors offered were satin white, sea foam green, turquoise, and dusty rose. The bird on the left in turquoise is unmarked. $125.00. The hand-decorated one on the right dates from 1940 – 1941 and is ink-stamped "Pacific Made in USA" in a circle. $175.00.

Padre bookend, 6" x 5¾". Padre began hand decorating some of its artware in the late 1930s, and the line that developed eventually became known as Padre Regal. New items were created specifically for the line in the early 1940s. This pouter pigeon bookend dates from about 1939 and has both an in-mold and painted mark. Painted mark: "Regal Calif Hand Painted by Virginia." $100.00.

Sorcha Boru birds, 5¼" x 10¾" (left) and 6½" x 9½" (right). Sorcha Boru was the professional name of Claire Stewart whose studio was located in San Carlos from 1938 to about 1956. She must have been associated with California Faience at some point because these large blue jays exhibit both the type of clay and the glazes commonly used there. Claire and her husband Ellsworth produced a variety of attractive artware and probably employed a few helpers during the 1940s when business was booming in California. Incised: "Sorcha Boru ©." $500.00+.

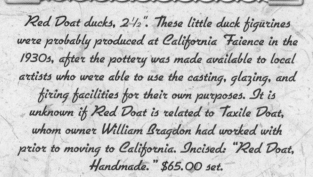

Red Doat ducks, 2½". These little duck figurines were probably produced at California Faience in the 1930s, after the pottery was made available to local artists who were able to use the casting, glazing, and firing facilities for their own purposes. It is unknown if Red Doat is related to Taxile Doat, whom owner William Bragdon had worked with prior to moving to California. Incised: "Red Doat, Handmade." $65.00 set.

Catalina plate, 12½". This hand-decorated Seahorse plate was one of several designs that were produced on Catalina Island as souvenirs and distributed to better stores throughout the country. Impressed: "Catalina Island." $1,500.00+.

Metlox shark, 6³⁄₈" x 5". About 1936, before production of the Metlox Miniatures series began in 1939, this hungry looking shark was made as an accent piece for the numerous low flower bowls the company made. Glazed satin turquoise. NM, $200.00+.

Washburn fish vase, 4³⁄₄" x 8¹⁄₄". Another ceramic artist associated with California Faience in the 1930s and 1940s was Jack Washburn. This hand-made vase shaped like a fish is glazed turquoise with the CF brown clay showing on the carved edges and is dated 1938. Incised "Washburn '38." NP.

Paper label on Pacific Sun Fish vase.

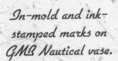

In-mold and ink-stamped marks on GMB Nautical vase.

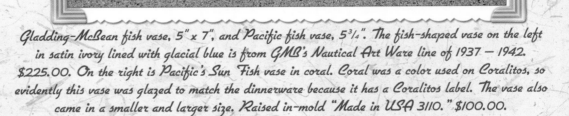

Gladding-McBean fish vase, 5" x 7", and Pacific fish vase, 5³⁄₄". The fish-shaped vase on the left in satin ivory lined with glacial blue is from GMB's Nautical Art Ware line of 1937 – 1942. $225.00. On the right is Pacific's Sun Fish vase in coral. Coral was a color used on Coralitos, so evidently this vase was glazed to match the dinnerware because it has a Coralitos label. The vase also came in a smaller and larger size. Raised in-mold "Made in USA 3110." $100.00.

Haldeman shell vases, 8" and 5". These seashell-shaped vases are different in size and style. The vase on the left is more formal in design with satin white on the outside and turquoise inside. In-mold: "Made in California" and incised "31-A USA." $45.00. The smaller vase is less fussy and more naturalistic and is glazed satin green inside and out. Incised "Calif 32." $35.00.

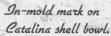

Catalina shell bowl, 5½" x 8½". This flower bowl resembling a nautilus shell was produced on Catalina Island circa 1936. It's glazed turquoise over white clay and has an in-mold mark. $250.00.

In-mold mark on Catalina shell bowl.

Padre shell vase, 6¼". This pointed shell on the crest of a wave is not only decorative; it functions well as a vase. Glazed satin ivory inside and out, it was produced about 1935. In-mold: "Padre 8." $175.00.

West Coast shell bowl, 2½" x 8⅝". This seashell-shaped bowl marked in the mold with only "California 21" is believed to be an early West Coast item. The West Coast Pottery was located in Burbank and operated from about 1940 to 1964. $50.00 (shells not included).

Padre ram's head vase, 6⅞". With this model, Padre must be credited with one of the first head vase designs. Because it has a low mold number, it undoubtedly was an early piece (c. 1935). In-mold: "Padre 43 Calif." $85.00.

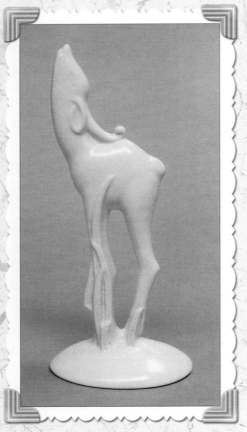

Cemar deer, 7¼". Fred Kaye modeled this figurine of a leaping deer about 1937. Deer figurines must have been very popular in the 1930s and 1940s because most pottery companies produced at least one. They remain popular with collectors. NM, $50.00.

Pacific deer, 9". This popular design was produced for several years in two sizes and was made in both solid colored glazes and a hand-decorated version. This is the large size. Ink-stamped "Pacific Made in U.S.A." $85.00.

Handwritten marks on Sorcha Boru fawn and fern.

Cemar deer, 4⅛" x 5⅜". Another attractive Fred Kaye deer in satin white, c. 1936, is seen here. NM, $45.00.

Sorcha Boru deer, 7" x 8". This lovely cast sculpture of a fawn sniffing a fern was modeled and produced by Sorcha Boru (Claire Stewart) about 1939. Glazed white over buff-colored clay, it is signed and titled on the bottom. $200.00.

In-mold mark on San Carlos deer.

Paper label on Padre deer.

San Carlos deer, 8¼" (left), and Padre deer flower holder, 6¼" (right). Two more deer; one from the north and one from the south. On the left is a San Carlos Pottery deer figurine. This company was located in San Carlos, which is situated between San Francisco and San Jose. Little is known about it, but the few examples seen have been distinguished by good design and quality workmanship. This example in an aqua colored glaze has an in-mold mark and paper label. $65.00. The Padre deer flower holder in pink also retains an original label. $60.00.

Paper label on La Mirada deer.

La Mirada deer, 11½". A white crackle glaze is used to good effect on this figure that features a standing and reclining deer. Produced by the La Mirada Potteries, it dates from about 1938. In-mold: "La Mirada" and paper label. $80.00.

Hamilton giraffes, 10³/₄". Sisters May and Vieve Hamilton were award-winning ceramic artists who produced handmade and slip-cast items in their Los Angeles studio in the 1930s. They are best known today for the artware and dinnerware they created for Vernon Kilns in the late 1930s. This figure of two intertwined giraffes was titled Neckers and dates from about 1934. Like most of their work, it exhibits the fashionable Art Deco flair of the times. Impressed "Hamilton" in a circle. $500.00+.

Brayton Laguna lemur, 9¹/₄". It is believed that owner Durlin Brayton created this one-of-kind ceramic sculpture prior to 1930. Few original works like this have been seen. It's quite heavy despite having a hollowed cavity. An interesting choice of glazes adds to the exotic look of an already exotic subject. Painted mark: "Laguna Pottery" (the original business name). $1,000.00+.

Ink-stamped mark on foot of Metlox lizard. This mark should not be confused with a similar Gladding-McBean stamped mark.

Metlox lizard, 1¹/₂" x 10". Speaking of exotic, this lizard from the Metlox series known as Oddities of the Animal Kingdom, qualifies. The bronze green glaze adds to its ominous appearance. George Skee designed this series of 1939, at least in part. His son Stan Skee made the molds. $300.00+.

Metlox elephant, 4" x 6³⁄₈". This elephant is from the Oddities of the Animal Kingdom series and was modeled after Baby the Indian elephant from MGM's classic Tarzan films starring Johnny Weissmuller. It was one of three poses of this star elephant produced in 1939. Ink-stamped "Metlox Made in U.S.A." $150.00.

Robertson Hollywood elephants, largest: 2½". It is believed that the Robertson Pottery produced these miniature circus elephants. The delicate crackled glaze is consistent as is the excellence of the modeling. NM, $150.00 set.

Painted mark on Burke-Winton squirrel figurine.

Haldeman monkey, 3", and bear, 3½". Here are two more animals associated with the circus. The quizzical monkey in satin white is impressed "Made in California." $65.00. The brown bear with arms folded is incised "376 USA." $50.00.

Burke-Winton squirrel, 2³⁄₄". Twin brothers Ross and Don Winton began the Twin Winton business when they were still in their teens. Walt Disney's cartoon characters were the inspiration for the small items produced in the early years (1937 – 1941). Helen Burke was an early partner in the business and did most of the hand decorating of the Don Winton models, like this rascally squirrel! $75.00.

Paper label on Brayton turtle.

Twin Winton bears, 2¾" (left) and 1¾" (right). This cute set of brown and white bears is typical of the early production of the Winton twins and dates from about 1940. Painted mark: "Winton." $65.00 set.

Brayton Laguna turtle, 1¾" x 4½" (left), and Padre turtle, 2" x 4" (right). The Brayton turtle is believed to have been modeled by owner Durlin Brayton, c. 1935. $175.00. The turquoise Padre turtle dates from about 1938. NM, $60.00.

Paper labels on Cemar horses.

Metlox horse, 7⅛" x 6". This is a very rare figure of a rearing horse, and in a rare glaze, produced c. 1937. Designer unknown. Ink-stamped "Metlox." $200.00+.

Cemar horses, 5"L (left) and 4¾"H (right). Both of these small satin white Cemar horse figurines have paper labels intact. $150.00 set.

Pacific horse, 4" x 4¾". Pacific Clay
Products produced this rarely seen
horse figurine in the late 1930s.
NM, $200.00.

La Mirada horse, 6⅝" x 9¼". An eye-catching rust red glaze
graces this horse figure from the La Mirada Potteries. Produced around 1939, it's unmarked but in all probability had a
paper label attached when it left the factory. NM, $100.00.

Roselane horse, 8¾". This striking horse with a pale
turquoise glaze proves that a humble cast figurine can
attain bona fide art status. Robert "Bill" Fields, who had
previously worked for Cemar, founded Roselane in 1938.
He designed everything including this horse until he was
drafted in 1942. His older brother William "Doc" Fields
subsequently assumed ownership of Roselane. In-mold:
"Roselane Pasadena." $150.00.

Brayton Laguna horses, 8¼" x 10¼". It's believed that this horse
was an early Kay Finch model sold to Brayton circa 1939 –
1940. Documented is the fact that she arranged to have some of
her equestrian and other animal models produced by the Laguna
Beach firm before her own business was well established in nearby
Corona del Mar. These two versions of the same model, in obvious
Brayton glazes, are not marked. NP.

Burke-Simmons rabbits (one at right, 2¼"). Following a falling-out with the Winton's in 1939, Helen Burke and Robert Simmons formed an alliance and items very similar to those produced by Twin Winton ensued. These diminutive bunnies bear an uncanny resemblance to earlier Burke-Winton items. Helen Burke eventually hooked-up with other local potteries. Painted mark: "B-S #10." $60.00 set.

Padre horse head vase, 6⅜". At first glance this looks like a purely decorative object, but on closer inspection a small opening for flowers can be seen. In-mold: "Padre Calif 31." $75.00.

Artistic cat, 6" (left), and Cemar cat, 6⅜" (right). Two similar cats demonstrate the difficulty of identifying unmarked California pottery figurines. The pink and aqua cat on the left is attributed to Artistic Potteries, but Knowles, Taylor & Knowles and West Coast used glaze combinations nearly indistinguishable from this one. $50.00. The cat on the right in satin-matte white (a common California glaze) is attributed to Cemar but Tudor produced similar cubist-styled animals. NM, $65.00.

Tudor dog, 6". George Skee, who had been one of the partners in the Tudor Art Tile business in Los Angeles in the 1920s, modeled this cubistic dog figurine for the Tudor Potteries. Tudor Potteries Inc. was situated at 2406 E. 58th St. and produced colored pottery patio ware, kitchenware, and artware from about 1929 to 1939. This dog figurine exhibits some of the same characteristics seen in the miniatures he would create after joining the Metlox staff. NM, $75.00.

Haldeman dog, 4¼" x 5⅜". An unusual gold colored glaze enhances this Caliente Pottery Scottie that dates from the late 1930s or early 1940s. Incised "359 USA." $75.00.

DeLee dog, 4". This black Scottie was named Laddie and although it's not visible, a small silver sticker with the printed name is attached. DeLee was the first company in California to use these nametags. The matching female was named Lassie. NM, $65.00.

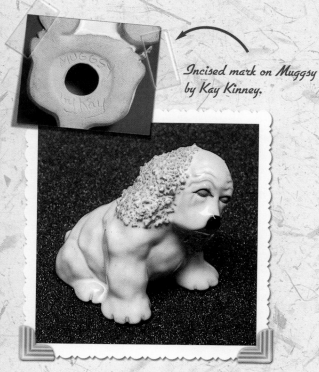

Incised mark on Muggsy by Kay Kinney.

Kay Kinney dog, 3⅜" x 4½". Kay Kinney, who often signed her work "Kay the Potter," modeled this sad looking pooch named Muggsy. I believe this item was produced about 1938 at California Faience. In the late 1940s, Kay Kinney designed numerous items for Brayton Laguna. $45.00.

DeLee cow, 3½" x 5". The name of this reclining cow is unknown as its name tag is now missing. A matching bull with the name Ferdinand has been noted. Jimmy Lee Stewart founded the deLee Art pottery in Los Angeles in 1937 and must be credited as the originator of the prototypical hand-decorated California figurine-flower holder. In-mold: "© 1938 deLee Art." $45.00.

Catalina ashtray, 3½" x 7½". A Mexican man at siesta is the centerpiece of this combination pipe holder, match holder, and ashtray in Toyon red with overglaze painted serape. The lore of Old Mexico provided its measure of inspiration for the potters in California in the 1930s and 1940s. The bright colored glazes connected with California pottery are one of the many design elements traceable to the Hispanic heritage of the state. Impressed "Catalina Island" in an oval. $450.00.

Catalina, Bauer, and Pacific ashtrays (left to right), each 2⅛" H. Are they sombrero or cowboy hat ashtrays? It's difficult to say with these three examples of an item produced by many of the California companies in the 1930s and 1940s. The cast Catalina hat in Toyon red is unmarked. $400.00+. The black glazed handmade Bauer hat is unmarked. $400.00+. The cast Pacific blue hat containing the legend: "America's Exposition San Diego 1935" was produced as a souvenir of the fair commemorating the opening of the Panama Canal. Paper label. $150.00.

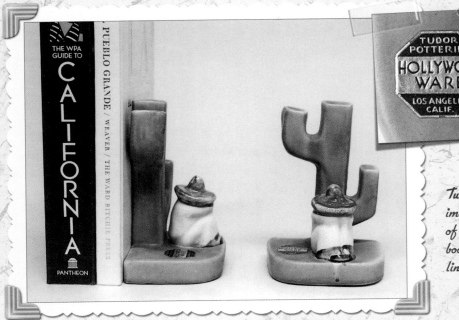

Paper label attached to the Tudor bookends.

Tudor bookends, 5⅛" x 3¼". The cliché image of a napping señor under the shade of a cactus is seen again in these novelty bookends from Tudor's Hollywood Ware line. NM, $100.00 set.

In-mold marks on dark blue Metlox candleholder.

Metlox candleholders, 7½". These candleholders with their distinctive spiral design were made in a wide assortment of glazes in the late 1930s. Various in-mold marks. $75.00 each.

Incised mark on Brayton candleholder.

Brayton Laguna candleholder, 3¼". Brayton produced this handmade chamber stick in burnt orange to go with its innovative handmade colored pottery dinnerware. Bauer produced a similar design. $300.00+.

La Cañada candleholder, 2⅞" (left), and Tudor candleholder, 1¼" (right). Flowers were the inspiration behind these two candleholders. The handmade La Cañada model repeats the device of overlapping clay found on their flower bowls and centerpieces. Incised "La Cañada Handmade 59." $40.00. The smaller Tudor model is more symmetrical and formal in feeling. NM, $30.00.

Catalina candleholder, 6¼" (left), and Haldeman cactus, 2¾" (right). Much of the terrain of Southern California is (or was) desert, and succulents are a large part of the native plant life. Not surprisingly, the cactus motif was employed with some regularity in the 1930s and 1940s. This cactus-shaped candleholder in Descanso green illustrates why the brown color of the island clay added distinction to the Catalina glazes. Incised: "Catalina." $500.00+. Alongside is a rarely seen Caliente Pottery cactus that combines two Haldeman glazes. Incised: "336." $75.00.

Winfield Pasadena trivet, 5⅞" x 6⅛". A highly stylized cactus motif graces this porcelain trivet produced in the early 1930s by the Winfield Pottery of Pasadena. Incised "Winfield Pasadena" (the lack of shape number may indicate a very early item). $200.00.

Unusual impressed mark on Pacific ashtray.

In-mold mark, "Padre 13 Calif" is appropriate for the lucky horseshoe base on the Padre cowboy boot vase.

Padre vase, 5⅛". Hollywood's version of the Wild West inspired numerous western-themed California pottery items like this tan colored cowboy boot vase with horseshoe base. $100.00.

Pacific ashtray, ⅞" x 4⅞". This rarely seen Art Deco ashtray in silver green has a mark that was used by Pacific Clay Products for a brief period, c. 1932. $200.00+.

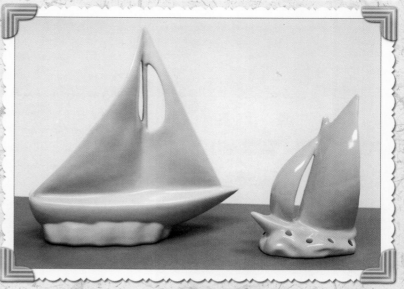

Catalina cigarette/match holder, 2" x 5". William Wrigley, Jr. was the owner of the Catalina Pottery and also owned the Chicago Cubs in the 1930s. The club held their annual spring training on the island and this rare baseball item in Monterey brown was created to commemorate the practice. Impressed "Catalina." $750.00+.

Roselane planter, 9⅛ x 9¼" (left), and Haldeman flower frog, 6¾" (right). Here are two items that catered to the weekend sailor or anyone who aspired to be one. The Roselane aqua glazed sailboat-shaped planter dates from about 1940. In-mold (raised): "Roselane Made In California." $65.00. The Caliente Pottery sailboat-shaped flower frog in pink is from the same time period. Impressed "Made in California" and incised "72 USA." $45.00.

Tudor cigarette/match holder, 2¾" x 3⅛". This matte-glazed cigarette or match holder has an image of a sailboat in low relief on the front. The Pacific Ocean inspired images of sailing and other marine-related activities by the local ceramic industry. Probably a Hollywood Ware item although the identifying paper label is no longer intact. NM, $50.00.

Vernon Kilns figure, 14½", and bust, 11". These sculptural pieces were produced during noted ceramists May and Vieve Hamilton's brief association (1936 – 1937) with Vernon. The figure of a woman is titled Sari and the bust is called Head with Hair. Both items with their commanding Art Deco design elements are attributed to May Hamilton. Both have an ink-stamped Hamilton logo. $1,000.00+ each.

Vernon Kilns figure, 11³/₄". This neoclassical female torso in satin white by May and Vieve Hamilton is titled Torse. Ink-stamped "May & Vieve Hamilton Pottery, Made in U.S.A. Vernon Kilns Calif" and "Torse" in a circle. $800.00+.

Padre diver, 8³/₄". Padre produced this unusual and well-balanced figure of a nude diver in satin ivory in the late 1930s. It was also made in a terra-cotta finish accented with a colored glaze. NM, $200.00.

Dan Daniels figures: 17³/₄" (left) and 17¹/₂" (right). These high-glazed attenuated figures with design elements in common with the WPA program of the Depression are marked in the mold "Dan Daniels © 1937." It is unknown whether the artist himself produced these or they were made by one of the local pottery companies under contract. NP.

West Coast figure, 16¹/₂". This is one-half of a set of figures that may have been modeled by Dan Daniels for the West Coast Pottery. There is a clear relationship between this model and the female figure in the adjoining photograph. The West Coast figure is somewhat shorter than the original and is glazed satin-matte white. In-mold: "West Coast Pottery California 302." $200.00.

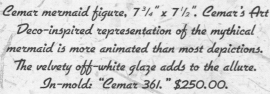

In-mold mark on Cemar mermaid.

Cemar mermaid figure, 7³⁄₄" x 7¹⁄₂". Cemar's Art Deco-inspired representation of the mythical mermaid is more animated than most depictions. The velvety off-white glaze adds to the allure. In-mold: "Cemar 361." $250.00.

Padre dancer, 10⁷⁄₈". Dancing lady figurines like this were popular during the Depression years and were inspired to some extent by the Hollywood musicals of the period starring Fred Astaire and Ginger Rogers. In-mold: "Padre California 24." $200.00.

Padre dancer, 10¹⁄₂". About 1940, Padre unveiled a hand-decorated line that became known as California Regal or Padre Regal. Like this dancer, many of the items in the line were previously released models. Her colorful flowered skirt and halter and black hair give the figure an entirely different look and, as was the custom, it bears the first name of the decorator. Painted mark: "Padre Regal Calif. Hand painted by Virginia." $175.00.

Cemar dancers, 7¹⁄₂" (left) and 8" (right). Cemar produced these two dancing ladies in satin white about 1938. The shorter figure on the left is marked in-mold: "Cemar 512." The one on the right is marked "Cemar 538." $150.00 each.

Impressed and incised marks on matte ivory Haldeman dancing lady.

Walker dancers (from left): 5" and 4"; and Haldeman dancers: 7", 4½", 6¼". The Walker Pottery of Monrovia produced the two female dancers on the left in the late 1940s — early 1950s, which confirms the enduring popularity of these figurines. The others were made during the 1930s and 1940s by the Haldeman Pottery of Burbank, which produced the greatest number and variety of these dancing ladies in California. The Walker figures are unmarked. $45.00 each. The maroon glazed Haldeman figure is incised "408 Cal." $175.00. The small pink Haldeman figure is impressed "Made in California." $75.00. The unusual matte ivory Haldeman figure is impressed "Made in California" and incised "411." $125.00.

Pacific dancer, 7". This figure of a ballerina in blue-gray glaze dates from the late 1930s. Ink-stamped "Pacific Made in Calif. USA." in a circle. $125.00.

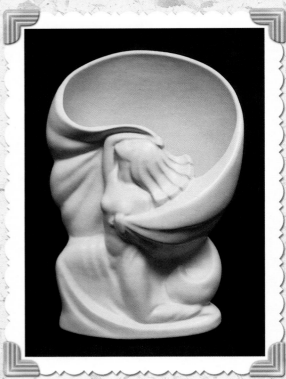

Cemar vase, 10½". Cemar produced this satin white vase that combines design elements of both Art Nouveau and Art Deco. In-mold: "Cemar 275." $200.00.

Painted mark on deLee figure flower frog.

DeLee figure flower frog, 8". Jimmy Lee Stewart modeled this very early (c. 1936) deLee figure that doubles as a flower-arranging frog. It very likely was paired with a low bowl when originally sold. Few of these very early figures have been noted. NP.

Gladding-McBean figures, 13¼," and 4¾" x 8". Dorr Bothwell, a noted California artist, designed these captivating Samoan figures for Gladding-McBean after a pilgrimage to the South Pacific islands in the mid-1930s. They were included in a line called Terra Cotta Specialties (1937 – 1940) and were produced using a brown-stained clay to simulate terra cotta. Both are marked with an ink-stamped "Made in U.S.A." The Samoan Mother and Child (C-807), $400.00+. Reclining Samoan Girl (C-808), $200.00+.

Will-George figure, 7⅜". Will Climes, one of the three Climes brothers involved in the Will-George business, modeled this figure of a young native of Samoa or other equally exotic locale. Produced in a combination of colored bisque and high glaze, this delightful figure was one of a series produced in about 1936. Incised "Will-George." $175.00.

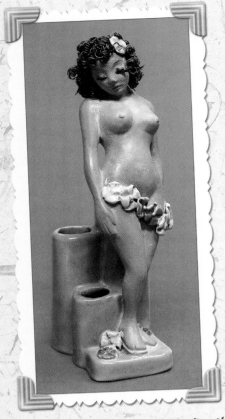

Hermione female head flower frogs, 7" (left) and 7¼" (right). The trademark curlicue wire hair and outlandish wire eyelashes give an ethereal look to these heads that double as flower frogs. They were produced at California Faience in the late 1930s. The redhead in pointed hat on the left is incised "Flora by Hermione" and "Pat. Pend." The brunette with a flower in her hair is incised "Gardenia by Hermione" and "Pat. Pending." $125.00 each.

Hermione flower holder figure, 9". This Hermione (she used only her first name) Palmer Hawaiian woman with coiled copper wire for hair and eyelashes was produced at California Faience in Berkeley, c. 1938. The red-brown California Faience clay was an ideal choice for this alluring figure, with the sectioned flower-holder base and flowers done in a contrasting gloss finish. Incised "Leilani by Hermione" and "Pat. Pend." $200.00.

Hermione head vase, 5". This Hermione Palmer design is functional as well as decorative. There is an opening on top of the woman's head to receive flowers. Incised "Susan by Hermione." $60.00.

Esther Shirey head vase, 8". Esther Shirey was another artist that probably utilized the production facilities of California Faience in the 1930s and 1940s. This head vase (c. 1940) has the glamorous look that film star Carmen Miranda popularized in the 1940s. Incised "E Shirey." $75.00.

Ink-stamped mark on Harry Bird corset vase.

Harry Bird vase, 4¼". William "Harry" Bird is best known for the dinnerware he hand decorated with brightly colored flowers for Vernon Kilns in the 1930s. He also had his own studio where he produced similar items as well as this unusual vase shaped like a Victorian era corset. $50.00.

Richenda Stevick flower holder figure, 6". Richenda Stevick was well educated in fine art when she established a small ceramics studio in Redwood City in the early 1930s. Early success prompted her to affiliate with California Faience; after 1935, most of her cast figures and figure vases were produced at the Berkeley facility. A lavender-glazed girl with fawn stands beside a tree trunk with openings for flowers. Incised "Stevick ©." $200.00.

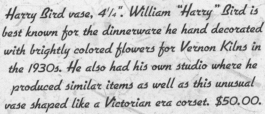

Incised mark on Esther Shirey flower holder figure. Hand-written "103" may be a shape number.

Kay Kinney figure, 8". Kay Kinney was another ceramic artist who utilized the facilities at California Faience. This figure (c. 1939) of a peasant girl with long braids carrying buckets was produced there and anticipates the designs she would create for Brayton Laguna in the late 1940s and early 1950s. Incised "Kay ©." $75.00. (Kirby W. Brown photo)

Esther Shirey flower holder figure, 5¼". The blanket this seated young girl is holding forms a shallow pocket suitable for an arrangement of small blossoms. Subtle polychrome glazes make this an exceptional example of Shirey's work at California Faience. $75.00.

Esther Shirey figures, 5³/₄" (left) and 5¹/₄" (right). These Shirey figures of a young girl with lamb and an angel holding a candle are typical of the pieces she produced at California Faience in the late 1930s — early 1940s. The seated girl with lamb is incised "Shirey." $85.00. The standing angel with tiny wings is also incised "Shirey." $75.00.

Hermione figural bottle, 6¹/₂", and figural bud vase, 4³/₄". These functional figures by Hermione Palmer are two more examples of the productivity of the California Faience works during the 1930s and 1940s. The drum majorette's hat is the stopper for a bottle that may have once held perfume. Incised: "Hermione." $85.00. The little Hawaiian girl holds a gigantic flower with an opening in the center for a single bud. Incised "By Hermione." $150.00.

Brayton Laguna figures: 8" (left) and 5¹/₂" (right). Could this be Laurel and Hardy as children? These early (c. 1935) Durlin Brayton figures are probably based on storybook characters. The older boy with pointed hat is carrying a black cat. Painted mark: "17-2." $200.00+. The little boy's pajamas have come unbuttoned in back, which may explain why he's crying. Painted mark: "17-6." $150.00+.

DeLee figures, 4³/₄". These two versions of the same figurine illustrate the subtle differences a decorator can make. Even though a form is repeated, the individual results can be very different depending on the skill level of the painter. This little girl holding flowers is an early (c. 1938) deLee model and both versions have retained their circular paper label. $60.00 each.

DeLee figure, 4". The startled expression on this little girl's face suggests that she's just had a great fall. Early deLee figurines like this one (c. 1938) are the most difficult to find. Many of them have open eyes. Paper label. $80.00.

DeLee figure flower holders, 7". Both of these deLee figurines can function as flower holders. The boy toting a basket is named Buddy. Paper label. $45.00. Patsy is the name of the girl with basket and parasol. Patsy can be found with either open or closed eyes. In-mold: "deLee Art." $60.00.

Pacific figure flower holders, 5". This pair of matte-glazed figural flower holders named Jack and Jill are typical of florist ware designed for new or expectant parents. They date from about 1935. In-mold: "Pacific." $45.00 each.

The 1930s

Incised mark on Hermione flower holder mask.

Hermione flower holder mask, 6⅝". This Hermione mask of a young woman has small openings at her neckline for placement of petite flowers. It will stand on its own or can be hung on the wall. $65.00.

Incised mark on Hermione profile mask named Joan.

Hermione profile mask, 6½". This woman's head in profile, produced at California Faience c. 1939, is named Joan, but probably isn't a representation of Joan Crawford because of the hair color. $100.00.

Padre mask, 9". Primitive African tribal masks helped shape the iconography of Art Deco (and later Modernism) and its influence is seen in this female mask that is believed to be a Padre piece, c. 1938. NM, $125.00.

Unidentified figure, 10³/₄". Simply incised "Calif," this very stylized Madonna and Child has characteristics common to a number of early manufacturers. NM, NP.

Brayton Laguna figural candleholder, 6¼". A kneeling woman holding a bowl forms the base of this graceful candleholder with Art Deco nuances. Incised "© Brayton Laguna Pottery." $100.00.

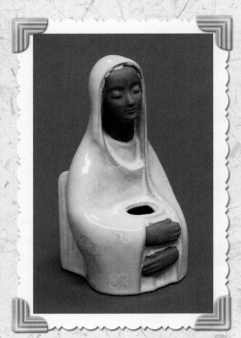

Brayton Laguna figure, 13⁷/₈". This version of the Madonna and Child theme is believed to be the work of founder Durlin Brayton and dates from about 1937. The understated decoration is an outstanding feature. Incised "Brayton Laguna Pottery." $300.00+.

Hermione flower holder figure, 6¼". Hermione Palmer's respectful depiction of the Virgin has a small opening that would accommodate a display of tiny blossoms. Incised "Madonna of Flowers by Hermione." $50.00.

Incised mark on Will-George pair of figurines.

Richenda Stevick figure, 4¹/₂". Richenda Stevick modeled this Art Deco angel figurine. It was produced at California Faience, c. 1935. Incised "Stevick ©." $250.00. (Kirby W. Brown photo)

Will-George figures: 4¹/₈" (left) and 5¹/₄" (right). Will Climes modeled these whimsical yet sophisticated depictions of priests. They date from about 1938 and have luster glazed robes contrasted with matte glazed faces and hands. $200.00 set.

SAINT FRANCIS. (Shown on cover) 11½ in. high. Robe of gray glaze, birds white, face and hands of unglazed terra-cotta. Or the entire figure in white glaze. $12.00

PRELUDE. 10 in. high. White or Persian blue glaze. $16.00

SAINT FIACRE. (Patron saint of gardens.) 9 in. high. Robe of gray glaze, flower white, face and hands unglazed terra-cotta. $12.00

PEASANT GIRL AND BABE. 10½ in. high. Bright peasant-color glazes with face and hands of unglazed terra-cotta. $17.50

Undated California Faience Co. promotional brochure showing items modeled by Richenda Stevick.

ELEPHANT JAR. 7 in. high. Persian blue, white, black, red or gray glaze. $10.00

BOWL. 9½ in. wide. White or black glaze. $5.00
LEAPING LAMB. 8½ in. high. White or black glaze, with or without holes for flowers in the base. $5.00

LITTLE ANGEL 4½ in. high. White or Persian blue glaze. $2 each
BOWL. 9¾ in. wide. White, Persian blue, red, black or yellow glaze. $5.00. Candle holders to match, 3 in. high. $1.25 each

ORDER FROM: CALIFORNIA FAIENCE COMPANY • 1335 HEARST AVENUE, BERKELEY, CALIFORNIA

The 1940s witnessed a ceramic giftware explosion in California with imports cut off during World War II. Domestic ceramic production boomed in Southern California as a whole new industry arose to fill the void and provide department stores and gift shops with artistic wares on a twice-a-year basis. The figurines that emerged in Northern California in the 1930s were fully developed during the 1940s. Now-familiar names like Kay Finch, Hedi Schoop, and Florence Ward lead the pack. A fascination with Hawaii and all things foreign ensued at war's end.

Weil vase, 8". Weil of California was located in Los Angeles at 3160 San Fernando Road. Owner Max Weil, formerly with Gladding-McBean, purchased molds and leftover bisque ware from GMB's Catalina Pottery artware series after it was discontinued in 1942. He put several shapes into production at his plant, some of which were hand painted, like this vase with Bird of Paradise decoration originally from the Encanto line. It can be compared with the original on page 22. The production of these items by Weil was noticeably inferior to the lofty standards set by Gladding-McBean. NM, $85.00.

Weil vase, 6". This is another example of the reuse of a Catalina Pottery shape (from the Polynesia line) by Max Weil. This vase has a hand-painted Hibiscus design. The decoration resembles the type of painting found on figurines Weil produced at the same time as well as his earlier California Figurine Company production. Ink-stamped "Weil Ware Made in California" mark with the outline of a burrow in the center. $75.00.

Ink-stamped mark on undecorated Weil Ware vase. The burrow became Weil's trademark.

Weil vase, 6³/₄". A Weil Ware vase made by reusing an original mold from Gladding-McBean's Floral Artware line. It dates from about 1945 and combines one glaze on the outside and another inside with no hand decoration. In-mold: "702." $50.00.

Barbara Willis vases, 7³/₄" (left) and 6⁷/₈" (right). Barbara Willis established her prosperous and influential pottery business in Los Angeles in 1942. It was later relocated to North Hollywood where these two vases were produced. The cone-shaped vase on the left is a fine example of her characteristic use of crackle glaze in combination with areas of stained and textured bisque. It dates from the late 1940s. Incised signature of Barbara Willis. $400.00. The slightly later cylindrical vase on the right has a white crackle glaze on the inside and free-hand squiggles of the same glaze around the outside. Incised "Barbara Willis." $300.00.

Authentic incised signature of Barbara Willis on turquoise glazed vase. Not all early signatures were by her hand. Workers also signed much of the ware.

Barbara Willis at the window at her first location in Los Angeles, c. 1942. Note early ware on ledge.

Wilmer James vase, 8". Wilmer James got her start in the pottery business as one of Barbara Willis's employees. In an oft-repeated scenario, James departed, believing she would enjoy the same success as her employer. Although she produced some respectable ware in the Willis manner, she did not make it big, and being a black woman may have had a negative effect on her career. She eventually formed an alliance with Tony Hill, another black ceramist, and together they attained a degree of success, although finding many examples of their work today would be difficult. This cylindrical vase with textured exterior and crackle-glazed interior shows that she learned from her experience as a Willis apprentice. Painted mark. NP.

Advertisement for Tony Hill-Wilmer James studio from the October 1947 issue of <u>Arts & Architecture</u> magazine.

for

contemporary interiors

ceramic lamps

bowls — ash trays

colors matched to order

available through decorators and better stores everywhere

tony hill — wilmer james
3121 west jefferson blvd
los angeles 16
rochester 5110

Phyllis Lester bowl, 17³/₈". Little is known about Phyllis Lester. Purportedly a student of Glen Lukens at USC, she was a member of Registered California in 1948 but no mention of her is found in later years. The business was located at 3481 W. 71st St. in Los Angeles, but this could have been her residence. Vases, bowls, and cigarette sets have been observed. This large shallow bowl (c. 1948) with its lively pattern of white crackle glaze set against a red-stained background is quite dramatic. Incised signature: "Phyllis Lester." $150.00.

Chalice vase, 8¼". The pottery of husband and wife team, Charles and Alice Smith, although rarely seen, is one of the most interesting developments in California in the 1940s. Apparently free-spirited artists, they were somewhat ahead of their time with the unconventional ware they originated and produced in their Los Angeles studio during the 1940s. The hand-painted and carved decoration as well as the grainy matte texture seen on this Chalice of California vase are characteristic of much of their work. Incised "Chalice." $75.00.

Incised mark on bottom of Chalice bottle vase.

Chalice vases, 10½" and 5½". Here are two more examples of the quirky artware of Charles and Alice Smith. On the left is a bottle shaped vase with a grainy matte glaze on the outside and glossy glaze inside, $80.00. The rectangular vase on the right has the same surface treatment on the outside, but is glossy both inside and at the base. Both items are incised "Chalice." $65.00.

Barbara Willis vases, 5½" x 6" (top) and 4" x 6" (bottom). Barbara Willis received her schooling in ceramics at the University of California at Los Angeles where she studied with Laura Andreson. This group of Barbara Willis pillow vases of the 1940s and 1950s illustrates her resourceful reuse of a shape over several seasons by the addition of new colors and surface treatments. All vases are incised or ink-stamped "Barbara Willis." Top row, $250.00 – 300.00; Bottom row, $200.00 – 225.00. (Larry Gill photo)

Catering to the Demand for the Unusual...

Green Thumb Planter Lamps

Ceramics used in these lamps are by California's Barbara Willis. They may be lifted from the lamps to permit watering the plants conveniently without removing the lamp shade or discoloring furniture with spilt water. Bases are custom designed in mahogany. Each is grooved to fit the base of the removable ceramic planter. ‡All shades are exclusive designs in modern textures, fabric lined and covered—

Lamp 200-1. Flared ceramic bowl. Coolie shade and planter in chartreuse. Shade trimmed in chocolate. Also available, white crackle bowl with coolie shade in assorted colors. Shade dia. 22", lamp 26" high.

Model 400-1. Two staggered modern pillow vases topped with tailored rectangular shade. Other lamps in this model, not shown, are 400-2 with chartreuse planter and shade, trimmed at top with burnt sugar hand pleated trim, and 400-3 with contrasting shade. Shade 17", lamp 21" high.

Model 100-1. White crackle ceramic cylinder. Fabric lined and covered shade trimmed with shirred welt or tied ruching (100-2). Lamp 100-3 has modern cone shaped shade in various colors. Shade 100-3 is paper parchment. Shade 17" lamp 26" high.

Lamp 500-1. Square tapered vase. Awning shade box pleated at bottom, edged in assorted colors. 500-2, not shown, carries tied ruching at top of awning shade. Shade 13", lamp 24" high.

Model 300-2 features single pillow vase, white crackle, with tailored shade in assorted colors. Planter also furnished in chartreuse with matching or contrasting shade (300-3). Lamp 23" high, shade 13".

ALBERT ARKIN COMPANY
504-505 BRACK SHOPS • 527 WEST 7TH ST. • LOS ANGELES 14, CALIF.

This full-page ad for the Albert Arkin Lamp Co., from the October 1946 issue of The Gift and Art Buyer, pictures a selection of Barbara Willis vases incorporated into lamps. They were removable for ease of watering.

Workers finishing ware in Barbara Willis's North Hollywood pottery, c. 1947.

59

The Bennetts vase, 6" x 3¾". The considerable success that Barbara Willis enjoyed resulted in numerous imitators. Imitation may be considered the sincerest form of flattery, but when it comes to business, it's another matter. Most potteries did not patent their designs, so it was relatively easy to produce and market outright copies. This pillow vase by The Bennetts, basically a husband and wife team, has characteristics in common with Willis, but is not a blatant copy. Incised "The Bennetts California 605." $60.00.

Incised mark on Adelle vase.

Adelle vase, 6¾", and Stahl vase, 3¾" x 7". The paradigm that Barbara Willis set in motion in the early 1940s ultimately became a California pottery methodology as these two vases reveal. The vase on the left, by Adelle of Laguna Beach, is a rather brazen copy of the Willis style with its glazed interior overlapping a combed and stained bisque exterior. $40.00. The Stahl piece represents a refinement of the technique and manages to stand on its own. In-mold: "Stahl California 801A." $50.00.

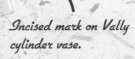

Incised mark on Vally cylinder vase.

Vally vases, 7¼" x 7" and 7½". The Vally Werner Ceramic Studio was a business begun in the late 1940s. It was located at 441 S. La Cienega Blvd. in Los Angeles and specialized in terra cotta vases such as these with crackle glazes not unlike those of her former employer, Barbara Willis. She later added simple sgraffito-like figurative patterns to the plain shapes and produced a line of octagonal dinnerware. Both vases incised "Vally." $100.00 each.

Incised mark on bottom of McAfee pillow vase.

McAfee set of planter-vases, 3⅜" (largest). McAfee Gardens of San Gabriel was owned and operated by sisters Grace and Ruth McAfee and was a combination small pottery and nursery. Much of the pottery was designed for potting and display of native flora. Starter cactus and diminutive succulents were a feature of the nursery so many of the ceramic items were small scaled, like this nesting set of glazed terra cotta pillow vases that could also function as planters. $75.00 set.

McAfee planter, 3¾" x 6". This angular Art Deco planter, in terra cotta with pale green glazed interior by McAfee, was suitable for either displaying cut flowers or for planting. In-mold: "McAfee" and paper label. $75.00.

Paper label on McAfee planter.

Early ink-stamped mark on burgundy with light rose William Manker vase.

William Manker vases, 8" and 7½". These William Manker vases are the same design from different decades. The vase on the left in pale turquoise blended with rust brown dates from the late 1940s and is ink-stamped "William Manker California U.S.A." It is slightly taller than the burgundy with light rose vase on the right. William Manker Ceramics was located in the Padua Hills arts center north of Claremont. $200.00 each.

Covina vases, 6" x 4" and 4³/₄ x 4½". The Covina Pottery of Covina was founded in 1943. A change of ownership occurred in the 1960s. It was one of the oldest established potteries in California when it finally closed in the mid-1990s. The business special-ized in ceramic planters but in the early years vases, like these two with shapes and glazes similar to those of William Manker, were made. Vase at left is incised "Covina Calif 59." $50.00. The vase at right is incised "Covina Calif 79." $45.00.

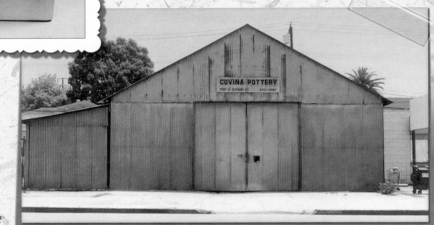

View of the Covina Pottery.

Incised mark on one of the Dick Knox vases.

Dick Knox vases, 9" x 5½". Understanding California pottery can be difficult because many of the people involved in the industry wore more than one hat. For instance, Dick Knox started out as a manufacturers' representative and ended up a manufacturer himself. He counted among his clients Sascha Brastoff, Hedi Schoop, and Barbara Willis, but in the early 1940s, he decided to tackle producing, and selected Laguna Beach as the ideal location for his business. These two eye-catching vases with overglaze gold and silver bases speak volumes about their place in history, the post-war 1940s. Incised marks. $100.00 each.

Harold Johnson vase, 3¾". After working at Pacific (with his father Fred), Catalina (on Catalina Island), and briefly for Bauer, Harold Johnson established his own business in Glendale in 1940, which he called the Hacienda Pottery. By then, he was a well-trained potter who was adept at throwing on the wheel, making models as well as molds, and formulating clay bodies and glazes. His refined, semi-porcelain flower bowls and vases were popular both during and after the war years of the 1940s. This ball-shaped bulb vase has two sections and is often found without the top part that holds the bulb. Incised "Harold Johnson." $125.00.

Harold Johnson vase, 10½". This Harold Johnson vase with fanciful Art Deco cartouche has two contrasting glaze colors, a design feature characteristic of his ware. The inside is chartreuse. This same shape can be found marked "West Coast Pottery" because they purchased the mold after Johnson closed his pottery in 1952. Incised "Harold Johnson." $150.00.

Harold Johnson low bowls (clockwise from top), 3½"H x 8½"W x 15½"L, 1¾"H x 7¼"W x 11¼"L, and 1⅜"H x 5⅝"W x 6½"L. Harold Johnson was best known in the 1940s for his elegant low flower bowls. They also adapted well as fruit bowls and reportedly were even used by a candy company to package their candy. The bowls were modeled after a variety of tropical flora, and when the business closed, Cemar purchased some of the molds. All incised "Harold Johnson." Large bowl, $125.00; medium bowl, $85.00; small bowl, $50.00.

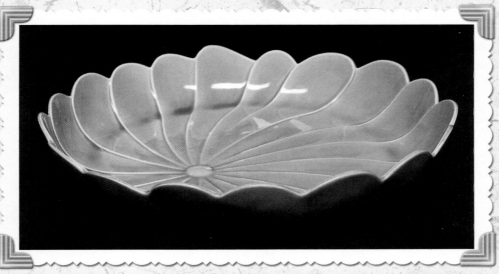

Harold Johnson low bowl, 3" x 15³/₄". This large flower bowl, resembling a lily pad, is glazed pink inside and gray outside and would make a spectacular centerpiece. These bowls can be used to float flowers and also make great platforms for a cluster of oversize candles. Incised "Harold Johnson." $150.00.

West Coast vase, 12". This vase by the West Coast Pottery of Burbank has some Art Deco touches and considerable movement in its top-to-bottom linear pattern. The pale turquoise color adds to the aquatic feel of this good-looking vase. In-mold: "West Coast Pottery California 307." $85.00.

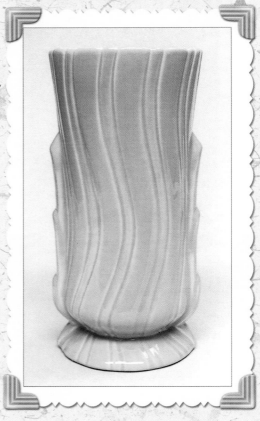

West Coast vase, 10". This West Coast Pottery vase also displays a strong sense of movement and has a fairly contemporary design for its time, c. 1949. The combination of colors hinted of things to come in the 1950s. In-mold: "West Coast Calif 705." $85.00.

In-mold mark on square West Coast vase.

Paper label on square West Coast vase.

West Coast vase, 7¼" x 5". The West Coast Pottery was established about 1940. It was located at 724 N. Victory Blvd. in Burbank and the owners were Lee and Bonnie Wollard, who had previously been associated with KTK. Floral artware and figurines were the stock in trade of the business, some of which was hand decorated and artist signed. Many of the company's designs included plant forms, like this square vase with subtle coloration. $65.00.

West Coast vases, 10⅛" (average height). These four vases formed by tropical leaves are representative of the glaze colors made available to the West Coast buyer of the 1940s. There were other blends and solids produced. In-mold: "West Coast Pottery 446." $85.00 each.

In-mold mark on West Coast peacock vase.

West Coast vase, 12¼". This vase is from a West Coast series of 1946 called Vain Peacock that incorporated peacocks in relief. Most examples observed have had this mingling of lavender and turquoise or a glaze akin to it. $75.00.

West Coast wall pockets, 12". These feathery wall pockets are an eye-catching pair. West Coast Pottery produced a number of wall pocket designs, this being one of their best. The company remained active until the mid-1960s. In-mold marks. $75.00 each.

Knowles, Taylor & Knowles vase, 13⅝". The Knowles, Taylor & Knowles (KTK) plant, located in Burbank, produced this striking vase with its energetic pattern. Homer Knowles, a member of the Knowles family of Ohio potters responsible for the celebrated Lotus Ware, came west and founded a California business in the late 1930s. His son John, as well as other family members, participated in the production of vases, low bowls, and figurines. In-mold: "K.T.K. S-V China 805." $100.00.

Knowles, Taylor & Knowles vase, 7¼". This vase, in a blended glaze of turquoise and dark blue, resembles a horn of plenty but could also represent a seashell and waves. It has a rather dynamic profile with Art Deco nuances. In-mold: "KTK, S---V China, Calif 509." ("S---V" is an abbreviation for semi-vitreous.) $65.00.

Incised markings on bottom of the KTK wall pocket.

Knowles, Taylor & Knowles vases, 5½" (average height). These three cast vases and one wall pocket started out as plain cylinders. By manipulating them while still green they have been transformed into four different objects. Rims were rolled and fanned out slightly, then details like leaves, fruit, and a large bow were added. The four glazes give an idea of the color combinations that KTK produced. Some are similar to other companies' glazes, so familiarity with marks is important. Incised marks. $60.00 – 80.00 each.

*Incised mark on KTK
planter-vase.*

Knowles, Taylor & Knowles planter-vase, 5" x 5½".
Another example of the handmade pottery of KTK is
seen here. A simple rectangle was trimmed and hand
formed into an entirely new shape while still pliable but
not too wet (known as the leather hard state). This
added detail is interesting and was only possible because
the cost of labor was reasonable in the 1940s. $75.00.

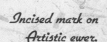

*Incised mark on
Artistic ewer.*

Artistic ewer, 10⅝". Artistic Potteries began operations about 1940 in
Whittier. It evidently changed its location twice, first in 1942 to 829 W.
Olympic Blvd. and later in the decade to 3421 Fernwood Ave., both Los
Angeles addresses. J. Barney Ordin was the owner of the business, which
employed about 70. The ware produced was similar in many ways to both
KTK and West Coast. In fact, some of their glazes, like the one seen on
this pitcher-vase, are dead-ringers for the blended glazes produced by
these other companies. Not all Artistic Potteries ware was marked, so
difficulties in attribution can be expected. $50.00.

Printed markings on
Claire Lerner porcelain vase.

Claire Lerner porcelain vase, 8". This interesting vase with applied flowers and leaves is an example of Claire Lerner's original porcelain line. Claire, with husband Sidney's help, began producing ceramic costume jewelry at their Los Angeles residence in 1941. Demand for their clever lapel pins required a factory and staff, and the business was relocated to 1009 W. 7th St. in Los Angeles, where the porcelain line was eventually developed. During the war years, it was a common practice in California to produce facsimiles of various types of ware previously imported from Europe and Asia. The buyers for the big department stores were generally favorable to them and many were good sellers. Items such as this vase were essentially a re-creation of something no longer available to the giftware buyers. $85.00.

Giftwares
TOYS *and*
HOUSEWARES
MAGAZINE

JUNE, 1946

Cover of the June 1946
Giftwares featuring a
selection of Claire
Lerner's porcelain ware.

Mark on Freeman-Leidy covered dish.

Freeman-Leidy covered dish, 6³/₄" x 5¹/₂". Freeman-Leidy of Laguna Beach was another pottery that did their best to reproduce some of the suspended foreign imports during WWII. This covered dish with lid heavily festooned with sculptural fruit and leaves accented with overglaze gold appears to be an Italian Majolica replica. Freeman-Leidy was owned and operated by C. Leland Freeman and Russell L. Leidy. At some point, the name of the company was changed to Ceramic Originals. $85.00.

Freeman-Leidy bowl, 3³/₄" x 7¹/₂. The intended purpose of this item is unclear. It may have been used on a dresser to deposit earrings, keys, or other small objects. The inner dimensions are rather small and much too shallow for an arrangement of flowers. The outside is entirely composed of three-dimensional representations of fruit and leaves that have been accented and outlined graphically with overglaze gold. This tour de force is incised "Freeman-Leidy." $85.00.

Freeman-Leidy shell dish, 4¹/₄"H x 7¹/₂"W. Another item with an esoteric purpose is seen here. Perhaps the open shell was designed as a soap dish or to hold small objects on a lady's vanity. The base is decked out with smaller shells and the entire piece embellished with gold gilding. Incised "Freeman-Leidy." $75.00.

Hermione vase, 5½". This Hermione item could also be used as a jardinière. The glaze color on the inside is a deep burgundy. Hermione Palmer produced it after she relocated to Glendale in the early 1940s. Chauncy Thomas of California Faience became affiliated with the business following the move. The Glendale address of the Hermione Pottery was 321 W. Los Feliz Blvd. In-mold: "Hermione." $60.00.

Landaker vase with lizard, 5⅛". Landaker has to be one of the most interesting of the obscure production potteries of the 1940s. A new venture for painter-turned-potter Harold C. Landaker, the business began in metropolitan Los Angeles but eventually relocated to unhurried Pacific Grove on the central coast. Landaker's interest in ancient glazes combined with a sense of humor led to some very imaginative and unconventional items, like this vase with a lizard perched on one side. The widespread stain and crackle glaze combination has been kicked up a notch or two here. Incised "Landaker Original Ceramics." $100.00.

Paper label on red Brad Keeler vase.

Brad Keeler vase, 9". After Gladding-McBean's successful development of an authentic red glaze, other California companies began to replicate their achievement. One of the first to do so was Brad Keeler, with help from one of the GBM chemists. Keeler called his red glaze Ming Dragon Blood and used it to good effect on many items including this cylindrical vase. Like the Ox Blood line of GMB, this vase has a whitish contrasting interior. Ink-stamped "636" plus paper label. $100.00.

Batchelder vase, 6³⁄₈". Ernest A. Batchelder is well known for the Craftsman era tiles he produced in Pasadena and later Los Angeles. An even later business, Batchelder Ceramics — also located in Pasadena — is less familiar but no less interesting. Spurred on by William Manker's success and essentially following his example, Batchelder imbued his line with an even more palpable Asian sensibility. His cast ware was thin-walled and delicate and the combinations of colors were refined and understated, like this Chinese style vase, c. 1942. Incised "L.A. Batchelder Pasadena" and "42." $175.00.

Roselane footed bowl, 4¹⁄₈" x 8⁷⁄₈". Chinese Key is what Roselane called its line of Chinese inspired designs of the 1940s. Chinese Modern interiors had become quite fashionable in California and items like this footed console bowl in contrasting period colors were indispensable decorative accessories. Ink-stamped "Roselane California 310" plus paper label. $65.00.

Roselane ad in the July 1948 issue of Giftwares.

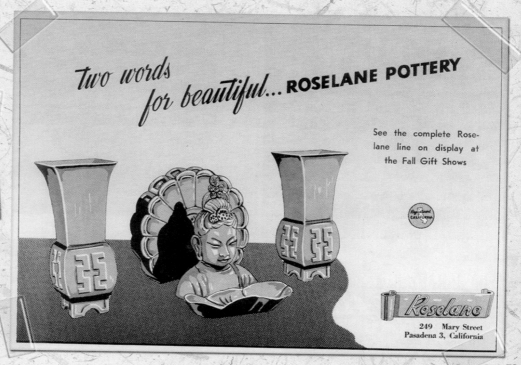

two words for beautiful... ROSELANE POTTERY

See the complete Roselane line on display at the Fall Gift Shows

Roselane
249 Mary Street
Pasadena 3, California

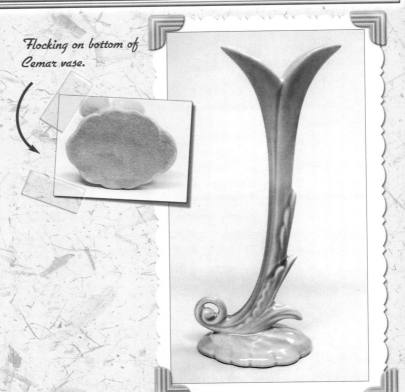

Flocking on bottom of Cemar vase.

Weil vase, 8". Max Weil also recognized the need for Asian-styled accessories and this vase with hand-painted scene with added coralline-like decoration was part of a large assortment produced in the 1940s. Ink-stamped "Weil Ware Made in California" and "Pat. Applied For" plus paper label. $60.00.

Cemar vase, 10½". This Cemar vase with its towering cornucopia design is from a series that straddled the mid-century mark. Elements common to both decades can be seen here. The gray and pink colors belong to the 1950s while the attenuated form is more characteristic of the 1940s. Unmarked but with added flocking. Cemar is believed to have been the only California pottery that flocked the bottoms of items. $85.00.

Incised mark on La Mirada vase.

Cemar vase, 6⅝" and La Mirada vase, 6⅛". These two vases are at opposite ends of the design spectrum but both were tailored to harmonize with design developments of the 1940s. The Cemar vase with it outlandish drapery design is all glitz and glamour. Unmarked flocked base. $75.00. The lotus shaped La Mirada vase, on the other hand, is more restrained and Asian in mood. $50.00.

Incised mark on bottom section of large Kellems planter.

Kellems planters, 3½" and 5¼". Kellems of Pasadena, operated by Edgar E. Kellems, was known in the late 1940s — early 1950s for their self-watering planters. These are just two of the many styles produced. They have two components; the top contains the plant, and the bottom holds water. Technically, a fiberglass wick attached to the base of the planted section draws water into the plant a little at a time. Apparently it worked, because many were sold. The dark-green planter is incised "Kellems Calif. USA" and "Pat. Pend." Shape numbers are also included on these items. $35.00. The larger gray planter is incised on both sections. The top part reads "Kellems Pasadena USA Pat-Pend." $45.00.

Handwritten underglaze mark on Sorcha Boru covered dish.

Sorcha Boru covered dish, 3¼" x 6". Covered dishes and boxes with life-like flowers on their lids were popular in the 1940s. Round ones are generally considered to be candy dishes. The leaves and petals on this Sorcha Boru example were formed by hand as separate components and then attached to the cover prior to firing. The cover itself is quite heavy. $125.00.

Haldeman covered dish, 3½" x 6". This Caliente Pottery candy dish has a leafy branch and a single white rose bud attached. The Haldeman pottery produced a variety of items with added rosebud embellishment. The roses and leaves were cast separately and attached to the lids with slip. Only recently has it been learned that the Claire Lerner Studio acquired the Caliente line in 1948 and continued its production until 1958. They used the same molds, glazes, and paper labels that were used by the Haldeman Pottery. This now makes the origin of Caliente Pottery items difficult to determine. Incised "Calif 214." $65.00.

Paper label on
Johannes Brahm
covered box.

Johannes Brahm covered boxes, 4"H x 7"L. The handmade roses and leaves that adorn these Brahm boxes appealed to the woman of the house in the 1940s. They probably held cigarettes but did so with élan. Unlike today, smoking was considered socially acceptable in the 1940s and 1950s. Johannes Brahm's business was located in Reseda. The gray box on the left has an intact paper label in addition to the in-mold mark. The burgundy box is marked in-mold "Johannes Brahm California U.S.A." $75.00 – 85.00 each.

Johannes Brahm covered box, 5" x 6½". Johannes Brahm produced many of these covered boxes with flowered lids, but this one is exceptional because of the color. It actually dates from the early 1950s, when brilliant red glazes became readily available to the industry. But by then, interest in the boxes had begun to wane so relatively few red ones were produced. In-mold: "Johannes Brahm California U.S.A." $150.00+.

In-mold mark on
Wildwood covered dish.

Wildwood covered dish, 3½" x 5¾", and covered box, 3⅛"H" x 4½"L. Wildwood Ceramics was located in Pasadena. Joseph A. Galley and his wife Hazel established it in the early 1940s. In the early 1950s, Dale Kennedy of the Los Angeles Pottery assumed ownership. Semi-porcelain items like these were the specialty of the business. The celadon glazed candy dish with wild rose at left is marked in the mold. $60.00. The gray cigarette box with daffodil is marked with a circular ink-stamp reading "Wildwood Ceramics Pasadena." $50.00.

Paper label on backside
of Wildwood plaque.

Wildwood wall plaque, 8³⁄₈" x 6¹⁄₈". Wildwood Ceramics, in addition to its covered dishes bedecked with flowers, produced decorative wall plaques with flower and/or fruit motifs. The frame and background of his oval plaque consists of a single unit that was fired separately from the fruit and leaves. The three-dimensional grapes and leaves were hand painted then attached before the second firing. A third and final firing (at a lower temperature) was required for the added gilding to bond with the glaze. $50.00.

West Coast vases, 7¹⁄₈" (left) and 6½" (right). These two West Coast vases show the evolution of a design. The vase on the left with narrow opening and subtle blend of pink and turquoise dates from about 1945. In-mold: "West Coast Pottery California 121." $75.00. The other vase with the wider opening is only a slight modification of the original shape with added hand decoration on the embossed butterfly. In-mold: "West Coast Pottery California" and painted mark: "021D." (The "D" stands for decorated.) $60.00.

Padre butterfly, 6". Padre started hand painting some of their existing shapes about 1940. New designs were eventually added and the line became known as Padre Regal. This butterfly was in all probability an item made specifically for the Regal treatment. Painted mark: "Padre Regal Calif." and in-mold: "66." $75.00.

Claire Lerner butterfly, 10¼". The Claire Lerner Studio was relocated to 2406 E. 58th St. in Los Angeles (Huntington Park) in 1946, where an earthenware line was added to the earlier porcelain line. This butterfly decoration in emerald green, an example of the earthenware line, was produced c. 1950. $65.00.

In-mold marks on Claire Lerner butterfly.

Sid and Claire Lerner in their Huntington Park factory, c 1949. Note Caliente Pottery on shelves. The Lerners took over production of the Caliente line from the Haldemans in 1948.

William Manker leaf-shaped bowl, 2½" x 26½" x 11½". This shallow leaf-shaped bowl or serving tray is one of the largest items produced by William Manker during his remarkable ceramics career and illustrates why his work was held in such high esteem in the 1930s and 1940s. Ink-stamped mark. $200.00+.

Incised mark on leaf-shaped tray by Maxine Cloud.

Maxine Cloud, Winfield Pasadena, and Eugene White leaf-shaped items. Shown here are only a few examples of the diverse ways the California potters transformed leaves into useful and attractive objects for the home. On the left is a leaf-shaped tray by Maxine Cloud with dark green glaze on the top portion and the unglazed bottom and sides stained brown in the Barbara Willis manner. $45.00. In the center is a shallow handled leaf tray by Winfield of Pasadena in an autumn brown glaze. Impressed mark. $50.00. On the right is a large leaf-shaped handled bowl with a sea green glaze inside and unglazed terra cotta outside. Incised "Eugene White California." $75.00.

Eugene White in a photo taken in the 1980s.

Eugene White leaf-shaped dishes. Eugene White created some appealing items, both decorative and useful, during his foray into ceramic production. He was in business from 1941 to 1948 in Bell Gardens. He had studied ceramics at USC under Glen Lukens and his work reflected the influence of this distinguished ceramist and educator. White also was a teacher and headed the art department at Pepperdine University in Los Angeles before finally retiring in 1979. Here we have examples of his leaf-shaped terra cotta serving ware. On top is a 9" tray in sea green. $45.00. At bottom left is a 2¼" x 9½" bowl in cobalt blue. $65.00. At bottom right is a 9¼" tray in golden yellow. $50.00. All incised "Eugene White California."

Incised mark on
Eugene White creamer.

Eugene White utility ware: serving tray, 1½" x 13½"; coffee pot, 8"; open sugar and creamer, 3". Eugene White produced a varied and attractive assortment of items for preparing and serving food during his brief ceramics career. Crackle glazes, although not a particularly practical application, were sometimes used on these utilitarian items. The large handled tray with "bull ballet" had a hammered aluminum lid (not shown) to keep what was served in it warm. Incised "Handmade by Eugene White California" in a circle. $175.00. The coffee server has a yellow glazed interior with a clear glaze on the upper segment of the exterior. Ink-stamped mark. $125.00. The matching sugar and creamer are both incised "Eugene White California." $85.00 set.

Eugene White promotional photograph with a display of ware.

Eugene White casserole, 5" x 11¼", and covered bowl, 4" x 6¼". The large broad-brimmed casserole with flower finial was, like all Eugene White items, made with terra cotta clay and only partially glazed. Incised "Handmade by Eugene White California" in a circle. $250.00. The small covered bowl may have been intended for candy or condiments. Incised "Eugene White Calif." $175.00.

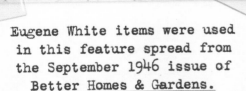

Eugene White items were used in this feature spread from the September 1946 issue of Better Homes & Gardens.

Knox China 10" dinner plate, individual coffee pot, cup, and saucer. These are examples of a very elusive dinnerware designed by famous California ceramist Beatrice Wood and manufactured by Dick Knox. With little to go on, it appears that it was only produced for a short period in the late 1940s. No one seems to know why this porcelain ware with such a pedigree failed to achieve wider acceptance. A possible marketing gaffe was the omission of the designer's name on the individual pieces. Not a single example noted has been marked in any way. The items produced were matte glazed; the examples pictured are in a color called sage. Dinner plate, NM, $300.00+; individual coffee pot, $750.00+; cup and saucer, $350.00+.

Knox China

10" Dinner Plate — $30.00 dz.
9" Luncheon Plate — 24.00 dz.
7½" Salad Plate — 18.00 dz.
7" Bread & Butter Plates — 12.00 dz.
Covered cream soup with 2 handles — 6.00 ea.

Creamer — $ 3.00 ea.
Tea Pot — 7.50 ea.
Coffee Pot — 7.50 ea.
Tea cup and saucer — 30.00 dz. sets
   Extra cup — 1.65 ea.
   Extra saucer — 1.00 ea.
Sugar bowl with cover for
   dessert or soup — 30.00 dz.

Dinner Plate (10" dia.) — $30.00 dz.
Chop Plate (13½" dia.) — 7.50 ea.
Cup and Saucer — 30.00 dz. sets

ALL PRICES QUOTED UNDER PICTURES ARE RETAIL

A page from the Dick Knox catalog of 1948 showing part of the Knox China line by Beatrice Wood.

Knox China teapot, 6½"H. This porcelain teapot designed by Beatrice Wood, one of California's most famous potters, speaks for itself. NM, $750.00+.

Ink-stamped mark on Riverside China cup.

Riverside China 9½" dinner plate, cup and saucer (saucer 7½"), 5" bowl, and 6" vase. The Riverside Ceramic Co. of Riverside produced an elusive set of fine china by noted industrial designer Eva Zeisel in the late 1940s. Thinly cast and delicate biomorphic shapes similar to those seen in earlier Zeisel sets (by other companies) are accentuated by attractive colored glazes in both solids and subtle blends. A few items included copper components. Shown here is a selection of items in the line's distinctive colors. Some pieces were ink stamped with the Riverside China logo and facsimile signature of Eva Zeisel, but many were not marked. Dinner plate, $75.00; cup and saucer, $150.00; bowl, $50.00; vase, $250.00+.

Riverside China carafe, 8¼", and sauceboat, 9¾"L x 4⅝"W. The carafe (on the left) is one of the highlights of the hard-to-find dinnerware that Eva Zeisel designed for the Riverside Ceramics Co. NM, $400.00+. The sauceboat, like many of the items in the line, has a curved bottom that allows it to rock slightly without spilling its contents. NM, $250.00. The Riverside Ceramics company has proved as furtive as the china it produced.

Maxine Cloud ashtray, 2¼"H x 6"W. The studio of Maxine Cloud was located in Hawthorne and was in operation from about 1945 to 1953. Cloud's combination of stains and glaze on pottery called attention to the contrast between the lighter wood-toned areas and a deep forest green. She also incorporated tangible woodland elements in her pieces. She has cleverly used oak leaves and acorns on one corner to form a cigarette rest on this square ashtray. Incised "Maxine Cloud Calif #22." $45.00.

Maxine Cloud coffee pot, 9½". This is another example of how Maxine Cloud used forest elements in her pottery of the late 1940s. The basic form of this coffee server, including the oak leaf clusters, was slip cast. The hand-made vine-like handle and finial in shiny dark-green glaze in contrast with the warm brown bisque add a rustic charm to the completed item. $65.00.

Incised mark on Maxine Cloud coffee pot.

Chalice coffee pot, 13¼". This high-rise Chalice of California coffee server combines Art Deco elements with a serious dash of imagination. The cone-shaped terra cotta body with a small amount of surface texture contrasts nicely with the turquoise-glazed handle, flattened top, and fish-shaped finial. Undoubtedly, there were cups or mugs to match this remarkable item, c. 1945. Incised "Chal." $250.00.

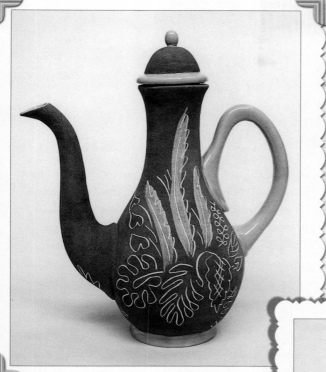

Chalice coffee pot, 14". Another whimsical coffee server from Charles and Alice Smith that epitomizes their penchant for coarse matte-finished surfaces accented with high-gloss glaze and sgrafitto decoration. Two other sizes of this pot along with matching cups were produced in 1949 – 1950. The largest size towered to 22". Incised "Chalice." $175.00.

Chalice 11¾" pitcher, 4" tumbler, 8¼" pitcher. These Chalice items all have the characteristic matte background accented with high glaze and sgrafitto decoration. The tall pitcher on the left and the tumbler are not an exact match even though they have similar hand-incised patterns. The pitcher is incised "Chalice." $90.00. The tumbler bears an incised "Alice" and may be a piece made by Alice Smith after the collapse of their partnership. $25.00. The cylindrical pitcher on the right is incised "Chalice." $85.00.

Chalice 3¾" dessert cup, 9" plate, 4¼" bowl, 4" coaster-ashtray. This pictographic Chalice of California tableware with mythological imagery is from a mixed set produced in the late 1940s – early 1950s. Triton is the title of this particular motif. The dessert cup is not marked. $30.00. The plate has a painted mark: "Triton" and "Chal." $50.00. The small bowl and coaster have the painted mark: "Chal." $25.00 each.

Painted mark on Guppy salad plate.

Guppy dishes: 14" chop plate, 3" mug, 8" salad plate. Harriet and Roy Guppy produced three closely related sets of casual dinnerware in the 1940s at their Corona del Mar pottery. Harriet Guppy's designs and patterns were utterly unique in concept and were particularly appropriate for patio dining. The line shown here was known as Western Way and a variety of color combinations was produced. This busy pattern with calm at the center (like the eye of a hurricane) is bold and energetic. The chop plate integrates black and pink brushstrokes. Painted mark: "Guppy's Calif." $75.00. The salad plate mixes splashes of green, yellow, and brown. $20.00. The cup with coiled base (no saucer was made to match) combines black with gray. NM, $25.00.

Guppy 4³⁄₄" shakers and 7" tumblers. More examples of Guppy's Western Way dinnerware showing various color schemes. The gourd-shaped shakers and tumblers have hand-coiled bases. The shaker sets are unmarked and are NM. Shaker set, $50.00. Tumblers, $35.00 each.

casual dining in the modern way

. . . ten color combinations

Created and Produced by
HARRIET GUPPY
Los Angeles, Calif.

Exclusive representative
SHARON MERRILL
712 South Olive St. Los Angeles 14, Calif.
Room 404

Guppy 10" dinner plate and teapot. This Island Ware dinnerware made by the Guppy's of Corona del Mar may be their most unconventional design. Bamboo was the obvious inspiration behind the line, and a table fully set with it was guaranteed to evoke the islands of the South Pacific. The examples pictured here were glazed a pale chartreuse edged with deep burgundy. The square dinner plate with wavy edges and wicker-like texture is marked with an overglaze painted "Guppy's Island Ware Calif." $35.00. The large bamboo-shaped teapot with its plated metal handle is not marked. $85.00.

Painted underglaze mark on Guppy tumbler.

Guppy dishes (left to right): 4½" sugar bowl, 6½" handled mug, 3" punch cup, 7" tumbler, creamer. More Guppy's Island Ware items in pale chartreuse with a burgundy drip are pictured here. A complete dinnerware set with numerous accessories was made during the 1940s. Some items in this exotic line were marked overglaze with some type of paint so it's not unusual to find them with the mark completely worn away. Covered sugar, $30.00; handled mug, $40.00; tumbler, $35.00; punch cup, $40.00; creamer, $25.00.

Guppy covered box, 4¾" x 7¾". This covered item is very likely a cigarette box because an ashtray matches its exact length and width. Glazed aqua with brown drip, it effectively exploits the bamboo shape. An interesting feature of the Guppy pottery was the tunnel kiln that Roy Guppy designed. This led to a side business that eventually saw Guppy tunnel kilns installed in many California potteries. NM, $85.00.

Roselane vases, 7" and 9½". These two bamboo-shaped vases from the Roselane Pottery of Pasadena were among the many items the company produced during the 1940s with an Asian theme. Bamboo is native to many lands and islands, but these vases were accessories for a trend in home decor that drew inspiration from the ancient wisdom of China. The small bamboo vase on the left is incised "Roselane Calif." $45.00. The larger vase on the right is incised "Roselane Pasadena Calif." $60.00.

Paper label on backside of
La Mirada wall pocket.

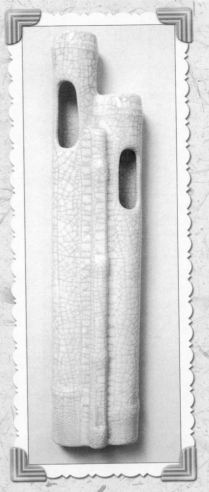

La Mirada wall pocket, 15" x 3½". La Mirada produced many interesting wall vases but this eye-catching bamboo design was probably their most successful. Originally sold in pairs marked "R" for right and "L" for left (the uppermost bamboo section of each unit would be in the center), it came in a variety of crackle glaze colors, but this colorless example called Cobweb is particularly lovely. $65.00.

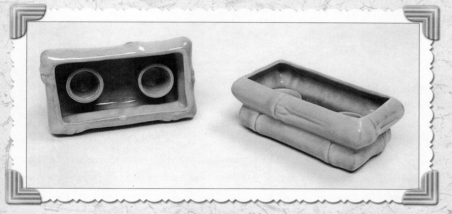

California Art Products candleholders, 1¾"H x 4½"L x 2⅝"W. Hollywood was almost as popular a tag line as California or Calif. It is believed that California Art Products, Inc. produced this clever set of bamboo-shaped double candleholders that can also hold cut flowers or leaves. California Art Products was a restructuring of Tudor Potteries that occurred in the late 1930s. Ink-stamped mark: "Hollywood Ware, Made in California." $30.00 set.

Ink-stamped mark on
Weil Ware Malay
Bambu dinnerware.

Weil dishes: 7" covered butter dish, 9¾" dinner plate, cup, and saucer. Weil's Malay Bambu dinnerware of the late 1940s was completely hand painted, so some variation is noticeable from piece to piece. All items pictured are back stamped as shown. The dinner plate has the additional information: "Design Patent 149606." Butter dish, $50.00; dinner plate, $25.00; cup and saucer, $25.00.

Weil dishes: 9¾" dinner plate, 6¼" bread and butter plate, cup, and saucer. Weil also produced the bamboo pattern on its square dinnerware. These examples were hand decorated on a white background. Both lines were popular but the round design was made for a longer period and is easier to find today. All items are back stamped with the familiar "burrow" logo bordered by the words: "Hand Decorated Weil Ware" and "Made in California." Dinner plate, $25.00; bread and butter plate, $10.00; cup and saucer, $25.00.

Weil promotional brochure of July 1, 1950, featuring another popular Malayan Ware pattern, Malay Blossom.

Tepco China 19" platter and 24 oz. teapot. Tepco China produced these heavy-grade Bamboo patterned items. Their chinaware was utilized by restaurants and hotels throughout the country and is very collectible today. The large oval turkey platter and small teapot are both transfer printed "Tepco China U.S.A." Platter, $500.00+; teapot, $200.00.

Tepco China 11½" chop plate and 8 oz. mug. Italian immigrant John Pagliero founded Tepco, short for Technical Porcelain and China Ware Co., in the northern California city of El Cerrito in 1918. Various members of the Pagliero family operated the company until it closed in 1968. This Tepco hotel and restaurant grade china pattern was called Palm and was produced in several colors over the years. It was widely used during the 1940s and 1950s. Both items are transfer printed "Tepco China U.S.A." The company called their 11½" plate (and an even smaller size) a chop plate. $75.00. The coffee mug in green did not require a saucer. $50.00.

Printed mark on Tepco China Palm pattern chop plate and coffee mug.

Tepco business card.

Technical Porcelain and China Ware Co.

HOME OF "TEPCO" AND "PAMCO" VITRIFIED HOTEL CHINAWARE

ANTONE A. PAGLIERO

MAIN OFFICE & FACTORY
6416 MANILA STREET
EL CERRITO, CALIF.
CONTRA COSTA COUNTY

WAREHOUSE & OFFICE
223 S. LOS ANGELES ST.
LOS ANGELES 12, CALIF.

WAREHOUSE & OFFICE
1706 CONGRESS AVENUE
HOUSTON, TEXAS

Wallace China 7½" pitcher and Tepco China 7¼" pitcher. Wallace of Los Angeles and Tepco of El Cerrito were the West's largest manufacturers of hotel and restaurant grade chinaware. They both produced similar shapes and patterns in the 1940s and the tropical leaf patterns seen on these two pitchers are proof. Wallace originated the pattern, which they called Shadow Leaf. Then Tepco introduced its Palm pattern to compete with it. The green Shadow Leaf pitcher by Wallace is ink-stamped Wallace China Los Angeles California. $350.00. The red Palm pattern pitcher is printed "Tepco China U.S.A." $500.00+.

Tepco China 13⅝" platter, 8 oz. individual teapot, and 32 oz. teapot. This busy Tepco China pattern featuring repeated hibiscus flowers was called Hawaiian and was made available in several colors. All printed "Tepco China U.S.A." Platter, $250.00; individual teapot, $250.00; teapot, $350.00.

Wallace China logo on protective shipping pouch.

Printed mark on the Wallace China Tropicana oval bowl.

Wallace China oval bowl, 2⅓"H x 11¾"L x 9"W. This is a seldom seen pattern of Wallace China called Tropicana, and also rare is the designer credit included on the ware. The backstamp includes "By Osmond." Pictured is an oval vegetable serving bowl in green with the tropical foliage pattern on the inside only. $150.00.

Tepco China punch bowl, 5¾" x 7¼". This tropical punch bowl, called the Scorpion Bowl, was produced for the Polynesian-themed Trader Vic's restaurants. The colorful decoration of tropical fish and seaweed was produced using an airbrush and stencils. There were other items made exclusively for Trader Vic's, including the Fog Cutter beverage tumbler, the Hula Girl and Tiki bowls, and the Skeleton Mug. NM, $200.00.

Roselane salad set: oil and vinegar cruets, 9½"; bowl, 14"; and fork and spoon, 12". It's unclear whether Roselane actually assigned a name to this salad set and the various accessories that were made. A vintage advertisement referred to it as Aqua Marine, but no other reference has been noted. In addition to aqua, the playful dolphin design was produced in pink, and dark blue has also been reported. The cruets are marked in-mold "Roselane 28." $75.00 set. The salad bowl is marked in-mold "Roselane Pasadena Calif. Pat. Pend. 25." $125.00. The utensils are unmarked. $75.00 set.

Vee Jackson footed tray, 3" x 8". The Vee Jackson business was originally located in San Gabriel and later relocated to Pasadena. The company produced decorative housewares such as this attractive shell-shaped tray with applied blossom and leaves. This item dates from the late 1940s and would be an early example. The business enjoyed exceptional longevity. Ink-stamped "Vee Jackson San Gabriel California" in a circle. $50.00.

Brad Keeler handled tray, 3" x 9½". It has been reported that this item and others like it were made by Brad Keeler to complement the various Santa Anita Flowers of Hawaii dinnerware designs. If true, it may be that Santa Anita commissioned them because a Brad Keeler backstamp has not been observed on any examples. Apart from this, the handled tray with three-dimensional Anthurium has definite eye appeal. NM, $175.00.

Santa Anita 10½" dinner plate. This is the Red Anthurium motif from the very popular Flowers of Hawaii dinnerware introduced by the Santa Anita Potteries in 1949. The line grew to include these nine diverse flora native to Hawaii: Bird of Paradise, Red Anthurium, Red Ginger, Yellow Hibiscus, Shell Ginger, Monstera Leaves, Croton Leaves, Night Blooming Cereus, and Cup of Gold. The line utilized the California Modern shape originally produced in solid pastel colors. Printed mark: "Red Anthurium" and "Santa Anita Ware, Copyright, Flowers of Hawaii, Made in California" in a oval. $65.00.

Printed mark on the night blooming cereus dinner plate and saucer by Santa Anita.

Santa Anita 10½" dinner plate and cup and saucer. Santa Anita added the Night Blooming Cereus motif to the Flowers of Hawaii dinnerware in 1950. This line was advertised with the footnote: "Styled by Iranda." Who Iranda was remains a mystery. The naturalistic images that grace the ware were accomplished using printed transfer decals. The dinner plate and saucer are marked as shown. The cup is not marked. Dinner plate, $35.00; cup and saucer, $25.00.

American Ceramic Products 10" dinner plate, and Santa Anita 10½" dinner plate. The American Ceramic Products Co. of Santa Monica acquired the manufacturing rights to Winfield China in 1946 and produced numerous dinnerware patterns using the name until the early 1960s. Winfield China's Bird of Paradise was entirely hand painted as were most of their dinnerware patterns. It was advertised as having been designed by Ayako Obuko. Ink-stamped "True Porcelain, Winfield Hand Crafted China, Made in U.S.A." $25.00. The Santa Anita Potteries' Bird of Paradise decal design was added to their popular Flowers of Hawaii line in 1950. Ink-stamped "Bird of Paradise" and "Santa Anita Ware, Copyright 1950, Flowers of Hawaii, Made in California." $65.00.

Wallace China dishes (left to right): 7" salad plate, 6½" soup bowl, 10½" dinner plate, and cup and saucer. After the success of the Westward Ho line of barbeque ware featuring Western artist Till Goodan that the M.C. Wentz Co. had commissioned and distributed, Wallace China produced additional dinnerware lines with a Western theme. The El Rancho pattern pictured here is one of them. It's a printed transfer pattern in brown on a saddle tan ground, but was not designed by Goodan because it does not include his signature. El Rancho was a complete hotel and restaurant service introduced in 1949, but it may also have been marketed through selected outlets directly to the public. The dinner and salad plates are back stamped "Wallace China Los Angeles California" and "El Rancho Pattern made exclusively for Dohrmann Hotel Supply Co." The bowl and cup and saucer bear the printed Wallace China logo. Salad plate, $65.00; soup bowl, $85.00; dinner plate, $150.00; cup and saucer, $120.00.

Printed markings on El Rancho oval platter by Wallace China.

Wallace China 15½" oval platter. Two sizes of oval platter were made in the "El Rancho" pattern and this is the larger size. The smaller size measures 13½". A printed transfer design depicting a bustling Wild West town of the 1800s is surrounded by brands and other Western imagery. $250.00.

Printed markings on Tepco China's Western Traveler chop plate.

Tepco China 10½" chop plate. The Tepco China Co. answered Wallace China's successes with Western-themed ware of their own making. This chop plate picturing a Wells Fargo Pony Express rider is an example of their Western Traveler line. Any plate larger than 9¾" was called a chop plate by Tepco. This would be considered a large dinner plate in most commercial dinnerware sets. $150.00.

Tepco China plates, 7¼" and 6¼". Here we have two more examples of Tepco's Western-themed china. The small (dessert size) plate with white background on the left pictures a cowboy on horseback hunting buffalo and has rifles all around its narrow rim. This could have been an exclusive for a hotel or restaurant, however the pattern name is unknown. Ink-stamped "Tepco China USA." $45.00. The small (bread and butter size) tan colored plate picturing a cowboy on bucking bronco surrounded by branding irons, etc., is from the Branding Irons pattern. Transfer printed "Tepco China U.S.A." $50.00.

Tepco China 11" grill plate. This grill plate with six sections has "The 49er" emblazoned on its crest and depicts scenes of the fabled gold rush of 1849 including an early view of the Port of San Francisco. This item was an exclusive for the National Corporation of America. Transfer printed "Tepco China U.S.A." and "Patents Pending, Mfg. Exclusively for The National Corporation of America by Tepco China, U.S.A." $145.00.

Tepco China oval platter, 13" x 8¾". Another exclusive design for the National Corporation of America, this oval platter commemorates a rather grisly event of the California gold rush. At its crest is the title, "Early California" but below a wagon train scene are the words, "Donner Party 1846." The Donner party gained notoriety after these gold-seekers became snowbound in the Sierras and resorted to cannibalism in order to survive. Printed mark: "Tepco China U.S.A." and "Patents Pending, Mfg. Exclusively for The National Corporation of America by Tepco China, U.S.A." $175.00.

Vernon Kilns dishes (left to right): 6½" bread and butter plate, 10½" dinner plate, and cup and saucer. Not to be outdone, Vernon Kilns introduced its Winchester 73 dinnerware in 1950 as a tie-in with the release of the movie, Winchester 73. After the Winchester Firearms Co. raised objections, the name was changed to Frontier Days. Every piece had a different printed design on it and they all required a certain amount of hand tinting. Paul Davidson created the original drawings that were used and his signature appears on each one. Note the attention to detail in the dinner plate. All items except the cup are back stamped "Hand Painted Under Glaze, Frontier Days, Vernon Kilns California U.S.A." in a circle with Western scene in the center. Bread and butter plate, $35.00; dinner plate, $75.00; cup and saucer, $50.00.

In-mold mark on Lane divided platter.

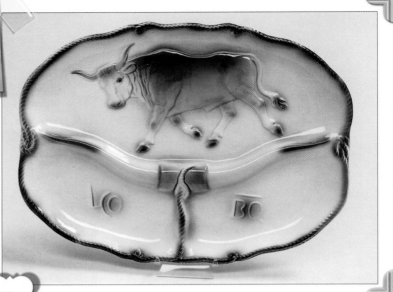

Lane divided platter, 13⁵⁄₈"W x 18¼"L. This popular divided serving platter with airbrush-decorated Western motifs in relief was introduced in the 1950s and continued to be made for a number of years. Many were used to bring grilled meat to the dinner table in those bygone lazy days of summer. $50.00.

Sascha Brastoff 10" plate. This hand-painted Sascha Brastoff plate was part of a complete dinnerware service introduced in 1950. The Western square dancers motif is consistent with themes Brastoff explored in the late 1940s and early 1950s. Because it is signed "Sascha B," it probably was painted by an assistant rather than by Brastoff himself. The backside in unmarked. $65.00.

Hand-painted mark on Hedi Schoop square dancers.

Hedi Schoop figure, 10½". This remarkable and rarely seen Hedi Schoop figure of square dancers in Western garb is especially distinguished for its colorful hand-painted decoration. It probably dates from the late 1940s. Although Hedi Schoop's business was located in North Hollywood, she slyly included the word "Hollywood" in many of her marks, but not this one. $250.00+.

CLUBS
Los Angeles Times

| PAGE 6 | TUESDAY, JULY 23, 1940 | PART II |

"You'll find it at Barker Bros."

We
Discover
a brand new young artist

We searched out the creator of these appealing flower and candle holders, and found a young lady from Switzerland, looking remarkably like her own wistful little flower girls. Her name is Hedi Shoop (you probably know her famous dancing sister, Trudie Shoop) and she designs the most wistful, charming little pottery figures we've ever seen. She tells us she not only designs the pieces, but does all the molding and coloring...so that each decorative is very much her own creation. She makes pottery trays, too, shaped like a huge slice of apple, very whimsical and smart. She's Barker Bros. own discovery, and you'll find her decoratives and trays only at Barker Bros., priced from $1.50 to $7.

FIRST FLOOR

BARKER BROS.
SEVENTH ST., FLOWER AND FIGUEROA

This Barker Bros. advertisement in the <u>LA Times</u> of July 23, 1940, announces their discovery of Hedi Schoop. An interesting note is that Trudie Schoop was the more famous of the Schoop sisters at the time.

Injunction Won by Sculptress

Former Employee Accused of Copying Her Creations

Suit for an injunction in which Hedi Schoop, sculptress, complained that a former employee had copied her line of statuettes, figurines and other bric-a-brac to compete against her commercially was decided in her favor yesterday by Superior Judge Arthur Guerin.

The court granted Miss Schoop, a sister of Trudi Schoop, ballet dancer, an injunction restraining Miss Katherine Schueftan, described as the former employee, from displaying and selling the line which Miss Hedi Schoop complained is like or very similar to hers.

Originally, Miss Hedi Schoop also had asked for $10,000 damages but the monetary plea was dropped during the trial.

Painted mark on bottom of one of the Kaye of Hollywood figures.

Clipping from the <u>Los Angeles Times</u> of April 25, 1942, reporting the outcome of Hedi Schoop's lawsuit against Katherine Schueftan.

Kaye of Hollywood figures: 11¼" (left) and 10½" (right). Katherine Schueftan, who had been one of Hedi Schoop's decorators in the late 1930s, decided in 1940 to use the knowledge gained to launch a competitive business under the fictitious name of Kim Ward. Her husband Peter joined her in the enterprise, which was located in North Hollywood, not far from her former employer's factory. These figures, of a guitar-playing cowboy and cowgirl, are representative of her derivative output that prompted a landmark lawsuit in 1942 by Hedi Schoop forcing Schueftan to cease and desist. She complied, but by 1945 had regrouped and reopened under a new name, Kaye of Hollywood. Much confusion has surrounded this situation but these seem to be the true facts of the matter. $150.00 set.

Roselane figures (left to right): 10¼", 10", 9", 9¼". Roselane produced a group of square dancers in the late 1940s or early 1950s and these are some of them. It's difficult to determine which figures were meant to be partners, and it probably doesn't matter. The rather bland glaze does nothing to enliven these rather stiff and colorless figures. Compare them with Hedi Schoop's colorful and animated depiction of the same subject. All marked in-mold "Roselane" plus individual shape number (combination number and letter). $35.00 each.

Metlox figures: cowboy, 10¾", and cowgirl, 9⅝". Here are the fore-runners of all the cowboy and cowgirl figurines produced during the 1940s and 1950s in California. Sculptor Carl Romanelli created these models for the Metlox Potteries of Manhattan Beach in 1940. The cowgirl was issued first and is seen much more frequently than her counterpart. Both have been hand decorated under glaze, but which one is faster on the draw? Cowboy is marked in-mold "Poppytrail, 1836, Made in California U.S.A." $400.00+. Cowgirl is marked in-mold "Poppytrail, 1819, C Romanelli, Made in California U.S.A." $250.00.

Metlox brochure promoting the company's artware of the late 1930s included this picture of Carl Romanelli.

ROMANELLI AT WORK

The creative genius of seven generations of Florentine sculptors lies behind the masterful skill of C. Romanelli . . . whose notable contributions to the modern world of art have been hailed by connoisseurs. Metlox is proud to present Mr. Romanelli's masterpieces in Art Pottery.

Brayton Laguna cowboy on bull, 9½" x 11½", and cowboy on horse, 11¼" x 11". Bill Dickenson, one of the many talented artist-designers that Brayton worked with, modeled these rodeo riders. They were produced in basic woodtone or, like these examples, in woodtone with hand-painted riders and are not easy to find. NM, $125.00.

Incised mark on unglazed bottom of Esther Shirey figure.

Esther Shirey figure, 8½". This cowboy figure in polychrome-glazed terra cotta is standing on a horseshoe-shaped base. It's a charming piece by Esther Shirey, a California ceramist who is not well known and deserves more recognition for the quality work she produced in the 1930s and 1940s. $125.00.

Ivar of Hollywood bookends, 9⅞" (left) and 10¼" (right). Little is known about this individual or his business, but these skillfully modeled and nicely decorated figures of cowboys almost certainly date from the 1940s. The fences that hold the books upright also support these dudes. The felt covered bottoms of the bookends have attached paper labels reading "Ivar of Hollywood." NP.

Robaul wallpocket, 7½" x 9½". Robaul of California is another enigmatic company that produced a variety of giftware. Seen most often are modern designs, but this item with a comical cowboy sitting on a fence may be an earlier design, c. 1949. Behind the figure is a simple rectangular planter with a hole for hanging on the backside. In-mold: "Robaul of California C-7." NP.

Billee Vier figure, 5", and Hagen-Renaker horse, 3⅛" x 3". Though separate companies produced these two small figurines, they look like they were made for each other. The cowboy holding a rope is simply incised "Billee Vier" and appears to be an item produced at the California Faience works in Berkeley, probably in the mid-to-late 1940s. NP. The horse is an early (c. 1949) model by Tom Masterson. Masterson was one of the first designers hired by Hagen-Renaker, which got its start in Monrovia in 1946. NM, $85.00.

Esther Shirey flower holder figure, 6½" x 6". Another appealing terra cotta model by Esther Shirey, of a Mexican boy seated on an oxcart with a colorful serape over his shoulder, is seen here. An enclosed space in back is provided for planting or for a small arrangement of flowers. Incised "Esther Shirey." $100.00.

Crowell figure, 8¼". This figure of an Indian standing next to a large wagon wheel is the likeness of one of the lead characters in the famous outdoor pageant *Ramona*. Produced annually in the desert community of Hemet, this ill-fated love story between a young lady of means named *Ramona* and a Native American suitor named *Alessandro* takes place during the fabled early days of California. The production runs for a limited time every year and has been going on for decades. Apparently, figurines of *Alessandro* and his lover *Ramona* (and perhaps other characters) were produced in the 1940s by a small pottery in Hemet as mementos of the pageant. *NP*.

Painted mark on bottom of
Alessandro figure by Crowell.

Cleminsons figures: Indian boy on donkey, 7⅛", and Indian girl, 3⅝". The California Cleminsons did not make many outright figurines as most of their items were conceived with a practical purpose in mind. These Native American children were based on the popular Canyon Kiddies comic strip by James Swinnerton that appeared in *Good Housekeeping* in the 1920s. The original series chronicled the activities of several Navajo kids on their reservation near the Grand Canyon. In the early 1940s, Betty Cleminson modeled four figures plus a three-piece set of dishes for children based on the Swinnerton characters, and these are two of them. All the kiddies had names. On the left is *Tee Hotte*, who seems unconcerned that his mule appears less than sure-footed. $150.00. The name of the shy little girl is *Neeta See*. *NM*, $100.00.

Page from a Cleminsons sales brochure of the early 1940s picturing the Canyon Kiddies.

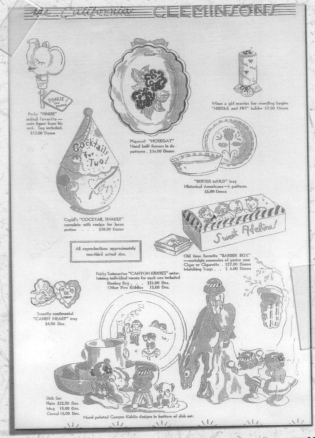

Gilner vase with figure, 6⅞". Although unmarked, this totem pole-shaped vase with small Indian boy attached is believed to have been made by the Gilner Potteries of Culver City. Gilner was owned and operated by Beryle Gilner and his son Burt. Gilner produced similar articles in the late 1940s and early 1950s in the same dark green glaze. NM, $45.00.

Poinsettia Studios miniature bell, 2½". Poinsettia Studios was known in the giftware business for its small hand-decorated figural shakers and other novelty items. Some items came with a ribbon attached, like this pint-sized bell in the shape of a teepee. Paper label on inside. $35.00.

Hedi Schoop flower holder figures, 8⅜" (left) and 8" (right). These Hedi Schoop angels are normally found with white faces. These dark-skinned examples are curious as well as unusual. Only the skin color has changed; the hair remains white. Angels apparently have a style all their own. As an émigré from a country with no ethnic variety (Switzerland), Hedi Schoop must have been moved by the diversity she found in Los Angeles and that perhaps explains these altered angels. They were designed to either sit or hang on the wall. Openings for flowers are in their wings. Painted mark on both: "Hedi Schoop." $200.00.

Incised mark on bottom of McCarty Bros. black boy figurine.

McCarty Brothers figure, 4³⁄₈". The McCarty brothers, Lee and Willard, established a pottery business at their home in Sierra Madre about 1941. Lee made the original models and Willard attended to their production. This figurine of a little black boy holding a watermelon (c. 1945) is somewhat unusual for the McCarty Bros since most of their production consisted of boy and girl planter sets of various nationalities. Depictions of African Americans were generally cliché laden at the time and this one is no exception, although cute and nicely decorated. $65.00.

West Coast advertisement from the December, 1945 issue of Giftwares.

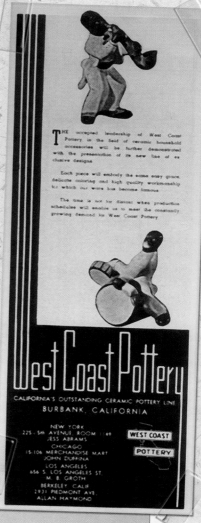

West Coast figures (left to right): 7¹⁄₈", 6¹⁄₂", 6⁵⁄₈", 5⁵⁄₈". Ray Murray was the designer of this fabulous jazz ensemble. The four amusing (without being derogatory) black musicians in their white tuxedos are a classic representation of the swing era. Often mistaken for Brayton Laguna, these hand-decorated West Coast figures are marked only with their inventory number: "1014D." $125.00 each.

Unidentified figure, 2⅝" x 5⅞". This delightful figure is signed "Mortashed" but the implication of the signage remains speculative. It's another mystery for the readers to hopefully solve. Other figures (both black and white) by the same modeler, who may have been associated with a Los Angeles company called Rick's Figurines, have been noted. Rick's Figurines were made from a composition material. Painted mark: "Mortashed." NP.

Kenny Dills figures, 3⅝" (left) and 3¼" x 4" (right). Controversy seems to swirl around these cute little figurines. Originally known as the Twinsies, Kenny Dills modeled them and Edward R. Darvill distributed them beginning around 1945. Darvill was also a manufacturer so he very likely produced them as well. The controversy stems from the fact that some of these figures turn up wearing (besides their diapers) a Dorothy Kindell sticker. This is one of the things that can make California pottery a researcher's nightmare. What probably transpired at some point is the sale or transfer of the molds to Kindell. NM, black, $75.00; white, $45.00.

Josef Originals figures, 4¾" and 4¼". Muriel Joseph George, the creative force behind Josef Originals, is responsible for these charming native African children. The girl's name is Congo and the boy's Bongo. They date from about 1950 and were among the early successes that Josef Originals of Monrovia enjoyed. Besides paper labels that read "Josef Originals California" they also bear individual name tags. Congo, $90.00; Bongo, $120.00.

Freeman-McFarlin miniatures, 2⅝" and 2". These unmarked miniatures are believed to be products of the Freeman-McFarlin Potteries of El Monte. They are crude, comical depictions of native African women and perhaps represent cannibals. This was a popular subject in the late 1940s and early 1950s for pottery manufacturers and is representative of the ethnic stereotyping common to the period. NM, $35.00 each.

Incised mark on Landaker humidor reads "Landaker Original Ceramics."

Landaker humidor, 6¾". Harold C. Landaker produced this tobacco humidor at his Pacific Grove studio, c. 1950. A former painter, Landaker apparently embraced ceramics after the medium became so commercially viable in California during WWII. Like many others at the time, he integrated unglazed areas that were stained brown with a variety of colorful crackle glazes. Many of his items were humorous but this head of a native African man is unusually commanding. $200.00.

This ad from an early 1950s issue of <u>Giftwares</u> was placed by Landaker representative W.A. Curie, and pictures items similar to the humidor.

Will-George figures, 11" and 11½". These marvelous and rarely seen African natives by The Claysmiths date from about 1950. Their exaggerated poses and speckled glazes are somewhat atypical of the work of Will Climes. Speckled glazes eventually became widespread during the 1950s. Incised "Will-George." $500.00+ set.

Brayton Laguna figures, 7⅛" (left) and 6⅞" (right). Frances Robinson designed these attractive Dutch children, part of a series of international kids she modeled for the Laguna Beach business. Brayton can largely be credited for the proliferation of figurines in California during the 1940s and 1950s. The company started making figurines in the mid-1930s and none other than Walt Disney took notice. In 1938, Brayton was the first company licensed to manufacture three-dimensional likenesses of his famous cartoon characters. The pottery's early successes gave rise to a host of hand-decorated sets like this Dutch boy and girl in the 1940s. Ink-stamped marks. $150.00 set.

West Coast figures, 6⅝" (left) and 5¾" (right). Figurines proliferated during the 1940s and it appears that every California producer rushed to market with a version of the Dutch boy and girl. These are the West Coast Pottery models, designed by Thelma Kyn. The girl holds an open basket for flowers. The boy is simply a figure. Besides the Dutch interpretation, they could also be seen as Swiss or Tyrolean children. I will let the reader decide. Incised mark on girl: "West Coast Pottery, Original Design by Thelma Kyn." Incised mark on boy: "Original by Thelma Kyn." In addition, both have the painted shape number: "1041D." $90.00 set.

Rarely seen paper label on bottom on Jean Manley female figure.

Jean Manley figures, 7¼" (left) and 8" (right). Jean Manley created this charming set of Dutch kids. Manley, a Canadian-born self-taught artist who started modeling in clay while still in her teens, produced her initial line in North Hollywood in a home-based studio. Increased demand for her handmade figures that resembled rag dolls dictated that molds be made and many of her most popular items were cast. This slip-cast set dates from about 1940. Sometime later, she relocated her business from the San Fernando Valley to the San Gabriel Valley. There is a paper label on the female figure but labeled or marked examples of her work are scarce. $200.00 set.

Weil figural flower holders, 7¼" (left) and 6⅞" (right). These Weil Ware hand-decorated Dutch children carry baskets that can accommodate a few dried or fresh flowers. They date from about 1948 and are more refined than the average example of Max Weil's earlier California Figurine Co. line. Ink-stamped with the Weil Ware logo plus handwritten numbers, on boy: "3040" and girl: "3041." $90.00 set.

S-Quire figures, 6½" (left) and 7" (right). Zaida was the designer of the figurines produced by S-Quire Ceramics of Los Angeles. Del Squire Jonas, formerly associated with the California Figurine Co, established the business, located at 2822 Benedict St., in 1943. Zaida had an interesting background. She was the daughter of Al Sears, a silent movie personality, and became a dancer and figure model before turning to art. She later married Larry Grannis, a radio personality in the 1960s. Her version of the popular Dutch children theme includes potted ceramic tulips. The sophistication and attention to detail of the decoration elevated S-Quire figures well above the average in California. Both ink-stamped: "S-Quire Ceramics California by Zaida." $150.00 set.

Painted mark under the glaze on backside of Modglin plaque.

Anton and Tanya
Modglin's
Original

Modglin plaque, 9¾". The Modglin Co. was in the pottery business for only about five years. Established in 1940 by A. Lois Modglin and her husband William, and located at 3809-17 Eagle Rock Blvd. in Los Angeles, the facility was purchased by Stewart B. McCulloch in 1945. While it was working, the pottery specialized in figurines, of both animal and human kind. This plaque with dancing Dutch peasant kids is unusual. Two shades of a velvety ribbon were woven through holes pierced in the clay and tied at the top. $40.00.

Yona

Yona plates, 11". These decorative wall plates were hand painted by Yona Lippin, another former Hedi Schoop decorator who opted to go into business for herself during the prosperous war years. Her early flower holder figures, which differed little from the work of her mentor, are much more commonly found than these painted plates that exhibit her spirited graphic flair. $50.00 each.

Painted mark on backside of Yona plates.

This photo of Yona appeared in the February 1946 issue of Ceramic Industry magazine.

Florence flower holder figures, 6¾". Florence Ward of Florence Ceramics of Pasadena modeled these figures that also function as flower holders. They appear to be Northern European, perhaps German peasant girls holding baskets. They demonstrate how the same model can be quite different in appearance depending on the hand decoration applied to it. Ink-stamped "Florence Ceramics, Pasadena California, Copyright" in a circle. $150.00 each.

La Mirada figure, 9³/₄". The La Mirada Potteries were one of the first to feature Oriental (Chinese) style figures in their line. They produced many different models over the years they were in business. This proper Mandarin gentleman with large storage jar is glazed in the turquoise crackle that Cecil Jones developed with the help of George Robertson of the Robertson Pottery. It dates from about 1940 and is unmarked. $60.00.

Poinsettia Studios figures, 7¼". Items made by the Poinsettia Studios are usually small, even miniature, in scale, so these larger figures of children of the Swiss Alps are unusual. Their hand-painted details have a distinctive European look that adds authenticity to the subjects depicted. Both of these innocent-looking children have mountain goats with them. Paper label reading "Poinsettia Studios." $150.00 set.

Roselane figures (left to right): M, 7¼"; W, 6⁷/₈"; M, 5²/₃"; W, 5⁷/₈". Roselane was another company that produced numerous Chinese figures as well as associated bowls and vases. Robert "Bill" Fields modeled these very authentic looking statuettes in the late 1940s after returning from war duty. The glazes integrate muted tones of brown and gray and impart a refined dignity to the figures. Most bear paper labels. $25.00 – 50.00 each.

Hedi Schoop figures, 13⅝" (left) and 13⅜" (right). Hedi Schoop produced a variety of Chinese figures, in pairs, of both children and adults. The marketing strategy of producing pairs or sets of figures traces its origins in California to the Brayton Laguna Pottery. In the mid-1930s, Durlin Brayton, Andy Anderson, and other designers created entire ensembles of figurines at Brayton. This matter raises some interesting questions. For instance, is there any value to purchasing only half of a pair of figures? And does owning a complete set add value to its individual components? Naturally, it's preferable to purchase an already matched pair. But since this is not always an option, I believe the answer depends on how rare the set is. If they're scarce, it might be better to continue looking because sooner or later, a complete set will turn up. Value is increased to some extent by having both halves of a pair, but if a set consists of many figures and it's complete, the value is increased greatly. Each figure in this matched pair by Hedi Schoop holds an open box allowing for the insertion of cut flowers. A liberal amount of overglaze gold has been used. Ink-stamped "Hedi Schoop Hollywood." $75.00 each; $180.00 set.

Stewart B. McCulloch figures, 14". A pair of these large Chinese figures was used on the set of the popular I Love Lucy television series of the 1950s. They sat on either end of the mantle in the Richardos' New York apartment. Stewart B. McCulloch, who got his start in the business with Modglin, produced them after purchase of the Modglin pottery facility in 1945. It isn't known whether he actually designed or modeled any of the ware he produced, including this set that dates from about 1950. The faces are nicely painted but the hands are rather cartoonish. In-mold: "© Stewart B. McCulloch, 2620, Authentic California." $150.00 set.

Joy Thompson figures, 11³⁄₈" (left) and 12¹⁄₈" (right). Joy Thompson titled this pair, Cathay Lovers. Thompson shared workspace in Ernest A. Batchelder's Kinneloa Kilns factory in Pasadena in the 1940s. Their wares coordinated well and were often displayed together at the gift shows. Joy Thompson was an accomplished ceramic sculptor who produced some of her work commercially to make it more affordable. However, with all the hand detailing and painting required, her figures were not particularly cost effective and were marketed to a discriminating clientele who could afford them. This demure yet regal-looking Chinese couple with blossoming tree forms in back demonstrate her modeling skills. Written under-glaze: "Joy Thompson" along with "Cathay Lovers." $500.00+ set.

Undated photograph of Joy Thompson.

Handwritten underglaze mark on Joy Thompson figure with faun.

Joy Thompson figure, 5¹⁄₂" x 4¹⁄₂". This seated woman in Mandarin attire with a fawn at her side is another figure of exceptional quality produced in Pasadena in the 1940s. A listing of Southern California pottery manufacturers of the 1940s has Joy Thompson located at 99 S. Raymond Ave. Evidently, she relocated sometime in the mid to late 1940s. It's been suggested that Thompson studied with Susi Singer. There are noticeable similarities in their work so it may very well be true. $200.00.

Joy Thompson figure, 10⅞". This attenuated figure by Joy Thompson of a woman playing a concertina is a tad unexpected. It's not the usual way she modeled the human figure and has certain characteristics in common with fashion illustration. Notice that the colors used on this curious figure are the same as those seen on the seated figure with fawn. Handwritten mark: "Joy Thompson." $250.00.

Ink-stamped mark on Stewart B. McCulloch figure.

Stewart B. McCulloch figure, 5½" x 9½". This alluring figure of a stylish Asian woman is almost certainly the likeness of Chinese film star Anna May Wong, who appeared in numerous Hollywood pictures in the 1920s, 1930s, and 1940s. $150.00.

Painted mark of Walter Wilson flower holder figure named Toy Ming.

Walter Wilson flower holder figures, 9" (left) and 8⅞" (right). Walter Wilson's business was located in Pasadena at 721 N. Los Robles Ave. Walter Wilson was another individual who fits in that gray area between distributor and manufacturer. He started out as a jobber and eventually established his own line of goods. Whether he designed any of the items produced is unknown. The exact dates when Wilson conducted business are also unknown, but he was well established by 1950. Toy Ming and Ho-Jai are the respective names of these Chinese figures attached to stepped bases. Each one holds an object that serves as a container for flowers. First-rate modeling and hand painting distinguish this pair. $100.00 set.

Walter Wilson planter with figures, 7¼" (left) and 8" (right). These young-looking Chinese figures have large containers with them that can function either as vases or planters. The female figure holds a parasol with a white plastic handle. These figural planters are similar to those produced by the McCarty Brothers, which Walter Wilson distributed. It's probable, but unproven, that Lee McCarty modeled them for Wilson. Paper label on female figure reads "Walter Wilson Pasadena California." $90.00 set.

Kaye of Hollywood flower holder figures, 10⅜" (left) and 9" (right). These Chinese figures carrying large baskets suspended from yokes demonstrate how Katherine Schueftan had begun to find her own style by the time these items were produced in 1945. The lawsuit her former employer, Hedi Schoop, initiated and won had made it a necessity. Her work here is no longer as overtly derivative of Schoop but has unique features that are convincing and noteworthy. Painted mark on man: "Kaye 328," and woman: "Kaye 329," plus she is dated "7/48." $125.00 set.

Full-page Kaye of Hollywood ad in The Gift and Art Buyer of November 1945 announcing the Ebeling & Reuss Co. as her new distributor. Note Chinese figures.

115

Painted mark on Hedi Schoop flower holder figure.

Hedi Schoop flower holder figure, 8½". Hedi Schoop originally called this flower holder figure of two Chinese kids, China's Children, but later changed it to Young China. Both hold baskets for flowers. Although the boy seems to be having a bad hair day, it's a charming piece and one of Schoop's bestsellers. $135.00.

Page from a Hedi Schoop catalog of the early 1940s with her renderings of the various models. Note China's Children.

No.107
AMERICAN GIRL
13"
Price $5.00

No.108
JOSEPHINE
13"
Price $5.00

No.108T
JOSEPHINE - *TEXTURE*
Price $6.00

No.109
DEBUTANTE
12½"
Price $5.50

No.109T
DEBUTANTE - *TEXTURE*
Price $6.50

No.110
CHINAS
CHILDREN
8½"
Price
$5.00

S-Quire figures, 6³/₄" (left) and 6⁵/₈" (right).
Superb modeling by Zaida and subsequent hand
decoration add greatly to the appeal of this set of
Chinese children. He holds a bowl of handmade
flowers. She wears flowers in her hair made from
delicate strands of extruded clay. $135.00 set.

The bottoms of the S-Quire
figurines reveal their various
ink-stamped markings.

Brad Keeler planter with figures, 5¼" x 10".
Ethnic stereotyping can be seen in this figural
planter of two Chinese kids posed with a
large laundry basket. The Ming Dragon Blood
glaze was used on the coolie hats. $85.00.

Ink-stamped mark on unglazed
bottom of Brad Keeler figural
planter. Notice that this design
was copyrighted.

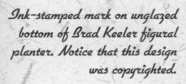

"Cholly" say—
"More better sprinkle
BOTTLE
WAY—
than squirt through
TEETHEE
All the day."

Cleminsons laundry sprinkler bottle, 8¼". Here's another example of the notion that equated the Chinese in America with laundries at the time. Known as Sprinkle Boy, this device was used to dampen clothes prior to ironing them and was a big seller for the Cleminsons. The backside of the original hangtag with a Betty Cleminson verse is shown. Ink-stamped Cleminsons logo plus "Hand Painted." $120.00 with tag.

Betty Cleminson modeling the
Sprinkle Boy laundry sprinkler.

Josef Originals figures, 4" (left) and 3½" (right). Two versions of the same figurine are seen here. Pity Sing was the name given by Muriel Joseph George to her first commercial success in 1946. These small figures were originally produced in her garage, a familiar launching pad in the history of California pottery. The hat proved troublesome and two different styles were ultimately produced. The red on the feet and hat was, in industry jargon, cold painted. In-mold marks plus paper labels. $50.00 each.

Yona figures, 5³/₄" (left) and 5⁵/₈" (right). The popularity of Chinese figures during the post-war 1940s must be apparent by now. This small set by Yona Lippin, which dates from about 1945, is representative of her early approach with its obvious debt to Hedi Schoop. Painted mark: "Yona 35." $65.00 set.

Incised mark on bottom of the McCarty Bros Hindu Boy. Note the date of manufacture, a common feature of McCarty Bros ware.

McCarty Bros. flower holder figures, 8" (left) and 8¹/₄" (right). These McCarty Bros. children were known as Hindu Boy and Hindu Girl. Lee McCarty modeled this set in 1944 but these particular examples were produced in 1946. By 1948, as reported in the trade, the McCarty brothers had severed ties with Walter Wilson and begun handling the distribution of their own line. Sets of children of various nationalities were produced in the 1940s. $65.00 set.

Full-page Walter Wilson ad in the August 1947 issue of The Gift and Art Buyer features the American children, Billy and Betsy, by the McCarty Bros.

The 1940s

Weil figures, 6¾" (left) and 4¾" (right). These Burmese dancers are something of a departure for Max Weil's California Figurine Company. They probably are eleventh-hour items, produced about the time (1946) he renamed the business to Weil of California. Their angular modeling and abbreviated decoration hint of things to come in the 1950s. $75.00 set.

Back views of the Burmese dancers showing intact paper labels. These labels were put on all California Figurine Co. items but most of them have been lost to time.

Dorothy Kindell figures, 13½". Dorothy Kindell became well known in the 1950s for her audacious nudes. These Balinese performers are the largest and most spectacular examples of her modeling skills. They have an abundance of overglaze gold and were also produced as lamp bases. The figures depicted in California pottery by the late 1940s were becoming more and more exotic. In-mold: "© Dorothy Kindell." $300.00 set.

Knowles, Taylor & Knowles wall pocket, 7¼". This figural wall pocket by KTK of Burbank of an androgynous Asian with elaborate headdress makes good use of one of the company's skillfully blended glazes. These were achieved by spraying one color over another prior to a final trip through the kiln. Incised "KTK Calif 417" and "L," which may indicate that this was the left half of a pair. $45.00.

Vadna miniature masks, 2¾". These unusual Vadna Ware mini masks appear to be depictions of East Indians and their matte brown glaze helps to reinforce the notion. Vadna was located in Leucadia, which is on the coast north of San Diego. Ink-stamped "Vadna Ware Leucadia California." NP.

Interesting mark on the backside of Pat and Covey Stewart plate.

Pat and Covey Stewart plate, 8¾". Pat and Covey Stewart's pottery was one of many that sprang up in the artist colony of Laguna Beach in the 1940s and 1950s. Inspired by the successes of the Brayton Laguna Pottery and the Kay Finch Studio (in nearby Corona del Mar) many artists who were basically oil painters or watercolorists turned to pottery production. A ready outlet existed in the Pottery Shack, a retail store and world-famous Laguna Beach landmark. Unfortunately, little is known about the Stewarts other than they managed to achieve technical excellence with their imaginative line. Superbly painted decorative plates like this one of a Russian Cossack were a large part of their output. Signed on the front, "Pat Stewart." $65.00.

All the colors in the spectrum appear in this pottery display at Laguna Beach, a town where nearly everyone has his own kiln.

DINING OFF THE RAINBOW

This photo was featured in the interesting article, "Dining off the Rainbow" by Frank J. Taylor, that appeared in the November 19, 1949, issue of The Saturday Evening Post. It pictures shoppers in the outdoor section of the famous Pottery Shack in Laguna Beach where seconds were typically sold.

Painted mark on S-Quire Russian man. The woman is similarly marked but the model number is 102.

S-Quire figures, 10⅝" (left), and 11½" (right). This handsome pair of Russian peasants is just another example of the fine quality figures that S-Quire Ceramics produced from original models sculpted by Zaida. The company must have been very selective in the decorators they hired because the hand painting on their ware is consistently excellent. They frequently used a pink-tinted clay body. $200.00 set.

This S-Quire ad appeared in the Giftwares issue of August 1946.

Joy Thompson figures, 11³/₄" (left) and 12" (right). Russian nobles are the subjects of these exquisite Joy Thompson figures. The attention to detail is truly a hallmark of her series of figures of various nationalities produced in the 1940s. A pet Russian wolfhound accompanies the man. Handwritten mark: "Joy Thompson Calif." and "Russian." $500.00+ set.

Joy Thompson figures, 12⁷/₈" (left) and 11¹/₄" (right). These figures are representative of two of the four seasons. The male is titled Autumn and the female Spring. Both figures have intertwining vines with attached flowers. Again, the detailing is exceptional in these Joy Thompson figures. It's unclear why the bases have pierced openings. Perhaps they were meant to hold small flowers. Handwritten: "Joy Thompson Calif" with "Autumn" and "Spring" added. $500.00+ set.

Joy Thompson dancer, 12¹/₈". Here is an example of a Joy Thompson original. She modeled, glazed, painted, and signed it. Her ceramic sculptures may have been marketed differently than the cast pieces, and probably were pricier. They are understandably hard to find today but worth knowing about and keeping an eye out for. Handwritten signatures on bottom and backside of base. $500.00+.

Joy Thompson figure, 5", and base, 1¹/₄"H x 13¹/₂"W. This is an unusual Joy Thompson figure with separate base. The young woman's hands and face were left unglazed and the rest of the piece glazed satin-matte ivory. The base is reversible. The underside is a contrasting matte green, but this is the preferable arrangement as there's just enough of a lip on the base for adding a spot of water so small blossoms can be floated around. Incised "Joy Thompson Pasadena." $200.00 set.

Dubby of Hollywood dancer, 13³⁄₄". Dubby of Hollywood was a short-lived business located in Hollywood. It was owned by E.O. "Dubby" Davidson and his wife Eilene, both formerly associated with KTK in Burbank. The pottery only operated for a few years prior to its relocation to Texas (and change of name.) This appealing hand-painted figure of a dancer has a painted mark reading "Dubby of Hollywood." NP. (Chris Crain photo)

DeLee dancer, 11½", and drummer, 8". Jimmy Lee Stewart modeled this superb set of Cuban performers named Pedro and Panchita. Introduced about 1950, they represent the more polished and mature side of deLee Art's production. Overglaze gold and red cold paint were added to the figures as a final touch. Fewer of these figures were made, which makes them especially sought today. In-mold, on the dancer: "De Lee Art." The drummer is not marked (but both started out with paper labels attached). $450.00 set.

Jimmie Lee Stewart, on the left, and friend Barbara Willis, on the right, at a Registered California banquet, c. 1952.

Detail of an undated deLee Art price list that features Jimmie Lee Stewart's illustrations of some of her company's popular models.

Unidentified dancers, 12½" (left) and 13⅝" (right). The in-mold mark on this pair of animated dancers in exotic Arabian costumes is indecipherable. Hopefully, someone out there can shed some light on this extraordinary set of figures. NP.

Cole-Merris figure, 9½". Bob Cole and Herb Merris were the owners of Cole-Merris Ceramics, a small pottery based in San Gabriel. The young partners were just getting their artware line firmly established when they both were drafted in 1942. During the war, Will and George Climes agreed to continue production of their line. It's unknown when this uniquely styled figure was made. NP.

Raised in-mold mark on Cole-Merris figure. Note dark clay color.

Muriel busts, 11¾" (left) and 12" (right). These unmarked busts of stylish society ladies are consistent with items that Muriel Joseph George produced in Pasadena before the founding of Josef Originals. Apparently, Muriel of California was sold to Stanley Stocker, because he was the listed owner in the California Manufacturers Registers of 1948, 1949, and 1950. The business was located at 1242 N. Fair Oaks. NM, $150.00 each.

Florence bust, 6¾". This bust of a regal white-haired lady from a bygone era is not marked but is unmistakably the work of Florence Ward. Pompadour is the name of the piece but the exact date of production is unknown. The addition of lace, roses, other hand-applied trim, and gold gilding add value to Florence figures. NM, $300.00+.

Heirlooms of Tomorrow porcelain bust, 6¾". Heirlooms of Tomorrow was located in Manhattan Beach. The business was established in 1944 by William D. Bailey and specialized in Dresden and Meissen style figurines as well as decorative housewares with an abundance of lace trim, applied roses, and other trimmings as well as gold. At its peak in the early 1950s, HOT employed 135 people. Florence Ceramics of Pasadena was a direct competitor, but Heirlooms seemed to lavish more lace on their product line. The delicate lace was easily damaged and rarely is a completely intact figurine found today. This bust of an elegant elder was produced using pink-tinted porcelain. The wholesale price in 1952 was $15.00. Paper label reading "An Original by Heirlooms of Tomorrow Manhattan Beach Calif." $90.00.

This Heirlooms of Tomorrow ad appeared in the July 1948 issue of Giftwares.

Printed backstamp, painted name and shape number, and paper label on bottom of Heirlooms of Tomorrow Mabel figurine.

Heirlooms of Tomorrow porcelain figure, 5⅛". This demure young lady named Mabel in period attire dates from the late 1940s to the early 1950s and would be considered a miniature figurine. But even though small in stature, the company obviously did not skimp on the lace trim. Miraculously none of the delicate lace or other trappings has been lost to time. After the business relocated to nearby Torrance and changed its name to California Originals, Architectural Pottery occupied their original plant. $175.00.

Lee Wollard porcelain figure, 9½". Wendy is the name Lee Wollard assigned to this lovely porcelain figure. Lee and his wife Bonnie, the owners of the West Coast Pottery, purchased a property across the street from KTK (where they got their start in the business) at 1104 Chestnut St. in Burbank in 1946, and established Lee Wollard Ceramics. This second company specialized in Dresden type porcelain figurines with an abundance of hand-applied lace trim and roses, and remained in business until the mid-1950s. $85.00.

This Lee Wollard photo from the February 1953 issue of *Registered California Pictorial* shows a few its of its exquisite porcelain figurines. Wendy is on the right.

Exquisite china figurines by LEE WOLLARD CHINA COMPANY to satisfy the most discriminating customer. Perfect in every detail and beautiful to behold, these lovely ladies are in the tradition of fine craftsmanship. Write for catalog to LEE WOLLARD CHINA COMPANY, 1104 Chestnut, Burbank, California.

YONA
25B

Painted mark on Yona figure.

Yona figure, 9". Yona was one of the ceramists in California who added hand-applied lace and/or handmade blossoms and bows to her more elaborate figures, like this one of a smartly dressed young lady holding a bouquet of roses and a parasol. This attractive Yona piece dates from about 1948. $65.00.

Brayton Laguna figure, 9½". Walter Bringhurst was the designer of the company's Gay 90s line of the 1940s that included this flirtatious lass, her weight balanced on an elaborate parasol while discreetly revealing a shapely leg. It's an exceptionally well decorated example and is incised, rather enigmatically, "Bob's First Lady." $125.00.

Hand painted Regal Calif.

Painted mark on Padre Regal flower holder figure.

Padre flower holder figure, 10". This same piece has also been noted marked with a Weil Ware backstamp. This brings up another issue. Occasionally, molds originated by one company would be retired and sold to another company. Some of Gladding-McBean's Catalina Pottery molds were transferred to Max Weil around 1945. I believe Padre first produced this shape in various monochrome glazes. Later (c. 1939), the shape was added to the Regal collection and received the treatment seen here. Then sometime later, Weil acquired the master mold. This may have taken place in 1943, after a fire destroyed the Padre factory. In-mold: "Padre 607" plus painted mark. $70.00.

Modglin figure, 9³/₈". Here is another demure lady figurine, this one by Modglin, with a flowered dress and even flowers in her hair. A combination of airbrush and hand painting was used here. Painted mark: "Original," a common marking on Modglin items. $45.00.

Betty Lou Nichols figure, 9⁷/₈". Olga is the name of this peasant woman by Betty Lou Nichols. Besides her famous head vases, Nichols produced a variety of figurines and other giftware in her La Habra pottery. The business began, as so many did, in a home-based studio and relocated when the volume of orders demanded a larger facility and more workers. This doll-like figure, from the Pleasant Peasants series, dates from the late 1940s or early 1950s and is not hard to find. Painted marks include "Betty Lou Nichols" and "Olga." $60.00.

From a Ruth Sloan brochure promoting the Betty Lou Nichols line, this page pictures groups of full figures that Nichols produced in addition to the Pleasant Peasants.

129

West Coast figure, 8½". Thelma Kyn was the designer of this West Coast Pottery figurine of a young woman. After West Coast started producing hand-decorated items such as this, the designer's name was sometimes incorporated into the mark, giving them some recognition for their work. In-mold: "West Coast Pottery, Original Design by Thelma Kyn." $50.00.

Weil flower holder figure, 10½". This sophisticated lady, produced near the end of Weil's California Figurine Co. period, has more panache than many of the earlier models. Max Weil's lucrative pottery, which was located at 3160 San Fernando Road in Los Angeles, seems to have produced the greatest variety and volume of these flower holder figurines, and particularly female figures. NM, $80.00.

Weil flower holder figures, 10". Both of these Weil Ware lady vases are nicely painted and date from the late 1940s. The one on the left has the trappings of a country girl while the one on the right would be a city slicker. Ink-stamped Weil Ware logo on each one. $75.00 each.

A Hedi Schoop Original

Backside of the Hedi Schoop one-of-a kind plaque.

Hedi Schoop plaque, 11⅛" x 7¼". Ceramic artists recognized for their three-dimensional objects occasionally produced items with flat surfaces such as plates, plaques, or tiles. Hedi Schoop was no exception and she frequently hand painted and signed them. This female figure in a tropical setting combines brushed on color with incised graphics and is enhanced by its dramatic black background. Signed on the face: "Hedi." $150.00.

Hedi Schoop, c. 1948.

Dorothy Kindell figure, 10" x 10". Her nudes are what brought Dorothy Kindell to the attention of the majority of giftware buyers. Her daring portrayal of the female body in the 1940s and 1950s resulted in increased public awareness and sales at a time when nudity was almost unheard of in popular culture. These matching figures of a Polynesian woman with legs up may have been designed as bookends. When mounted on the wall, an individual figure could serve as a gentleman's tie rack. In-mold: "Dorothy Kindell ©." $175.00 each.

In-mold mark on bottom of Dorothy Kindell mugs.

Dorothy Kindell mug set, 5" (average height). This Eye Appeal Barware, as the set was billed, depicts a strip tease. A large matching pitcher was also produced. Dorothy Kindell's pottery business got started in the early 1940s in Laguna Beach but was relocated to 2721 E. Coast Highway, Corona del Mar about ten years later. Each mug is marked in-mold "© Dorothy Kindell." However, this did not deter knockoffs. $45.00 each.

In-mold mark on Dorothy Kindell sophisticated lady head vase.

Dorothy Kindell head vases, 7½" (left) and 7" (right). Dorothy Kindell created several head vase designs. The sophisticated lady on the left was one of her most popular. The one on the right is more stylized and has Art Deco traces. In-mold: "© Dorothy Kindell." Sophisticated lady, $50.00. Deco lady, $85.00.

Betty Lou Nichols head vases (left to right), 6³/₄", 5⁵/₈", and 5³/₄". Ermintrude is the name Betty Lou Nichols gave to the head vase on the left but it's marked Yvonne, presumably because of the blond hair. Painted mark: "Yvonne by Betty Lou." $450.00. That's Valerie in blue in the center. Painted mark: "Valerie by Betty Lou." $350.00. On the right in the candy-striped outfit is Candy. Painted mark: "Candy by Betty Lou Nichols." $350.00. Nichols initiated the head vase craze in the late 1940s with her Flora-Dorables.

Painted mark on Kim Ward head vase.

Kim Ward head vase, 10". This Hawaiian woman balances a flower/fruit bowl on her head. Applied flowers and leaves form the outline of a lei and openings have been cut for real flowers to complete it. One of the more inventive Kim Ward pieces. $175.00.

Dubby of Hollwood head vase, 9³/₄". Teresa is the name of this good-looking Dubby of Hollywood head vase. It bears a slight resemblance to certain Weil Ware lady vases. The handmade gardenias are a nice touch. All Dubby items can be considered rare. Painted mark: "Dubby of Hollywood, Teresa." NP. (Chris Crain photo)

Dubby of Hollywood head vase, 8³/₄". This sweet-faced country girl named Sunbonnet Sue is another rarely seen Dubby of Hollywood example. Excellent hand painting distinguishes this piece. Ink-stamped "Dubby of Hollywood, Sue." NP. (Chris Crain photo)

Florence figures, 8" (left) and 7¹/₄" (right). Although they seem to be a match, these well-dressed Florence Ceramics figurines of children are representative of entirely different eras. The girl is from the Gibson Girl series of the early 1940s that depicted fashions from the turn of the twentieth century and is unmarked, $100.00. The boy with dog is dressed in French Colonial attire of the 1700s and has a paper label attached. $175.00.

Ynez figures, 6¹/₂" (left) and 6¹/₄" (right). Ynez Ward (no relation to Florence Ward) was the creator of these sweet-faced semi-porcelain children outfitted in the trappings of a bygone era. Ynez and her husband Carleton Ward began production in the early 1940s and their claim to fame was "The first successful application of lace in domestic pottery in California." This quote was included in their listing in the Sixteenth California Gift and Art Show's Fall 1942 Buyers Guide. A daughter was also involved in the business, which was located in Inglewood. Unmarked except for the paper label on boy reading "Ynez, Personality Porcelains." $150.00 set.

Cleminsons wall pocket, 7¹/₄". Most wall pockets were intended for planting or cut flowers but this one was designed to hold potholders. Marie is a maid by trade and she originally came with potholders in her pocket, but they've all been lost to time. Ink-stamped with a very small Cleminsons logo (without the children on either side) and "©." $75.00.

134

Florence figures, 5½". Florence Ceramics' Wynkin and Blynkin from the popular children's story are seen here. The boy in blue with his teddy and the girl in pink with her dolly are idealized representations of childhood in the late 1940s — early 1950s. Paper labels. $125.00 each.

Lee Wollard porcelain figures, 4½" (left) and 3½" (right). Lee Wollard of Burbank produced these porcelain figurines of brother and sister at bedtime. The boy's name is Tim, the girl's name is Pam, and the pink coloration on their bedclothes approximates a luster glaze. These well-behaved youngsters date from about 1950. $85.00 set.

Markings on bottom of Lee Wollard figure of boy. Note the well-defined feet.

Lee Wollard ad from the February 1952 issue of <u>Giftwares</u>.

178A—THORA
5" Tall . . . $8.50

189A—BARBARA
5" Tall . . . $5.00

New costume figurines in fine porcelain, appropriately decorated in dark or pastel colors.

AT ALL GIFT SHOWS

Lee Wollard

1104 CHESTNUT   •   BURBANK 12, CALIFORNIA

Brayton Laguna figures, 6³⁄₈" (left) and 4" x 4¹⁄₈" (right). Lietta Dowd was the talented artist who modeled these figures of children for the Brayton Laguna Pottery. They're from a wide assortment that proved popular during the 1940s and continue to be so today. The cute boy holding the elephant is named Arthur and is ink-stamped "Arthur, Brayton Pottery." $250.00+. His unruffled girlfriend's name is Dorothy and she is ink-stamped "Dorothy, Brayton Pottery." $150.00.

Brayton Laguna figure group, 6¹⁄₂" x 6¹⁄₂". This group of figures from the Lietta Dowd childhood series by Brayton is extraordinary. The complexity of the model may have proved difficult and limited production. The ensemble consists of three little girls and either a little boy or doll. Very nice and very rare. Paper label. $1,000.00+. (Jean Oberkirsch photo)

Jessie Grimes flower holder figure, 7¹⁄₄". Very little is known about Jessie Grimes. Located in the San Francisco Bay area, the company produced some quality figurines, like this one of a young girl holding up her apron to form a pair of openings for flowers. Excellent hand decoration adds to the appeal of this piece. Painted mark: "Jessie Grimes California." $50.00.

Kaye of Hollywood flower holder figure, 7⁵⁄₈." This endearing figure of a youthful bellhop toting containers by Kaye of Hollywood (Katherine Schueftan) dates from about 1948. Painted mark: "Kaye 358." $85.00.

Painted mark inside body cavity of girl with dog by Susi Singer.

Susi Singer figure, 3⅝". The little girl holding a dog is by the distinguished Austrian émigré Susi Singer. Her studio was located in Pasadena and her favorite subject was childhood. Melancholy seems to infuse her subjects and could have been an unintentional expression of the artist's own disability. She commonly signed her pieces with her initials. $350.00+.

Susi Singer flower holder figure, 9⅛". This may have been Susi Singer's most successful production piece since it is seen more often than any other. Singer was essentially a studio ceramist who produced cast editions of some of her ceramic sculptures. This figure of a mandolin-playing boy has a flower holder attached to its boxy base. The piece has a definite European feel. Painted mark: "SS." $150.00.

Susi Singer figures, 8½" (left) and 6" x 6" (right). Two more Susi Singer figures of children. The girl on the left holding a large doll is marked with the painted mark "SS 106." $350.00+. The girl on the right is sitting on an open book with a small space suitable for holding pocket change or jewelry. Painted mark: "SS." $300.00+.

Jane Fauntz figures, 2⅞" (left) and 3½" (right). Jane Fauntz was the creator of these cute figures. Her early creations were done in affiliation with California Faience, but she later established her own complete ceramics studio in Berkeley. Her specialty there was small-scale figurines of childhood that were similar in spirit to those of Jean Manley. An ink-stamp reading "Jane Fauntz Original" is the typical mark. Boy in sailor suit, $75.00. Baby girl, $85.00.

Jean Manley figure group, 7⅜". Young girls with ducks or geese must have been a favorite theme of Jean Manley's. Here, two girls and two ducks were combined to make a single figure group. The four components were cast separately and while still damp were joined with slip, which is often used as a form of glue. Handmade trim was attached before firing. NM, $175.00.

Jean Manley figures (left to right): girl, 2⅞" x 3⅞"; geese, 1" x 2" (average); and girl, 1⅝" x 4⅛". These Jean Manley pieces were handmade and signed by the artist. The two girls have been slip decorated and given a matte finish but no facial features. The finish on the three geese matches the girls. Painted mark on girls: "Jean Manley." Painted marks on geese: "JM." Girls, $100.00 each. Geese, $50.00 each.

Karl Roma clock, 7½" x 9". Karl Roma is an unfamiliar name but his figures of children are very reminiscent of Jean Manley. This whimsical clock with attached figures is an item undoubtedly designed for a child's room. Production date is indefinite but probably early 1940s. Incised "Karl Roma." NP.

Sorcha Boru flower holder figure, 4⅞". Twin girls dancing together form a central vessel suitable for planting or an arrangement of flowers. Sorcha Boru, the professional name of Claire Stewart, modeled and produced it during the 1940s. Incised "Sorcha Boru." $90.00.

In-mold mark on backside of circular base of Josef Originals girl with doll figure.

Brad Keeler figures, 5" (left) and 5⅛" (right). Brad Keeler produced a series of items for children called Pryde & Joy in the late 1940s – early 1950s. These small hand decorated figurines based on children's nursery rhymes are two examples. On the left is Mary, Mary Quite Contrary. Ink-stamped "Brad Keeler Made in USA" plus paper label. The other figure is Little Red Riding Hood. Identical mark and label. $85.00 each.

Josef Originals figures, 5⅞" (left) and 7⅛" (right). Two depictions of idealized childhood from Muriel Joseph George combine airbrush and hand decoration. Both marked in-mold "© M J George." The girl with doll is named Melinda. $150.00. The boy with dog is named Tommy. $200.00.

DeLee flower holder figures, 7". These figures that are also flower holders are representative of the style that Jimmie Lee Stewart developed and continually repeated during the 1940s. Most of the figures had closed eyes with amazing eyelashes. On the left is Kitty with her kitty. Her bonnet in back forms a vase. In-mold: "deLee Art Hollywood" and "© 1947." On the right is Kenny with his dog. He retains his nametag. Same in-mold mark as Kitty. $75.00 each.

Jimmie Lee Stewart, c. 1949.

Painted mark on bottom of Betty Lou Nichols's Jane figurine. Note that the name of the figure is fired on while the name "Betty Lou Nichols" is a handwritten signature.

Betty Lou Nichols figures, 3¼" (left) and 2¾" x 5" (right). Dick and Jane are the names of these delightful figurines. Jane is touching her toe and has an applied ribbon in her hair. Dick in sailor suit is admiring a pet worm. Painted marks: "Dick" and "Betty Lou." $100.00 each, without signature.

Painted mark on Carla by Ynez.

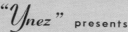

Ynez figure, 5". Carla is the name of this Ynez Ward figurine. She has a ruffled bodice made from actual lace that was dipped in slip and applied by hand to the figure. Her blond curls and the sheet music she holds were also hand applied. $45.00.

Ynez figures, 5½" (left) and 5¼" (right). Although Ynez figures can be found with paper labels indicating a porcelain body, her production was mainly earthenware. This matched set of Edwardian children is just one example of the many produced, and every figure was named. On the left is Edward, who holds his hat at his side and has a painted mark reading "Edward by Ynez." Eloise on the right is holding a petite bouquet. Painted mark: "Eloise by Ynez." $45.00 each.

This full-page ad appeared in the January 1947 issue of Giftwares. It was placed by the Paul A. Schmidt Co. on behalf of Ynez and announces new additions to her figurine line.

Photo of painted mark on Betty Lou Nichols Tom head vase.

Betty Lou Nichols head vases, 6⅛" (left) and 5⅝" (right). These are Betty Lou Nichols's representations of Mark Twain's fictional characters, Tom Sawyer and Becky Thatcher. Both have openings in their hats. Tom has a painted mark. Becky is marked in the same way but with her name in place of Tom's, $350.00 each.

Kim Ward flower holder figure, 11". This colorful depiction by Kim Ward of the famous Mark Twain character Tom Sawyer very likely had a matching Becky at one time. He has a large pocket for flowers and a smaller pocket with two emerging angleworms. The twig pole in not original. Is the pink straw hat a form of tomfoolery? Painted mark: "Kim Ward Hollywood, Hand Decorated, Tom." $120.00.

Robyn figure, 6¾". Mark Twain's Huck Finn character seems to have inspired this Robyn figure of a boy fishing. Robyn Sikking and her husband Bruce established Robyn Ceramics in Fallbrook in 1945. After the business was relocated to Idyllwild in 1955, rustic style figures like this were produced. Incised on the bottom of one foot is "Original Design by Robyn" with "Fishing Boy" incised on the bottom of the other. $125.00.

Robyn engrossed in modeling, in a photo from 1945.

In-mold mark on California Figurine Co. version and ink-stamped mark on Weil of California version of flower holder figures.

Weil flower holder figures, 7⅞" (left) and 8⅛" (right). These two figures of farm boys pushing wheelbarrows were produced only a year or so apart. The one on the left in the blue shirt was made about 1945 when Max Weil's business was still known as the California Figurine Co. In 1946, the name of the business was changed to Weil of California and the figure on the right was made shortly there-after. $65.00 each.

Hedi Schoop flower holder figure, 10⅛". The accordion this sailor is playing is also a flower holder. It was a topical item introduced in 1941, prior to the attack on Pearl Harbor. NM, $175.00.

DeLee figures (left to right), 5¾", 6", and 6". During World War II, the ceramic industry contributed in numerous ways to help the war effort. Most companies saw workers leave and join the fighting overseas. Some produced war-related items, and some produced patriotic items, like this deLee set of boys dressed in uniform. The young aviator on the left is named Jimmie. $120.00. In the center is Butch the sailor boy. $100.00. On the right, representing the army, with eyes wide open is Yard Bird. $100.00. All three figures are marked in-mold "deLee Art, USA. © 42."

Kenny Dills figures, 5½" (left) and 6" (right). Kenny Dills modeled these amusing figures of a sailor serenading a Hawaiian girl. Dills produced items for Edward R. Darvill, who was both a distributor and manufacturer. He also designed for Brayton Laguna, but these are more likely Darvill models, c. 1944. Sailor playing the ukulele is unmarked. Hawaiian native is incised "Ken." Sailor, $65.00. Hawaiian Girl, $100.00.

Block flower holder figure, 6⅝". Another example of a patriotic wartime item, this one is by Richard Block. The Block Pottery, located at 3208 Sunset Blvd. in Los Angeles, produced figurines, vases, bowls, wall pockets, banks, and baby novelties. Many of the California pottery figures in uniform offered comic relief and this one is no exception. On the back-side of the oversized shell casing is an opening for flowers or whatever. Raised in-mold: "Block Pottery Calif." $50.00.

These photos of very rare handmade Johannes Brahm figures were part of the estate collection of Jack Benny. On the right are two versions of a sailor with girlfriend, 9½". Braham's version of Lady Godiva, 9½" x 7," is on the left. Paper labels. NP.

Will-George figure group, 6¾". In Greek mythology, Pan was the god of flocks, forests and fields, but is most often associated with the forest. He was half human, half goat. This highly detailed model by Will Climes was produced in porcelain, c. 1946. Besides the young Pan, there's a bird, a rabbit, and a squirrel included in this piece. Pan's furry head and lower body were achieved by massing together hundreds of extremely fine strands of clay. Ink-stamped "Will-George, Porcelain, 103." $165.00.

Ink-stamped marks on Beth Barton miniature bugs.

Beth Barton miniatures, 2³/₈" (left) and 2" (right). Beth Barton produced whimsical small-scale figures in the late 1940s and early 1950s. Barton gained considerable notoriety for her anthropomorphic insects that acted out many of the rituals that humans are fond of. More than 120 different models were produced. The hefty bug in football gear on the left has over-glaze red-painted number, stripes, and helmet, and has an ink-stamped mark. $75.00. His petite admirer also has an ink-stamped mark. $50.00.

These photos appeared in the May 1951 issue of Ceramic Industry. One shows Beth Barton in her studio along with shelves filled with her ceramic bugs. The other pictures a few of her insect friends.

Beth Barton miniature, 2¹/₈" x 3¹/₄". Beth Barton, whose business was located in Fullerton, created a group of small Sea Urchins in 1949 and each one was individually named. This is Sleepy and, like most of the others, he wears a stylish starfish hat and has flippers for feet. NM, $65.00.

Beth Barton miniatures, 3⁷/₈ (left) and 3¹/₈" (right). These delightful veggie people are in all likelihood early Hey-Ho Dolls of Clay, which is what Beth Barton called her handmade miniature creations. They are surprisingly detailed for their size. On the left is a bashful young cauliflower. On the right is a roly-poly potato baby. NM, $100.00 each.

Paper label inside Poinsettia Studios mini bell.

Poinsettia Studios miniature bell, 2⁷⁄₈". Poinsettia Studios was another company known for its miniature scaled giftware. A variety of bells were produced; this caroler bell was a Christmas seasonal item. The sheet music Noel-Noel was printed with overglaze gold. $50.00.

Unidentified figure, 9½", and Betty Lou Nichols figure, 9½". The Santa Claus figure on the left is currently unidentified although it resembles the Santas of Robyn Ceramics. NM, NP. The Santa Claus figure on the right is the very popular model by Betty Lou Nichols that she produced over several seasons. There is a matching Mrs. Santa Claus figure. Painted mark: "S. Claus" on bottom of one foot. Ink-stamped "Betty Lou Nichols" on the other. $90.00.

Painted mark on Johanna Santa figure.

Betty Lou Nichols figure, 9½". This is another example of one company purchasing molds from another and extending the life span of a particular item. Johanna Ceramics of Costa Mesa was the originator of this large animated Santa Claus figure. When the Johanna business closed, Betty Lou Nichols bought some of her seasonal molds including this one. Produced in either white or red-painted versions with added overglaze gold trim, this item was carried for several seasons. NM, $120.00.

Johanna figure, 4³⁄₈" x 7½". This is an example of an original Johanna Ceramics Santa Claus figure. He seems to have slipped on the ice and cradles a shallow (empty) toy sack with one arm. $50.00.

This Betty Lou Nichols publicity photo displays more examples of her animated Christmas line.

Mackie figures, 8½". These large Santas were seasonal items introduced by Mackie Artware of Corona del Mar around 1950. The Santa figure on the left differs slightly from the one at right. The Santa on the right side has punched out buttonholes on the front of his suit along with hollowed out facial features and was possibly designed as a lamp. The other one has an opening in back for flowers. The red was cold painted. Claude Mackie Newton, a former Kay Finch mold maker, owned the business. Victor McNutt represented the line. They are both marked in-mold: "Mackies Calif." $100.00 each.

Jane Holland candy jar, 9". Before starting her own business, Jane Holland was employed by Padre as a designer and decorator. Padre Regal items with the painted mark "by Jane" on the bottom were decorated by Holland. The Jane Holland studio was located at 8981 Kendall in South Gate and opened sometime in the mid-1940s. It wasn't long before she attracted attention with her convincing American Toby jugs. This jolly Santa Claus candy jar captures the spirit of the season and is not easy to find. Painted mark: "Saint Nick by Jane Holland Calif." $200.00+.

147

Star-Angel "Aries" original design by Robyn

Ink-stamped and hand-painted marks on Robyn figure.

Robyn figure, 6⅛". This Robyn Ceramics figure is from of a series of angels representing the various astrological signs and is titled Star Angel Aries. The painted features on the faces of Robyn's angel figurines are quite distinctive. $75.00.

This photo of the Robyn staff was taken in the late 1940s when the business was still in its original Fallbrook location.

Susi Singer figure group, 5⅞" x 5½". This interesting Susi Singer piece features three female angels that seem to be blessing the masses. Behind them is a curious pretzel-shaped formation with a single bird perched on top. Painted mark: "SS." $450.00+.

Kay Finch figure, 6". This kneeling Madonna figurine was modeled by Kay Finch and was one of the many seasonal items she produced in the 1940s and 1950s. Popular items like this were made available season after season. NM, $85.00.

Joy Thompson figure, 12¼". Joy Thompson conveys a reverent feeling in this straightforward rendering of a Catholic priest or padre. A low-luster glaze was used on this figure. Incised mark: "Joy Thompson Pasadena 10." $125.00.

Betty Lou Nichols head vase planters, 7⅝" (left) and 9" (right). Each of these nun-like Madonna busts includes hands and has an attached planter in back. The medium sized Madonna on the left is ink-stamped "Betty Lou Nichols, Copyright." $65.00. The large size Madonna on the right is unmarked. $150.00. A small size (4") was also produced.

Clay Sketches (Ball Craft) vase with heron, 13⅝". Brothers Arthur and Howard Ball founded Clay Sketches (Ball Crafts) in Sierra Madre in 1940. They produced a limited line for a short period, selling the business to Cy Peterson in 1943. Later the same year, Arthur and Howard established Ball Brothers in Inglewood determined to produce animal and bird figures as fine or better than those that were imported from Europe prior to WWII. This impressive cylinder vase with attached heron was produced at the original business location in Sierra Madre, c. 1942. Less than 1,000 of them were produced. Ink-stamped mark: "Clay Sketches by Ball Calif." $250.00+.

Ink-stamped mark on Clay Sketches heron.

Clay Sketches heron, 12". This is an example of the heron that Clay Sketches produced after the purchase by Cy Peterson. Three of the original Ball Crafts molds were included in the sale and this is one of them. Economical airbrush decoration with minimal hand painting is seen here. $50.00.

Ball Brothers heron, 12¾". Arthur and Howard Ball produced this colorful heron in their Inglewood factory sometime between 1943 and 1948. In 1948, Howard left the business to accept a job designing for Brad Keeler Artwares. Howard Ball was the modeler while Arthur handled the production end of the business that employed at most 25 people. The fine modeling and attention to detail set the Ball Brothers apart from nearly all its competitors in California. Ink-stamped "Ball Brothers California" with an outline of the earth. $200.00.

Lucie Watkins candleholder with crane, 7¼" x 5¼". Lucie Watkins's introduction to the pottery business took place in the mid-1930s, when she was employed as a designer for the Catalina pottery on Catalina Island. Her handmade items stood apart from the company's ware at the time and presaged developments on the mainland during the 1940s.

Watkins moved to the mainland in the early 1940s and established a small business that produced items like this candleholder with crane. Most of her pieces incorporated handmade flowers or other organic elements. Incised "Lucie, Handmade, California." $180.00.

Will-George crane, 10½". Howard Ball was very likely the designer of this Will-George crane. Ball got his start in the pottery business in Pasadena as a designer for The Claysmiths. A refined fluidity has been captured for all time in this model, which is not an easy one to find. Ink-stamped "Will-George Pasadena." $150.00.

Will-George flamingoes, 10" (center), and bowl, 2"H x 14½"L. Will-George must be considered the first and foremost manufacturer of flamingoes in California. Their models have an elegance and grace like no other's, and many companies made competitive versions of this colorful and exotic bird.

The low bowls were produced to provide a vessel for a complementary floral arrangement. Each item ink-stamped "Will-George" or "Will-George Pasadena." Flamingoes, $150.00 – 200.00. Bowl, $75.00.

Padre flamingo, 10³/₄". This Padre Regal flamingo compares favorably with the Will-George flamingos. It may not have the naturalistic detail of The Claysmiths models but what it lacks in that regard is made up for in panache. I believe that Jane Holland, who later started her own pottery business, performed the hand decoration. This item has an in-mold mark and a painted mark reading "Hand Made Regal J.C.H." $150.00.

Brad Keeler parrot on perch, 15¹/₈". This large and colorful parrot is believed to be a model created by Brad Keeler about 1946. He was known for his birds and modeled many varieties and sets of them in the 1940s. This is one of the larger models produced and is rarely seen today. In-mold: "Brad Keeler no 27." $225.00.

William Maddux parrots, 8³/₄". William Maddux began modeling birds for production in the late 1930s in a small workshop at his home in Los Angeles. He relocated to a larger facility on San Fernando Rd. in 1941. In 1944, he and partner Jimmie Webster (who had earlier been associated with Brad Keeler) purchased a property at 3020 Fletcher Drive, where an even larger and better-equipped plant was constructed. Birds were the specialty of William Maddux Ceramics and many varieties, including flamingoes, were produced with the help of about 15 workers. Maddux sold the business in the late 1940s, and it continued to do well for many years under the name Maddux of California. These parrots probably date from the late 1940s. One is unmarked and the other is incised "William Maddux." $85.00 each.

Ball Brothers cockatoos, 11½" (left) and 11" (right). These naturalistic and colorful cockatoos perched on stalks of corn were modeled by Howard Ball and produced at the Ball Brothers pottery in Inglewood between 1943 and 1948. Incredibly detailed work was a hallmark of Ball Brothers and these life-like birds are stunning examples. Ink-stamped Ball Brothers mark. $200.00 each.

Howard Ball at work, c. 1948.

William Maddux cockatoos on perch, 11¼". Cockatoos, like flamingoes, proliferated in the 1940s and 1950s in California but the groundbreaking models by William Maddux were seldom equaled in beauty or workmanship. This piece incorporating two birds and a handmade floral accent is a case in point. In-mold: "Wm Maddux." $225.00.

153

Mackie parakeets, 6¼", with cage, 8¾" x 5½". Mackie Artwares of Corona del Mar produced this unusual set of two parakeets and cage with hook for hanging. The hand-decorated birds are individual units that can be positioned in the cage in slightly different ways. The birds are not marked but the cage has an in-mold mark. $100.00 set.

In-mold mark on Mackie parakeets' cage.

Cemar roosters, 18" (left) and 6½" (right). Fred Kaye designed the giant rooster on the left as well as his little brother. Cemar produced a large assortment of animals and birds in the polychrome glaze treatment seen here during the 1940s. The various colors were sprayed on the bisque ware and refired with a coating of transparent glaze. This 18" high rooster is possibly the largest of the bunch. In-mold: "Cemar 568." $250.00. The baby rooster is unmarked. $65.00.

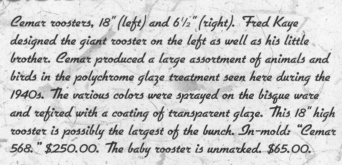

Ball Brothers rooster, 12½". In contrast to the Cemar roosters, this model is very naturalistic. The attention to detail is impressive. I believe the Ball brothers, Arthur and Howard, achieved their goal of equaling and even surpassing the quality of the birds the Europeans were importing prior to the war. The early Ball pieces tended to be finely cast and lightweight. Ink-stamped Ball Brothers logo. $175.00.

The Ball Brothers crew. Arthur Ball is in the center of the picture toward the back.

In-mold mark on tall poly-chrome Cemar peacock.

Cemar peacock, 17³/₄". Here is another very large bird model by Fred Kaye. It's interesting to compare this bird with its tail feathers at rest with the fanned-out plumage on the nearby Fred Kaye designed peacock vase. Cemar's sprayed-on polychrome glaze treatment is used to good effect on this large and distinctive bird. $200.00.

Cemar peacock vase, 9¼" x 9¼". The understated satin-matte glaze on this Cemar peacock manages to tame the vibrant natural colors of these male birds. It's a nice compliment to the imaginative modeling. A pocket-like vase in back allows for an arrangement of flowers or actual peacock feathers. In-mold: "Cemar 135." $125.00.

West Coast dove on perch, 10⅛". The similarity between Padre's Regal ware and West Coast's hand-painted items can be uncanny. It's likely that Helen Burke is behind this situation. After her break with the Winton twins in the late 1930s, Burke worked with several Southern California potteries, both encouraging and showing them how to add slip-decorated items to their lines. I believe that it was her direct or indirect influence that resulted in the slip-decorated West Coast bird seen here. Slip decoration involves painting with watered down clay mixed with various colorings. A final clear glaze usually follows to protect and intensify the colors. In-mold: "West Coast Pottery California 403" and painted "403D." $60.00.

Clay Sketches bird on perch, 8¼". This bird resembles the nearby Brad Keeler model but the tail is much shorter. Clay Sketches of Pasadena, which was owned and operated by C.A. "Cy" Peterson with wife Edna and partner William A. Hawkins, produced it. The location of the pottery was 30 S. Chester Ave., and airbrush decorated birds such as this one were a mainstay of the business. Ink-stamped "Clay Sketches Pasadena, Calif." $45.00.

Padre bird on perch, 9½", and Brad Keeler bird on perch, 9⅝". These two birds could induce an identity crisis without knowing the history of the companies involved. On the left is a Padre Regal long-tailed bird on flowering perch dating from about 1940. On the right is essentially the same bird produced by Brad Keeler (with the tail in front rather than in back, no flowers on the perch, and marked only with a number). Knowing that Brad Keeler worked for Padre for a short time in the late 1930s and had modeled the original Padre version solves the mystery. His model was ultimately added to the Regal family of hand-decorated items and the result is the bird on the left with painted mark reading "Regal Calif, Hand Painted by Virginia." $65.00. On the right is the altered version of the same bird, modeled by Keeler soon after the establishment of his own business. We know this because of the low number (#45). $65.00.

William Maddux birds on perch, 10¼" x 10". William Maddux modeled this attractive piece comprised of two short-tailed birds on a flowering perch. Many of the artistic Maddux birds of the 1940s incorporated handmade flowers and were decorated with a combination of airbrush and hand painting. Illegible in-mold mark. $75.00.

Brad Keeler swans, 16¼" (left) and 14⅛" (right). Howard Ball probably modeled these large and impressive swans during his association (1948 – 1952) with Brad Keeler Artwares. Designed in the Brad Keeler manner, they were somewhat less detailed than Ball Brothers models (a Ball Brothers swan can be seen below) In-mold: "Brad Keeler" along with shape numbers. $400.00 set.

Ball Artware swan, 8" x 13". Howard Ball's modeling skills are evident in this remarkably naturalistic swan produced about 1947. Mark obscured by felt pad on bottom. $300.00+.

Painted mark on backside of bases of pheasants by Freeman-Leidy.

Freeman-Leidy pheasants, 16⅜" (left) and 11" (right). Freeman-Leidy of Laguna Beach was a company that tended to lavish their product line with flamboyant detail and ornamentation. These Rococo pheasants are a good example of their over-the-top approach. Handmade roses and leaves and gold gilding were used in abundance in an attempt to dazzle the observer. Note the two chicks nestled under the female pheasant. $400.00 set.

Ball Brothers pheasants, 6¾" x 11½" (left) and 7⅛" (right). These Howard Ball pheasants are rather restrained in their use of color but their detailed modeling is unmistakable. Ink-stamped Ball Brothers logo. $235.00 set.

Ink-stamped Ball Bros logo on pheasants.

Painted mark on Freeman-Leidy bird on nest.

Freeman-Leidy bird on nest, 2⅞" x 4". To their credit, Freeman-Leidy could curb a tendency to get carried away, as this sweet little bird on nest demonstrates. A solitary bird perched on the edge of its nest, with only a leaf and snip of vine for added interest, can be more moving than a dozen gold-gilded peacocks. $75.00.

In-mold mark on Ross hen. Rooster is not marked.

Ross hen, 7⅝", and rooster, 8¼". The whimsical creations of Violet Ross of Ross Ceramics become easy to recognize once a few of them have been observed. Her popular chickens (and chicks) were produced for several seasons beginning in 1944. The rooster was named Sylvester and the hen Fannie. These examples would be later manifestations, dating from about 1950. A true red glaze, not cold paint, has been used here. DeLee helped distribute their line for a short time in the early 1950s. $120.00 set.

Ross chicks, 3⅝" (left) and 3¼" (right). These Ross chicks display the witty style of decoration that distinguished the company's figurines of the mid-1940s. Various animals and birds were given the Ross treatment that, not coincidentally, is reminiscent of Kay Finch, since Violet Ross was originally one of Finch's decorators. The Ross business began in Laguna Beach and was later relocated to Hawthorne. In-mold: "Ross © 45." $60.00 each.

Modglin chicks, 4⅞". Two very different color treatments on the same Modglin model are seen here. The black chick wearing a bonnet on the left is quite a contrast to the white and pale blue chick on the right. Both are charming. Painted mark: "Original." $50.00 each.

Knowles, Taylor & Knowles ducks, 3". Not the Easter parade, but a few small KTK ducks parading a few of the glazes that the company used on its wares during the 1940s. Some are unmarked while others have "KTK" in-mold. $30.00 each.

Padre fish bowl, 3" x 14". This is an extraordinary example of the Padre Regal line. Dating from 1942, this low bowl is composed of three colorful fish (salmon?) seemingly caught up into a swirling vortex of white-capped waves. It was introduced to the market less than a year before Padre's disastrous fire, so very few of these marvelous bowls were made. Painted mark: "Regal California Painted by Virginia." $300.00+.

Brad Keeler souvenir ashtray, 2½"H x 4⅜"W. The pottery on Catalina Island was the chief supplier of souvenir ashtrays and other novelties for the gift shops of Avalon during the 1930s. When the pottery closed in 1937, a souvenir void was waiting to be filled and Cemar was one company that rallied to the cause and began producing these items. Brad Keeler was another. This ashtray with legend, "Santa Catalina Isle," and a flying fish perched on it was produced in the post-war period. Ink-stamped "Brad Keeler 402." $165.00.

Cemar souvenir ashtray, 3⁵/₈" x 6³/₄". This is an example of a Cemar souvenir ashtray, although not one of Catalina Island. This would be a memento of someone's visit to Santa Barbara and dates from about 1949. In-mold: "Cemar 667." $85.00.

Knowles, Taylor & Knowles lambs, 5½" x 5". These lovable KTK lambs are somewhat unusual. This company was not known for its animal figurines and these two could prove difficult to corral. The only things typical of KTK here are the handmade bows around their necks. Resting lamb is incised "KTK Calif 419." Standing lamb is incised "KTK Calif 420." $90.00 set.

Pacific bear, 3". This bear and the author have crossed paths before. Don Winton was considered the probable model maker, but the company he made it for is uncertain. Pacific Clay Products, from 1940 to 1942, produced a large assortment of small hand-decorated figurines of animals and this cute little brown and white bear is one of them. Listed in their catalog as Inquisitive Bear, it is shape number 1377. There are other probable Don Winton models in this elusive collection. NM, NP.

1302 1303 1337 1338 1339 1340 1342 1344 1363 1364 1390 1391

1311 1312 1314 1315 1343 1345 1346 1347 1350 1351

1352 1365 1366 1367 1368 1369 1370 1371

1320 1323 1326 1328 1353 1358 1359 1372

1373 1374 1375 1376 1377 1378 1379 1380 1381

1357 1382 1383 1384 1385 1333 1334

1335 1386 1362 1387 1388 1389

PACIFIC

Page 6

HAND DECORATED BIRD AND ANIMAL FIGURINES
IN ASSORTED FINISHES

Stock No.	Description	PRICE
1302	Turtle, 3½" long	
1303	Small Resting Deer, 2¾" high	$ C
1337	Miniature Bird, 2" high	C
1338	Woeful Ducky, 2¾" high	C
1339	Surprised Bunny, 3¼" high	C
1340	Laughing Bunny, 3¼" high	C
1342	Miniature Bird, 2" high	C
1344	Little Red Fox, 2¼" high	C
1363	Chirping Dickey Bird, 2½" high	C
1364	Small Resting Faun, 3¼" high	C
1390	Airdale, 3" high	C
1391	Guppy, 3" long	C
1311	Standing Deer, 4¼" high	$ E
1312	Leaping Deer, 4½" high	E
1314	Girl Friend Ducky, 4½" high	E
1315	Boy Friend Ducky, 4½" high	E
1343	Miniature Horse, 3¼" high	E
1345	Contented Pup, 3" high	E
1346	Bathing Bird, Wings Spread, 3¾" wide	E
1347	Bathing Bird, 3½" long	E
1350	Lovebird on Perch, 5" high	E
1351	Futuristic Crane, 6½" high	E
1352	Futuristic Leaping Deer, 6" high	E
1365	Bashful Duck, 3½" high	E
1366	Bird on Perch, 3¾" high	E
1367	Swan, 4½" high	E
1368	Snail, 2¾" high	E
1369	Navy Goat, 4" high	E
1370	Woolly Sheep, 4½" high	E
1371	Happy Bear, 4" high	E
1320	Small Horse, 4¼" high	$ F
1323	Army Mule, 5" high	F
1326	Horned Deer, 3½" high	F
1328	Large Resting Deer, 5" long	F
1353	Bird on Perch, 6" high	F
1358	Cockatoo on Stump, 5½" high	F
1359	Bird on Perch, 4" high	F
1372	Sea Horse, 5" high	F
1373	Thrush, 4¾" high	F
1374	Bird on Limb, 5" high	F
1375	Small Parrot, 4½" high	F
1376	Squirrel, 3½" high	F
1377	Inquisitive Bear, 3" high	F
1378	Cub Bear on Stump, 3" high	F
1379	Crane Flower Holder, 5" high	F
1380	Pheasant, 3½" high	F
1381	Calf, 3½" high	F
1357	Large Parrot on Perch, 6" high	$ G
1382	Mallard Duck, 7" long	G
1383	Bird Vase, 6½" high	G
1384	Cub Bear on Hollow Log, 7" long	G
1385	French Poodle, 5½" high	G
1333	Ma Goose, 7" high	$ H
1334	Pa Goose, 7" high	H
1335	Large Horse, 6½" high	H
1386	Rooster Bud Vase, 8¼" high	H
1362	Tall Faun, 10" high	$ I
1387	Bird on Stump Flower Holder, 6½" high	I
1388	Saucy Squirrel, 4½" high	I
1389	Zulu Ash Tray, 5½" high	I

SEE PAGE 9 FOR PRICES

Padre squirrel, 7³⁄₈" x 6½". This hand-decorated squirrel dates from about 1941. It has an in-mold "Padre Calif" mark indicating it may have been a stock item that was given the Padre Regal treatment. Painted mark: "Regal." $60.00.

These two pages (above and on facing page) from Pacific's artware catalog of 1941 show the assortment of animals they produced in the early 1940s.

Ball Brothers squirrel, 10¼". Uncanny realism is about all one can say about this nearly life-size model of a squirrel and its small gathering of acorns by Howard Ball. His ability to mimic nature was unsurpassed in the ceramic industry. NM, $250.00+.

Betty Davenport Ford squirrel, 5¾" x 5¾". Betty Davenport Ford is probably better known today for the series of small porcelain animals and birds that she modeled for Florence Ceramics in the 1950s than for her own large-scale ceramic sculpture. She also made smaller items and this marvelous squirrel would be an example. There is no glaze on this hand-built terra cotta model. Impressed "B.F." $400.00+.

Bill Meyer goat, 10½" x 7½". William H. Meyer's line of animals, decorative bowls, figurines, boxes, and ashtrays were represented by Dick Knox. The business was located at 8729 Melrose Ave. in Los Angeles. This curious billy goat has been liberally layered with extruded spaghetti-like clay strands to simulate a fur coat, making it quite heavy. Painted mark: "Bill Meyer." NP.

Roselane antelope, 15½". The glaze treatment is the unusual feature of this large antelope by Roselane. The chocolate brown matte glaze on the body of the antelope has an atypical rough texture but the peculiar pebbly finish on the enormous horns and other elements is even more surprising. In-mold: "Roselane" and an unreadable shape number. $180.00.

Roselane deer, 5¼". Bill Fields modeled this popular deer figurine with oversized ears that was produced in nearly all of the Roselane glaze colors of the 1940s. A few of them are pictured here. Unmarked, with an occasional paper label. $45.00 each.

This photo that includes two West Coast Pottery deer figurines appears in the 1940 book, Flowers: Their Arrangement by J. Gregory Conway (see Bibliography.) It demonstrates how these small figurines were used to complement floral arrangements, a fashionable home accessory at the time.

Cali-Cali deer, 5¾". Cali-Cali Ware was a line of bowls, vases, and figurines introduced by the N.S. Guston Co. in 1947. Whether these were manufactured for or by Guston is unclear. Evidently, some molds were purchased by the Los Angeles Potteries at a later date because this deer figurine in a somewhat larger size appeared in their advertising. In-mold: "Cali-Cali F-4." $35.00 each.

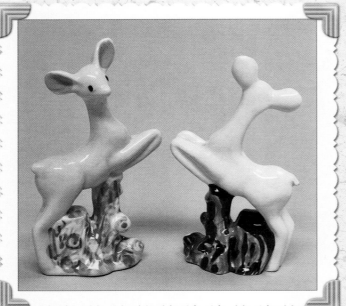

Walker deer, 7½". The Walker Potteries was founded in 1942 and was located at 900 S. Magnolia Ave. in Monrovia. Joseph, Frieda, Jessie, and other members of the Walker family were in charge. They made respectable popular-priced items for variety stores and similar outlets, like this deer figurine with its hand-decorated rustic base. NM, $35.00.

This photo of the Walkers was included in the company catalog of 1950.

THE WALKERS

Beth Barton deer, 4". Beth H. Barton was well known for her bugs and other small-scaled creatures but she also produced larger items like this amorous deer named Dear. Missing is her other half, a standing deer named Dearest. They were produced with and without the Christmas trappings, but were especially popular at holiday time. The deer on the left is ink-stamped "Beth H Barton ©" and includes the handpainted name "Dear." The identical model with added mistletoe, a red-painted harness, and gold bells is marked the same way. $75.00 each.

West Coast skunk, 2½", and deLee skunks, 2¼". Figurines of skunks must have been popular in the 1940s because so many potteries made them. On the left is a West Coast skunk that appears to have suffered a black eye. Painted mark: "1020D." $40.00. The acrobatic skunks on the right are from a troupe of diminutive stinkers known as the Skunkettes (a pun on the famous Rockettes). They were introduced in the early 1950s. DeLee produced more skunk figurines than any other California company. NM, $60.00 each.

A deLee invoice from 1953 with current items and prices. The Skunkettes were priced 50¢ each wholesale at the time.

Cleminsons monkey flower holder bank, 5½". Betty Cleminson created a small group of circus animals in 1950 that she called the Floralbank Circus. Each animal was designed to do double duty as a bank and a flower holder. This jovial monkey is holding a coin slot in front of him. His hat has an opening and the drum has holes all around to receive flower stems. Ink-stamped Cleminsons logo mark. $150.00+.

Robert Simmons zebras, 8½" (left) and 7¼" (right). Robert Simmons Ceramics was located in Los Angeles at 3269 Casitas Ave. The business specialized in animal figurines and both true-to-nature models and caricatures were produced. The natural models still left much to the imagination and each one had an individual personality and name. Nametags were routinely put on the animals before they left the factory. The zebra on the left is named Zig while the one on the right is Zag. Both have lost their nametags. NM, $120.00 set.

The cover of the Robert Simmons catalog of 1953.

Royal Hickman giraffe, 11⅞". It does not appear that Royal Hickman ever owned and operated his own pottery in California. He produced artware for the Sun Glo Studios of Los Angeles in the mid-1940s and he probably sold designs to distributors. That may be the case with this stylized giraffe with its cartoonish decoration. NM, $75.00.

Brayton Laguna giraffes, 12" (left) and 10" (right). Although these two giraffes were cast independently, when united they form a single unit and would be incomplete otherwise. They were introduced in the early 1940s and proved so popular that a larger set was produced. During the course of its lengthy run, they were produced in numerous glazes and decorative treatments. This simple tone-on-tone application was one of the first. NM, $230.00 set.

DeLee giraffes, 6½". These cute deLee giraffes have lost their original nametags. The male, on the left, with open eyes is named Tops. His mate with eyes closed is Topper. Paper labels. $200.00 set.

Pas Cal giraffe, 6⅜". Pas Cal was a popular priced artware line made by the Nipedal Manufacturing Co. of Pasadena. Vases, wall pockets, and figurines were produced. Caricatures of birds and animals, like this giraffe reminiscent of an early deLee design, are the most commonly found today. Paper label reading "Pas Cal Potteries Pasadena." $35.00.

Landaker bust of giraffe, 8¾". Harold Landaker produced this humorous head of a giraffe at his Pacific Grove location. The bisque-fired body is stained a dark brown but the eyes, horns, and mane have a blend of white and turquoise crackle glaze. Incised "Landaker Originals." $75.00.

Copa de Oro giraffe, 9¼". Mary Jane Hart called her limited Copa de Oro line a "menagerie in fantasy." These remarkable flights of fancy consisted of animals that she produced in terra cotta or white clay. She then added elaborate handmade embellishment that was usually gold gilded. Tiny handmade flowers were another addition. Dick Knox was her representative but these labor-intensive pieces were costly in their day (late 1940s) and are rarely seen today. Painted mark: "©MJH" (in lower case) plus a circular gold paper label reading "California, Copa de Oro, Hand Decorated Ceramics." NP.

Painted initials of Mary Jane Hart on her Copa de Oro giraffes.

Copa de Oro giraffes, 5½". These smaller giraffes by Mary Jane Hart are a little more restrained. Their looped golden manes are the only enhancement to the cast forms. The giraffe on the left was glazed black before the addition of gold. The white one is the unmodified clay color with a clear glaze over it. The application of gold required a separate firing at a low temperature to unite it with the glaze. NP.

Ross elephant bank, 4³/₄" x 5¹/₂", and Modglin elephant, 7³/₈" x 6¹/₂". Are you seeing pink elephants? The elephant on the left by Ross Ceramics is also a bank and is unmarked. $75.00. The Modglin elephant with trunk raised is just a figurine. The name "Lulu" has been printed on her ankle bracelet (not shown in photo) and on the bottom of one foot is the painted mark: "Original." $65.00.

Elzac elephant, 3³/₄". Elzac is the precursor of the Mattel toy company. Elliot Handler and a financial partner named Zachary Zemby (hence the name Elzac) started it in Los Angeles in 1941. In 1944, a new business partnership was formed when Elzac foreman Matt Matson and Elliot Handler founded Mattel in nearby Hawthorne. Handler, who was an industrial designer, was enamored of Lucite and its potential, and Elzac produced costume jewelry, figurines, and other giftware that incorporated Lucite until about 1947. This little blue elephant with pink Lucite ears is believed to have been designed by Ray Murray, who worked for Elzac after leaving Bauer. It has simple but nice hand-painted details and a paper label on the backside. NP.

Capistrano kangaroo, 8¹/₄" x 8¹/₂". John R. Stewart in association with Virginia Goodwin was the manufacturer of Capistrano Ceramics. Unmarked figurines produced by this San Juan Capistrano business are often confused with the work of Kay Finch. The similarities are less noticeable in this exceptional example of a mother kangaroo and her two offspring, titled Stralia and her Twins Melba and Sydney. It was not uncommon for one California firm to imitate the successful style of another. NM, $90.00.

Kay Finch dogs, 4½" (left) and 8" (right). Kay Finch's interest in dogs went beyond the modeling of various breeds for production. She also raised champion afghan hounds at her Crown Crest Kennels, which was registered with the American Kennel Club, and in later years, she became an AKC judge. These two perky cocker spaniels, from an extensive assortment known as The Dog Show, are essentially large and small versions of the same model. Both dogs are marked in-mold: "Kay Finch." Small dog, $350.00; Large dog, $750.00.

Kay Finch not modeling a dog.

Jane Callender dog, 5⅝" x 6⅛". Another ceramic artist who fancied dogs and is best known for her naturalistic canine models is Jane Callender. Established in Los Angeles in 1942, she later relocated to North Hollywood. Mary Ryan of New York represented the business, and a wide variety of breeds were produced including some that were one-of-a-kind. This Dalmatian is hand-signed "Jane Callender" along with "29B." $175.00.

Jane Callender modeling a dog.

Jane Callender dog, 4¾" x 6½". This realistic Jane Callender cocker spaniel is covered with hundreds of handmade clay strands. The moist clay was pressed through sieves of various size and the resulting "fur" was meticulously attached by hand prior to firing. Callender invented the technique, which has come to be known as spaghetti trimming. NM, $225.00.

No. 33

MARY RYAN *presents~*
"DOG SHOW"
by
Jane Callender

CHAMPIONS ALL — THESE FINELY MODELED CERAMIC DOGS DO CREDIT TO THEIR WELL-BRED PROTOTYPES — JANE CALLENDER'S LOVE OF DOGS PLUS HER TALENT AS SCULPTRESS LED HER TO DEVELOP A TECHNIQUE WHICH CLEVERLY STYLIZES THE COAT AND CATCHES THE CHARACTERISTIC MANNER OF EACH BREED. . . . EACH DOG SHOWN — WITH ONE EXCEPTION — WAS MODELED FROM THE "BLUE RIBBON" DOG WHOSE NAME IT CARRIES. "VERTE" HOWEVER IS PURE FANTASY! SHOWN ON THIS PAGE ARE ——

No. 33—KERRY BLUE "Gentleman Jim", blue-gray, 5½" high____ $20.00

No. 36—FRENCH POODLE "VERTE", white with green wheat and pink or blue bows, 6" high____ 12.00

No. 38—SCHNAUZER "Schnaps", gray and cream, 5¾" high____ 20.00

RETAIL PRICES

No. 36

No. 38

Jane Callender dog, 4" x 7¼". The fur on this exceptional reclining afghan from the early 1940s was hand shaped and applied to a cast bare-bones body. Because of this, every finished version of this particular dog was different from all the others. This example has a hand-painted mark, which generally indicates an earlier model; however it's difficult to accurately date Jane Callender dogs because many of them were made over several seasons. Painted mark: "Jane Callender, Afghan Hound 16." $300.00+.

A view of the Jane Callender studio of the early 1940s. Callender is second from the right.

Jane Callender dog, 17". This Briard (French sheepdog) has individually shaped clay tufts covering his imposing frame. A silky satin-matte glaze coats everything except the pink tongue. Not many dogs this big were produced. NM, NP.

The 1940s

Ink-stamped mark on Jane Callender pup, Tiny.

Jane Callender dogs (left to right): 2½", 2¼", 3", 2½". Pups like these dating from the early to mid 50s are the most commonly found Jane Callender models. On the far left is a brown and white cocker pup named Tiny. Next is a honey colored cocker pup named Rags. Algy is the name of the gray and black English setter pup. And on the right is a white schnauzer pup named Pepper. Different colors and combinations of colors can be found on these models. All of the smaller dogs have an oval ink-stamped mark reading "Jane Callender California" with the individual model number in the center. $100.00 – 150.00 each.

Hardie-Arnita set of dogs, 2½" x 3½" (largest). Hardie Albright and Arnita Wallace were husband and wife partners in Hardie-Arnita Gifts, which was initially located in Beverly Hills but later moved to El Segundo. The El Segundo address was 601 E. El Segundo Blvd. Hardie Albright was another canine specialist. His small-scaled Royal Family sets of three dogs (there were at least a dozen different breeds) included this Kerry blue family. A wide variety of other items were produced by the business. NM, $130.00 set.

This ad for the Hardie Royal Family of dogs in the February 1952 issue of Giftwares was placed by representative Robert L. Coslette.

175

Ink-stamped mark on Hardie-Arnita bulldog.

Hardie-Arnita dogs, 1³/₈" (left) and 1⁵/₈" x 3" (right). One member of this Royal Family of Hardie Albright bulldogs was not available for the photo session. These charming sets of three dogs of the same breed date from the late 40s to early 50s. Small dog, $30.00; Large dog, $50.00.

Painted mark of Freeman-Leidy dog.

Freeman-Leidy dog, 4¹/₄" x 5¹/₄". This is the only known Freeman-Leidy dog. It's a surprising departure from the elaborately decorated giftware this Laguna Beach pottery was known to produce. It may have been an exclusive for the famous Pottery Shack retail outlet. $75.00.

Ball Brothers dog, 5³/₄". Howard Ball produced amazingly life-like dogs. This bug-eyed puppy with his baby teeth bared combines both airbrush and hand painting. It was finely cast and is remarkably lightweight, as were many of the early Ball Brothers models. Ink-stamped Ball Brothers mark. $100.00.

Robert Simmons dog, 4³/₄" x 7⁵/₈". Major is the name of this Robert Simmons bulldog produced about 1950. His small silver nametag is on the opposite side. Exceptional details on this example include the studded collar and menacing facial features. Silver foil sticker (nametag) reading "Major III." $70.00.

Will-George dog, 13½". Howard Ball modeled this Great Dane for The Claysmiths in the early 1940s prior to formation of the Ball Brothers partnership. Like most of his work, the realistic detail on this model is uncanny. Not quite life-size but nevertheless imposing. Ink-stamped "Will-George Pasadena." $350.00+.

Robert Simmons dog, 6" x 6½". The only hand-painted details on this small Great Dane figurine are the facial features. The rest of the painting was accomplished quickly with an airbrush. The paper label barely visible on his belly reads "Hand Made Artware, Robert Simmons Ceramics, Los Angeles." $45.00.

Robert Simmons dog, 5⅛". This is Mama Boxer and there are two baby boxers (Toto and Coco) that are go-withs. Besides these, there were several other boxer models in the Robert Simmons line of the late 1940s and early 1950s. NM, $65.00.

Robert Simmons dog, 5". The name of this poodle is Suzette, although the small rectangular label with her name on it is missing. This model came in a choice of either white or black. NM, $75.00.

Paper label on Joseph Originals poodle.

Josef Originals dogs, 3¾" (left) and 3¼" (right). Josef Originals of Monrovia produced these two pampered poodles. On the left is Cherie. On the right is Coco, who is more sprawled out. Added spaghetti trim detailed in gold and tiny pink flowers and leaves add interest to these aristocratic canines. Both retain original paper labels. $90.00 set.

Robert Simmons dogs, 4⅞". These two dogs provide a glimpse of the other side of the Robert Simmons repertoire of more comical critters. Based on previously imported European models, these twin pooches were known as Pals. The wholesale price in the early 1950s for a dozen of these was $6.00. It was not uncommon for Simmons to copy models that were no longer being imported during and just after WWII. Both ink-stamped "2030." $70.00 set.

Paper label on Lagunita dog.

Lagunita dog, 4⅞". Lagunita Pottery was located in Oakland and was a business that distributed the ware of small potteries like Ross Ceramics. It isn't known if they eventually manufactured a line of their own like so many other jobbers did. It's conceivable that this hand-decorated cocker spaniel with applied collar is a representative of the company's own line. $40.00.

Landaker dogs, 7¾" (left) and 5⅛" (right). Harold Landaker's sense of humor is conveyed loud and clear in these bug-eyed dog caricatures. They are easy to recognize once a few have been observed, although they turn up rather infrequently. Dark brown stain on the unglazed portions is common as are the crackle glazes and the prominent eyes. Incised "Landaker Original Ceramics." Large dog, $120.00; Small dog, $80.00.

Guppy dogs (left to right): 4⁷/₈" x 5", 7¹/₈" x 8¼", and 4⁵/₈" x 6¼". Harriet Guppy of Corona Del Mar was the creator of these comical canines. It's unclear whether these animal figures predate her dinnerware lines of the 1940s or were produced at the same time. Considerable handwork went into their production, from the tooled surfaces that mimic fur to the hand-painted and applied bows. The Scottie on the left has a painted mark reading "Lassie by Guppy." $40.00. The large sheep dog in the center is unmarked. $75.00. The schnauzer at right is also unmarked. $50.00. Guppy animals were rarely marked.

Walker dog, 3⁷/₈", and Rio Hondo cat, 4½". The budget priced animal figurines produced by these two California companies have a similar look and are easily confused because they are seldom found with paper labels intact. The winking dog on the left by Walker Potteries of Monrovia is distinctive because of its brown glaze, a color not usually associated with Rio Hondo. Paper label. $40.00. The screwball cat has the look of a typical Rio Hondo animal, however Walker produced nearly identical models. Rio Hondo Potteries was located in El Monte and was founded in 1939 by Gerald McFarlin. One explanation for the resemblance is the fact that Frieda Walker designed for McFarlin prior to the establishment of Walker Potteries. NM, $35.00.

CALIFORNIA CERAMIC ANIMALS

Priced at $1.08—$1.35—$1.80 a dozen wholesale

RIO HONDO POTTERIES

EL MONTE CALIFORNIA

This Rio Hondo ad appeared in the August 1947 issue of The Gift and Art Buyer.

Guppy cat, 4⅛" x 5". Cats got the same whimsical Harriet Guppy treatment as dogs. This one with big polka dot covered bow and extruded spaghetti fur is unmarked. $50.00.

Pas Cal cat, 3½" x 4½". Pas Cal was a trademark of the Nipedal Manufacturing Co. of Pasadena. The name Elizabeth J. Smith accompanied its listing in China, Glass & Lamps' compilation of Southern California Pottery Manufacturers of the 1940s, but she may have been its representative rather than owner. The Pas Cal items seen most often are small animal figurines, like this cat with its tongue out. Paper label. $35.00.

Robert Simmons cats, 3½". Two variations of Tutsy are shown here. This fastidious little kitten had two companions, Wutsy and Putsy. All three are similar in style and scale. Only one of these Tutsys has its nametag intact. $25.00 each.

Beth Barton cat, 4⅜". Herbie is the name of this mischievous kitten by Beth H. Barton. There were several other Herbie models, including one that shows him in the process of unraveling a ball of yarn. These would date from 1949 to 1951. This example has considerable heft for its size. In-mold: "© Beth H Barton." $70.00.

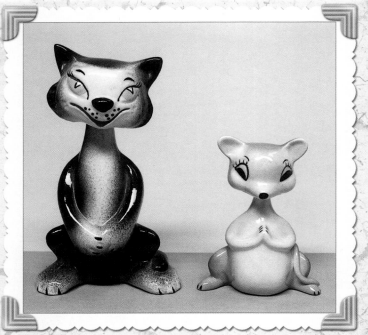

*Betty Lou Nichols nodders, cat, 7", and mouse, 4½".
Betty Lou Nichols, besides her fame as a head vase
producer, also created some clever sets of nodders (or
bobble heads, as they're commonly called today). Tom
is the cat's name and his head nods "yes." $200.00+.
The mouse's name is Twerpie, and he, of course, nods
"no." NM, $400.00+.*

This Betty Lou Nichols ad from the February 1955 issue of Giftwares shows two other sets of her witty nodders.

Paper label on Elzac cat.

*Elzac cat, 3¾", and horse, 5⅞" x 5⅜".
Here are two more examples of Elzac's
penchant for combining ceramic with
Lucite. The small yellow kitten is
showing off a big pink bow and pink
tail. The delightful horse boasts a
see-through pink mane and tail.
Paper labels. NP.*

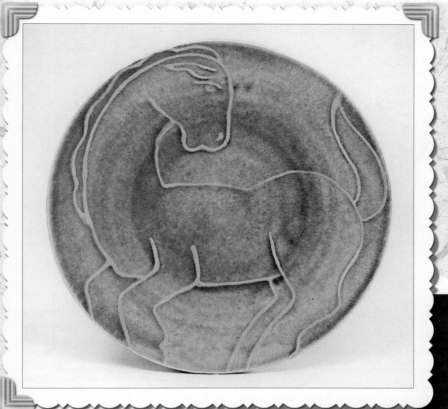

Eugene White chop plate, 16". Eugene White studied with Glen Lukens at the University of Southern California in the late 1930s and this eye-catching platter with barely raised outline of a horse exhibits his influence. Other related designs were produced on this scale in the early 1940s and all of them work well as purely decorative objects. Turquoise glaze with an extremely fine crackle covers the top surface of this example while on the backside the raw terra cotta clay is left bare. Incised "Eugene White California" in a circle. $250.00.

Roselane horse, 14¾". This powerful rearing stallion with extended neck by Roselane was produced sometime in the late 1940s. Glazed satiny white, the horse has a commanding presence and is amazingly well balanced despite its precarious posture. In-mold: "Roselane 283." $135.00.

Dorothy Kindell bookend, 7¼"H x 6½"W. The recognition gained because of her audacious nudes tended to overshadow Dorothy Kindell's equally well-modeled horses. This double horse-head bookend in dappled gray and white was produced at her original Laguna Beach location. It provides a glimpse of her wide-ranging equestrian output of the 1940s. Single horse-head bookends were also produced. In-mold: "D. Kindell, Laguna." $100.00.

Dorothy Kindell horses, 5³/₄" x 8" (left) and 4¹/₂" x 5⁷/₈" (right). These free-standing models of a colt and its attentive mother are also from Dorothy Kindell's equestrian line of the 1940s. The smaller horse was painted a slightly darker shade of brown than the large one. These figures were not marked so they have generally gone unrecognized in the secondary market. Large horse, NM, $100.00. Small horse, NM, $75.00.

Jean Manley horse, 4¹/₂ x 4¹/₂". This is an early handmade horse by Jean Manley and the artist has signed it. $135.00.

Guppy horse, 6" x 5³/₄". Harriet Guppy has lavished a great deal of attention on this fanciful horse model. Besides the spaghetti mane and tail, there are four hand-applied flowers, not to mention the hand painting. Only during the 1940s could the potteries afford to produce labor-intensive items such as this. The 1950s saw steady increases in the cost of labor and it became much less feasible to invest time on handwork unless extraordinary efficiency was possible. Paper label. $75.00.

West Coast horse, 4" x 6¹/₂". Possibly made for and sold as a souvenir of the famous Santa Anita racetrack in Arcadia, this downtrodden racehorse has a saddle blanket with the words "Santa Anita" and the number "2" painted on it. Next to the number is an original West Coast paper label. This is definitely one of the harder to find decorated West Coast figurines. $100.00+.

West Coast and Rio Hondo horses, 3". These two horse figurines demonstrate how one company could imitate the work of another. On the left is the original West Coast model. $45.00. The copy by Rio Hondo is on the right. Slight modifications to the shape and decoration are all that prevent it from being a carbon copy. NM, $25.00.

DeLee rabbits, 5½" (left) and 5" (right). The bunny with Easter egg-shaped flower holder on the left dates from 1941. No nametag. In-mold: "deLee Art, © 41 LA." $65.00. The coy bunny on the right named Cottontail is missing her mate, Hopalong (also 5" in height). No nametag, label, or mark. $50.00.

Ink-stamped mark and paper label on Bernard Studios rabbit holding vase.

Bernard Studios rabbits, 3¾" (left) and 6" (right). These rabbits have personality plus and they're both functional. The flirty one on the left is a cotton holder. She has a small opening in back. The Jackrabbit on the right has a rectangular slot in his back for handy disposal of used razor blades. Paper label. NM, $45.00 each.

Bernard Studios rabbit, 5". This cute bunny from Bernard Studios is holding an egg-shaped vase with no opening for flowers. The business was located in Los Angeles but no other information has been found. $40.00.

Ross pigs, 5" x 6½". These two Ross Ceramics pigs are exactly the same model but one requires feeding and the other doesn't. The gray piggy on the left is a bank. He has a slot in his head for coins. $85.00. The blue piggy is just a useless, yet amusing object, and guaranteed to raise a smile. NM, $75.00.

Paper label on De Forest pig shakers.

De Forest shakers, 3". Novelty salt and pepper shaker sets became big business in California in the late 1940s and it continued well into the 1950s. These large pig shakers are from the same mold; the only difference is the painted "S" and "P" on their foreheads. De Forest of California was located in Duarte and was known for its whimsical kitchen and bath novelties. $25.00 set.

Vallona Starr shakers, 3¼" (left) and 2" (right). Vallona Starr Ceramics produced these witty salt and pepper shakers named Drip (on the left) and Drop. Introduced about 1950, they were among the many clever sets this company turned out. Vallona Starr Ceramics was the trade name used by the Triangle Studios of El Monte. Triangle Studios got its name as a result of being a three-way partnership between husband and wife Everett and Leona Frost and friend Valeria de Marsa. Leona and Valeria were the creative forces and each had an individual style. Their ceramic line was manufactured from the late 1930s to the early 1950s. In-mold: "V. Starr, Pat-Pend." $75.00 set.

Vallona Starr shakers, 5³⁄₈". These Vallona Starr shakers were called Goose and Egg and were inspired by the nursery rhyme about the goose that laid a golden egg. A similar set, only smaller, was also produced. In-mold: "Vallona Starr." $35.00 set.

Poinsettia Studios shakers, 2⁵⁄₈" (left) and 2¹⁄₂" (right) with tray, 1¹⁄₄"H x 5¹⁄₈"L. These small-scaled novelty shakers of black crows wearing headgear and eyeglasses can be graciously classified as Black memorabilia. A tray shaped like an ear of corn completes the set. It's very likely that all Poinsettia shakers originally had trays of some sort. Paper label. $65.00 complete.

Treasure Craft shaker sets, 2¹⁄₂" (average height). Beginning in the late 1940s and into the 1950s, Treasure Craft of Compton produced innumerable sets of novelty shaker sets in which two related items were paired, like those pictured here. They have gone unrecognized for years because they are never marked. Distributor (and sometimes manufacturer) Edward R. Darvill billed himself as the "Salt and Pepper King" in part because he helped market them for Treasure Craft. These salt and peppers can easily be confused with similar sets made by Trevewood of Ohio. NM, $20.00 – 40.00 set.

Treasure Craft shakers, 4" (cactus) and 3½" (palm tree). Two charming sets of shakers by Treasure Craft are pictured. One is a desert horned toad pondering a cactus while the other is a monkey shading himself under a palm tree. After handling a few of these sets, it becomes easier to recognize them. Although unmarked, they do have certain characteristics in common if you look closely. NM, $25.00 each set.

Treasure Craft shaker sets, 1¾" (average height). These novelty salt and pepper sets with a transportation theme are a few more of the numerous sets made by Treasure Craft in the 1940s and 1950s. These sets will sometimes be found with the decal of a popular tourist destination because they were commonly sold as souvenirs in gift shops at these attractions. NM, $35.00 – 40.00 each set.

Arcadia miniature shakers, 1⅝" (book). The company that produced the most minuscule shakers that paired related objects was Arcadia Ceramics, which was located in Arcadia. Most of the items manufactured by the business were small but these salt and peppers are bona fide miniatures. The fine details are impressive given their size. The birthday cake looks delicious. Overglaze gold on these sets was common. NM, $45.00 each set.

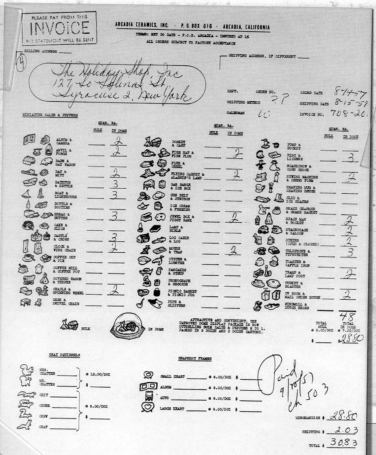

Arcadia miniature novelty shaker sets, 2³⁄₈" (bell). A few more of the dozens of sets of miniature shakers that Arcadia Ceramics produced are shown here. The detail on the schoolbook is remarkable. NM, $35.00 – 50.00 each set.

Elzac jewelry, 2⁵⁄₈" (left) and 2¹⁄₄" (right). In addition to producing figurines that combined ceramic with Lucite, Elzac of California turned out a large number and variety of pins and brooches that united these two and other odd materials in inventive ways. It is believed that Ray Murray was the designer of at least some of them. It's known that he designed for Elzac after leaving Bauer in 1941. The horse pin on the left is decked out with pink polka dots and a pink Lucite mane and tail. $75.00. The green fish pin on the left has amber colored Lucite fins. NM, $75.00.

Ink-stamped mark on backside of Kerry blue pin.

Jane Callender dog jewelry (left to right), pins, 1½"; medallion, 2¾"; pin, 1⅝". It was not uncommon for the smaller studio-level artware manufacturers in California to include some jewelry in the mix. Examples by several well-known names have been observed. Jane Callender made these pieces and they represent only a sampling of the ones produced. The two pug pins are the same model but have slightly different coloration. $45.00 each. The pink poodle medallion (or plaque) is one of the two similar designs. $65.00. The Kerry blue pin on the right has a twin airedale; only the color is different. $45.00. These dog heads were also sold without the pin backs or plaques attached. All ink-stamped "Jane Callender."

The name JANE CALLENDER is the now famous signature of this husband-wife team — Jane, the dog fancier and breeder, sculptor and painter — and David Rosen, teacher, artist. Throughout the world, in fine shops, department stores and discriminating homes one sees the unlimited canine ceramic creations of this pair.

Jane Callender PRESENTS...

PINS and PLAQUES

26 Dog Portraits in colorful ceramics available in Plaque or Pin design for your enjoyment. Your friends who love dogs will be more than delighted to receive their favorite's portrait as a pin to wear or plaque to hang on the wall.... Many will want the complete collection of 26 breeds to hang or to wear alternately. Dog Portraits are also available without pins or plaques if you wish to secure them permanently on the lid of a cigaret box, compact, handbag, front door, dog house, etc.

ANIMALS AT PLAY. Shown in this special Gift Catalog are selected breeds chosen from the Jane Callender Annual Catalog. On the cover are two of the famous Callender Poodles. A variety of animals at play are shown on the back page. Whatever you choose, your friends are bound to appreciate a gift created by Jane Callender.

PINS and PLAQUES—$1 each
10% discount on dozen orders
15% on complete set of 26

A   Kerry Blue
B   Chow
C   Boxer
D   Beagle
E   Dachshund
F   Chihuahua
G   Samoyed
H   Schnauzer
I   Airdale
J   Basset Hound
K   Pug
L   Scotch Terrier
M   Wirehair Terrier
N   Pekingese
O   Doberman Pinscher
P   Golden Retriever
Q   Poodle
R   Poodle
S   Dalmation
T   Boston Terrier
U   Cocker Spaniel
V   English Bull
W   Yorkshire Terrier
X   German Shepherd
Y   St. Bernard
Z   Afghan Hound

ANIMALS AT PLAY

#			
#C3	Mehitabel and Her Kittens	2.00	5½" high
#62	Miniature Schnauzer	5.00 ea.	3½" high
#12	Boxer Pup with Taped Ears	2.00 ea.	3" high
#02	Boxer Pup	2.00 ea.	3" high
#29	Boxer	5.00 ea.	5½" high
#1	Dachsy Set of 3 Puppies	3.00 set	2¾" size
#28	Collie	4.00	5" high
#6	Boston Terrier Pup	1.50	2½" high
#55	Boston Terrier	2.50	3½" high
#46	Poodle — "Frou Frou"	10.00 ea.	4½" high
#47	Sitting Up Poodle	8.00 ea.	6" high
#08B	Poodle	2.00	2½" high

NOTE: ALL Poodles and Chiuahuas are available in Standard Colors PLUS Pink and Turquoise. Please specify when ordering.

— ORDER BLANK —

JANE CALLENDER, Ceramics
5537 Vineland Ave., North Hollywood, Calif.

Please send me the following postage paid:

PINS (Indicate Numbers) _____

PLAQUES _____

Plaque Colors Desired _____

OTHER: _____

___ Please send me your Complete Annual Catalog (25c).

I enclose $_____ to cover the complete cost of the above order
(Add 10% Excise Tax for PINS)

NAME _____
STREET _____
CITY _____ STATE _____

A special Jane Callender gift catalog included her dog pins and plaques, and lists the various breeds included in the assortment and their original prices.

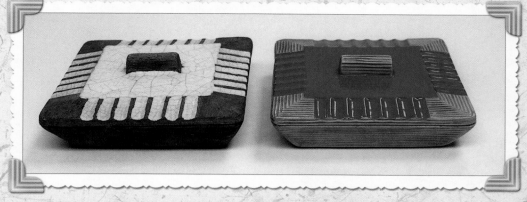

Barbara Willis cigarette boxes, 8". In the 1940s and 1950s smoking did not carry with it the social stigma of today and smoking accessories were a big item for most of the potteries in California. Barbara Willis pioneered and helped popularize the use of a single large (communal) ashtray and they found homes on countless coffee tables. The square-shaped cigarette boxes pictured here were produced to complement the design of the ashtray and came in many colors. The red one would date from the early 1950s. A smaller 5" size was also made. Ink-stamped "Barbara Willis." Green box, $200.00; Red box, $250.00.

Barbara Willis business card.

Barbara Willis

Terrene Pottery

STanley 7-3000

5535 Vineland Avenue
North Hollywood, Calif.

Barbara Willis ashtray, 5½". This is an example of the small (jack) size of ashtray that matches the Barbara Willis cigarette boxes. There were three sizes: king, queen, and jack. What makes this particular ashtray special? It's an example of a limited edition made exclusively for the Apple Valley resort located in the Southern California desert. The "AV" was handmade to resemble rope and compliment the Western decor of the resort. Incised "Barbara Willis." $300.00+.

Eugene White smoking accessories (left to right), ashtray, 7½"; cigarette holder and match holder, both 3" x 3¾". Eugene White produced this terra cotta smoker's set in the mid-1940s consisting of an ashtray, cigarette pack holder, and match holder. Ink-stamped marks. $60.00 each.

The 1940s

*In-mold mark on
Raymond Koechlin ashtray.*

*Raymond Koechlin ashtray, 3³⁄₈" x 6½". Raymond
Koechlin evidently operated a small pottery located in Los
Angeles in the 1940s. Not much is known about him or his
output. This bowl-shaped ashtray has a matte finish and
an unusual Raku-like texture and feel. The few pieces
observed have been marked in the same way. NP.*

*In-mold mark on
Walter Wilson ashtray.*

*Walter Wilson ashtray, 2¼"H
x 5¼"L and cigarette box,
3¾"H x 5½"L. This smoker's
set from Walter Wilson of
Pasadena includes an ashtray
with built-in matchbook holder
and a matching cigarette box
with hand-painted pheasant on
the lid and cutout bird designs
on the side. Both items have an
identical in-mold mark. Ashtray, $20.00; Box, $45.00.*

*Calpotter ashtray, 1⅛" x 4¼". Calpotter was one of the
numerous small potteries that sprang up in Laguna Beach
during the boom years of the 1940s. In the late 1940s, there
were as many as 65 individual pottery businesses in the
immediate area. There was even a local potter's association
established to preside over and help promote the variety of
wares. It can't be overstressed how much the success and
reputation of the Brayton Laguna Pottery was the catalyst
for much of the ceramic activity in this seaside town. Laguna
Beach's Annual Festival of Arts is commemorated on this
small Calpotter ashtray of 1949 — also the 100th
anniversary of the California Gold Rush. Incised
"Calpotter Laguna Beach California." $35.00.*

192

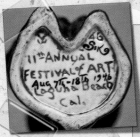

In-mold and painted marks on bottom of commemorative Yerbysmith Toby jugs.

Yerbysmith Toby jugs, 5¼". Yerbysmith Ceramics was another Laguna Beach firm that came into being during the 1940s when demand for pottery was great enough to support the many small businesses. Laguna Beach had long been an artist colony and many talented individuals, including Ernest A. Yerbysmith, turned to ceramic production for additional income. These three Yerbysmith Toby jugs are all from the same mold. The ones on the left and right were produced to commemorate the 11th annual Festival of Arts and are specially marked. $75.00 each. The one in the center is not a commemorative and is simply marked in-mold "Yerbysmith Ceramics Laguna Beach, Cal." $50.00.

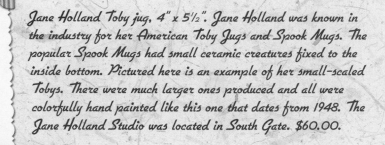

Jane Holland Toby jug, 4" x 5½". Jane Holland was known in the industry for her American Toby Jugs and Spook Mugs. The popular Spook Mugs had small ceramic creatures fixed to the inside bottom. Pictured here is an example of her small-scaled Tobys. There were much larger ones produced and all were colorfully hand painted like this one that dates from 1948. The Jane Holland Studio was located in South Gate. $60.00.

Painted mark on Jane Holland Toby jug.

Cleminsons covered mug, 5". This clown-faced coffee mug is suffering from a hangover. It has an ice-bag shaped cover and the hand-lettered phrase "Morning After" on its backside and "Never Again" on the inside bottom. This was a good seller for the El Monte based Cleminsons and is relatively easy to find today, although any without lids would be incomplete. Ink-stamped Cleminsons logo with "©" added. $45.00.

Ink-stamped mark on Decora wall decor.

Decora decor, 6½". Decora Ceramics was located in Inglewood at 136 N. Ash Ave. This company produced numerous items that were similar in concept and style to the Cleminsons. This decorated bottle-shaped piece is not a wall pocket but merely wall decor. Pictured is a man in period attire who has had a few too many. Most of the Decora items observed have been skillfully decorated. $40.00.

Brayton Laguna bookend, 6½" x 4⅞" and figure, 5⅞" x 5⅜". These clowns are from a circus set introduced by Brayton in 1948. Included in the collection were a cookie jar, a circus wagon with horses, clown with dog shakers, an elephant planter, and more. The clown bookend can be positioned sitting up or lying down. $75.00. The clown with pointed hat had only one function: to add a cheerful accent to any room. $85.00. Ink-stamped marks.

Marc Bellaire cigarette box, 2⅛"H x 7¼"L. This cigarette box with circus clown decoration is a preview of the fabulous fifties. Bellaire, a protegé of Sascha Brastoff, produced this item in the mid-1950s. It is signed "Ingle" on the cover. Ingle may have been a Bellaire artist who, in addition to decorating, originated the clown pattern. Incised "Bellaire Calif." $65.00.

Sierra Vista cookie jar, 10½". Reinhold F. Lenaberg founded Sierra Vista Ceramics in the mid-1940s. Two sons, William and Leonard, were also involved in the business and Leonard later assumed owner-ship. The business was located in Pasadena, at 1237 N. Fair Oaks. Muriel of California was just across the street. The company produced many items, including this clown head cookie jar, for Walter Starnes, a distributor who had a showroom at the Brack Shops in downtown Los Angeles. Starnes distributed a variety of California-made cookie jars and some of them were exclusives. NM, $60.00.

De Forest cookie jar, 13". De Forest of California got a rather late start. Another family affair, it was started by Margaret and Jack De Forest in 1950. Their sons also became active participants in the enterprise that remained in business until about 1970. This delightful clown cookie jar may have been designed by Don Winton. A free-lance designer at the time, Winton was an occasional contributor to their line. In-mold: "De Forest of Calif USA, © 5-24-57." $150.00.

This ad appeared in the August 1946 issue of The Gift and Art Buyer. It pictures a child's serving dish and mug with whimsical circus clown decoration by Sara Hume. The greater part of Hume's line dealt with items for children and items derived from children's folklore. Examples are not easy to find.

"Beppo" BABY PLATE AND CUP (BLUE OR PINK)~ by sara hume of California

REPRESENTED BY: William S. Frazier
152 S. Mission, Los Angeles, California

The 1950s

The leading light during the 1950s was Sascha Brastoff. His fabulous Los Angeles factory financed by pal Winthop Rockefeller became no less than a must-see tourist attraction. In the 1950s, the dominant and opposing styles in home decor were Modern and Provincial and most companies catered to both trends, sometimes attempting to marry the two with dubious results. The decade also saw the return of imports and the slow decline of the California pottery industry as products from abroad began to dominate the market once again.

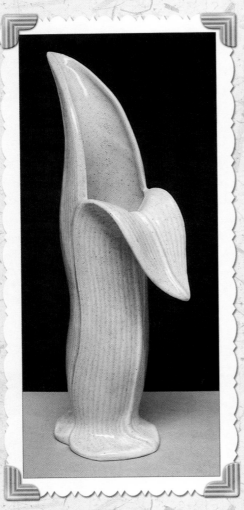

Cemar and Bauer vases, 7½". Here are before and after versions of the same shape from Cemar and Bauer respectively. The dark maroon glazed bud vase on the left has a chartreuse interior. $50.00. The Bauer revision in speckled pink has a slight tilt. $65.00. The Cemar vase has flocking on the bottom. The Bauer vase is not marked.

Bauer vase, 13½". In the mid-1930s, two employees of the J.A. Bauer Pottery left and formed a competitive business known as Cemar Clay Products. The Bauer management was of course miffed and they eventually got a payback when Cemar closed and sold molds and equipment to Bauer two decades later. This interesting tropical leaf-shaped vase was produced from one of the molds Bauer acquired. An actual example of this shape produced by Cemar has not been observed. The speckled glaze seen here is typical of Bauer in the 1950s. NM, $125.00.

Bennetts vases, 5½" x 5¼". The Bennetts were a husband and wife team that produced attractive floral artware and decorative accessories in the late 1940s and 1950s. Caroline and Dud Bennett were the owner-proprietors and their business was located at 7413 Varna Ave. in North Hollywood. Although their early efforts were essentially variations on the Barbara Willis method, later ware such as these two vases was more distinctive. The vase on the left is from their series called Rag Rug, introduced in 1949. Incised "The Bennetts California 403." $70.00. Serpentine, also from 1949, is the name of the series that included the vase on the right. Incised "The Bennetts California 203." $80.00.

Bennetts low bowl, 1½" x 15½". This large multi-purpose low bowl from The Bennetts' Rag Rug line of the late 1940s — early 1950s is an excellent representation of the line name. Incised "The Bennetts California 401." $85.00.

This ad from the February 1952 Giftwares features the Rag Rug line by The Bennetts.

"RAG RUG" Original by THE BENNETTS

Popular California-made home accessories for modern or provincial homes.

"Rag Rug"—"Serpentine"—"Autumn Ivy" these original, distinctive, top selling ceramic lines for the better stores are being presented at all major gift shows by THE BENNETTS.

Complete price list available on request.

THE BENNETTS
7413 VARNA AVENUE • NORTH HOLLYWOOD, CALIF.

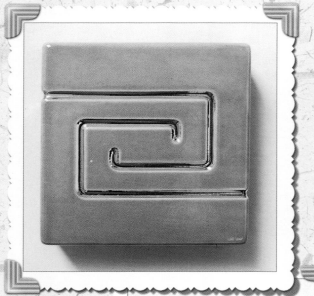

Robaul wall pocket, 6" x 6". This square shallow Robaul vase can either sit on a table or hang on the wall. It's a typical example of the company's good-looking up-to-date ware of the 1950s. In-mold: "Robaul of California." $45.00.

Johannes Brahm vase, 7³/₄"H x 8"W. Chinese Modern was a fashionable trend in home furnishings in the late 1940s — early 1950s and this bright red Johannes Brahm vase would have been a striking accent in such a setting. Not until the 1950s was a genuine and reliable red glaze commercially available. In-mold: "Johannes Brahm, California USA, 1460." $85.00.
(Photo courtesy of Yale University Art Gallery)

Jaru vase, 23½". This very tall and rather bizarre vase has two openings, one at its narrow top and a slightly larger one on the backside about half way up. The designer was Edmund Ronaky, a Hungarian-born artist who produced ware for Jaru Art Products. Ronaky's items generally bear his incised name, which is atypical of Jaru. The hand-painted decoration has an unmistakable 1950s feel. Incised "Ronaky Calif 110." $225.00.

Jaru vase, 6¼" x 19". This Jaru vase resembles a submarine. The crackle glaze and unusual proportions add up to a stunning example of 1950s design, although the designer is unknown. Jack and Ruth Hirsch established Jaru Art Products in 1950. The first two letters in their names were used to coin the name of the business. The Hirsch's were essentially jobbers in the beginning, contracting with various artists and artisans to produce their line. When Victor Houser and Robert Red left Bauer in 1951 and established Houser & Red Ceramics, it became the manufacturing arm of Jaru. Houser likely formulated the quality glaze seen on this example. Jaru price tag. $125.00.

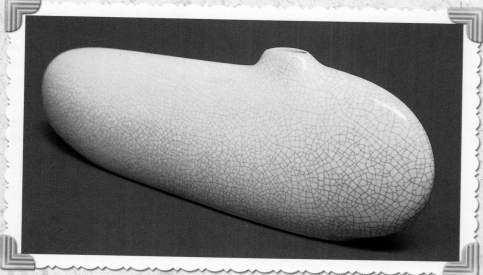

Jaru vases, 7" (left) and 9" (right). The vases on the left provide a sampling of the glazes that can be found on this Jaru shape with the distinctive bowl-like opening. There were two taller sizes produced. Triangular paper label. $50.00 each. The matte-glazed bottle vase on the right was decorated with horizontal brushstrokes while it was revolving on a decorator's banding wheel. Jaru paper label reading "A California Decorative Original by Jaru." $65.00.

Jaru set of vases (left to right): 7", 11", 18". These three ultramodern Jaru bottle vases were originally marketed as a set. It was a successful promotion in the 1950s and the set was produced for many seasons in various solid and speckled matte glazes. It's not uncommon for the individual units to be found and sold separately today. Paper labels. $200.00 set. Medium vase, $60.00; Small vase, $40; Large vase, $80.00.

The 1950s

Freeman-McFarlin vases (left to right): 10½", 20⅜", 3⅝". I don't believe these three Freeman-McFarlin vases were originally sold as a set, but they nevertheless are similar in style to the nearby Jaru threesome. Their matte glazes have a pebbly feel that is a familiar attribute of mid-century modern ceramic production. The colors are typical of the 1950s as well. Small oval paper label. Medium vase $50.00; Large vase, $90.00; Small vase, $30.00.

Cleminsons vase, 15¾". The Cleminsons produced the ultramodern vase pictured here in the mid-1950s. By then, George Cleminson had concluded that the best way to compete with the growing deluge of imports was to diversify. The Cleminsons were not known for contemporary ware, but the company went boldly in this direction and produced items like this vase in addition to their homespun line until finally closing in 1963. The decorative pattern on this tall vase and the various other household items in the line was based on a successful Jaru precedent. It's easy to confuse the two lines because neither one is usually found marked. Examples of the original Jaru design can be seen father along in this section. NM, $100.00.

Cleminsons footed bowl, 5¼"H x 9¼"W x 11½"L. Here is another example of the modernistic line produced by the Cleminsons in the late 1950s. Note that the decoration on this footed freeform bowl features a double arrow or feather motif. This pattern differs only slightly from the pattern originated by Jaru. NM, $60.00.

Cleminsons vase, 14⅝". This vase is from another contemporary line created in the 1950s by the Cleminsons. Hedi Schoop and Barbara Willis, whose businesses had closed in 1958, aided its creation. Both contributed molds, but the Jackson Pollack-like decoration was produced by means of a technique Schoop had devised yet never used on her own ware. The line was christened Happy Talk because owning an example would provide its owner with an instant conversation piece. NM, $120.00.

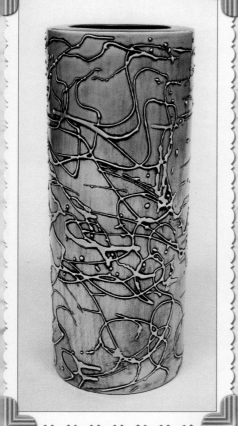

Are you a person who SEES THINGS? In clouds? In a crackling fireplace? Do you see a face on the moon? Then you will enjoy: "HAPPY-TALK" THE NEW FINISH BY Hedi Schoop

Fascinating ceramics where you can "SEE THINGS" with friends. Guaranteed to fill the lull in ANY conversation with: "HAPPY-TALK" MANUFACTURED BY The CALIFORNIA CLEMINSONS P.O. BOX 630 EL MONTE

"Happy Talk" hangtag crediting Hedi Schoop with the new finish.

In-mold mark on one of the Jenev vases.

Jenev vases (left to right): 12½" (pair), 11¾", 11¾", 11". Jenev was another small business operated by a husband and wife team. Owners Jerome and Evelyn Ackerman each contributed to the design and decoration of the various items that they produced. Like Jaru, the name Jenev was derived from their first names. This group of vases is representative of the sophisticated output of the business. The two slender vases on the extreme left are the same shape in different glazes while the third vase from the left is a slightly shorter version of the shape. The vases on the right with the bulbous bottoms are also slightly different in size. The shorter one on the extreme right has an attractive rutile glaze. In-mold marks. NP.

Jenev bottle with stopper, 14¾". This tall Jenev bottle has an incised decoration by Evelyn Ackerman. The business was located at 2207 Federal Ave. in Los Angeles and was essentially a studio-level operation. The Ackermans, besides being award-winning ceramists, went on to other, successful commercial ventures after Jenev's closing. Because the business operated only between 1953 and 1960, Jenev pieces are not easy to find. Jerome Ackerman continues to pot and produces outstanding hand-thrown vessels in the Japanese tradition. Evelyn Ackerman is the author of several books on collectibles. Incised "A Jenev Original by Ackerman." NP.

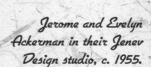

Jerome and Evelyn Ackerman in their Jenev Design studio, c. 1955.

Jenev bird bowl, 4" x 6¼". A whimsical abstract bird design enlivens this small multipurpose Jenev bowl. It was produced in various colors and combinations. Incised "Jenev." NP.

Sascha Brastoff vase, 11" x 16¼". This is an extraordinary and early (c. 1949) cast vase personally decorated by Sascha Brastoff. His imaginary mythical scene was achieved using the sgrafitto method of incising through the top layer of color to expose a contrasting layer below, prior to firing. Somewhat related to etching, it can produce very interesting results such as this. Signed "Sascha Brastoff." $750.00+.

Sascha Brastoff at work, c. 1953.

Sascha Brastoff vases, 8". Multi-talented Sascha Brastoff was without question the most celebrated figure in California pottery during the 1950s. His architect-designed factory and galleries located on Olympic Blvd. at Barrington in West Los Angeles became a popular tourist attraction after it opened in 1953. Brastoff, after obtaining financing from Winthop Rockefeller, produced an astonishing array of decorative household items and several fine china dinnerware patterns. He employed a group of skilled artists to duplicate the items he designed and those items always bore the faux signature "Sascha B." These two cylindrical vases are from his Abstract Originals line. The Sascha Brastoff gold backstamp that included his trademark chanticleer is on both items. If an "X" has been incised through the backstamp, that piece was deemed a second and was sold in the factory's seconds yard. $100.00 each.

The award-winning Sascha Brastoff Products Inc. factory was located at 11520 W. Olympic Blvd. in Los Angeles.

Interior view of the plant showing some of the decorators at work.

Madeline Originals vases, 9⅛" (left) and 9⅛" (right). The success and celebrity of Sascha Brastoff was an inspiration to many. Madeline Originals produced these two vases that bear a resemblance to Brastoff's Abstract Originals line. Produced in the late 1950s, the bands of color were applied while the vases revolved on a banding wheel. After this, they were sponged with a neutral shade to create an interesting overlay pattern. Finally, a matte glaze was applied. This same treatment can be found on various household items produced by Madeline Originals including ashtrays. Ink-stamped "Madeline Originals Made in U.S.A." $50.00 each.

Madeline Originals vase, 9⅛". Another Madeline Originals vase with Sascha Brastoff parallels is seen here. Like Brastoff, Madeline applied different designs to the same shape. On this vase, the abstract flower petals have a faux crackle effect outlined with gold. Madeline and Paul Johnson established the business in Pasadena in 1948. Madeline had previously been a Cleminsons decorator. For ten years her ware was marked "Madeline Ceramics" but a jobber she did business with suggested Madeline Originals was a better name and subsequent items, like this vase, were ink-stamped "Madeline Originals Made in U.S.A." $60.00.

Madeline Originals plate, 14¾". This large plate has the same abstract floral design and matte finish as the neighboring vase. Presumably, it was intended for decorative purposes rather than for food service. Ink-stamped "Madeline Originals Made in U.S.A." $75.00.

Ann Cochran Originals plate, 16⅝". Ann Cockran Originals was located in North Hollywood but little else is known about the business. Evidently in operation in the early to mid 1950s, the ware consisted of hand-painted accessories like this large matte-glazed plate with tropical flowers. Overglaze gold was used to accent the blossoms. Signed "Ann Cochran" on the front. Stamped mark: "California Original." NP.

Jean Goodwin Ames plate, 8¼". Jean Goodwin Ames produced decorative enamels on copper and decorated ceramic plates in the 1950s, like this one, that were hand painted and signed on the back (and sometimes on the front as well). White crackle glazed backgrounds were common. Painted mark: "Mama Mermaid, Jean Goodwin Ames, Claremont Calif." $85.00.

Jean Goodwin Ames plate, 12". Jean Goodwin Ames studied art at the Chicago Art Institute and ceramics with Glen Lukens at USC. She located her studio in the industrial arts complex known as Padua Hills where William Manker Ceramics was already established. She and artist husband Arthur Ames shared the space and both produced decorative tile and enamel on copper work, some of which was undertaken on commission. This plate with a white crackle glaze depicts a fanciful circus scene and is signed on the backside "Funicula, Jean Ames, Padua Hills Calif." $150.00.

This photo of Jean and Arthur Ames accompanied an article about them in the December 1955 issue of <u>American Artist.</u>

Painted mark on De Maray 5" porcelain vase.

De Maray porcelain vase, 6⅞". There were many obscure California companies that produced distinctive ware. De Maray was a porcelain line made in the 1950s by the M & L Manufacturing Company of Azusa. Vases, bowls, and related items in addition to a dinnerware line reportedly designed by Ben Seibel were produced. This egg-shaped vase has a deeply crackled surface and gold trim added at the top. Incised "De Maray." NP.

De Maray porcelain vase, 5". This De Maray vase combines alternating glossy and matte colored bands. The pale yellow is a gloss finish and the brown is matte. The striated brown has the look and feel of raffia. NP.

Marc Bellaire vases, 10⅜" (left) and 10¾" (right). A cloak of mystery seems to surround Marc Bellaire's early years in the business. Sascha Brastoff had employed Bellaire (who's birth name was Donald Fleischman) as one of his personally trained decorators prior to the opening of his Olympic Blvd. factory in 1953. Around the same time as Brastoff's relocation, Bellaire established a competitive business in nearby Culver City. Bellaire evidently designed and decorated items for the Harper Pottery of Santa Monica, in between, using the fictitious name Charles Le Richeux. Adding further intrigue, Tom Hamilton of La Mirada purchased the Le Richeux line from Harper in 1953. The vase on the left has a Harper Pottery backstamp and is signed "Le Richeux." $150.00. The vase on the right was produced at Bellaire's Culver City plant and is incised on the bottom "Balinese Dancers, Marc Bellaire" and also signed on the side "Marc Bellaire." $250.00.

The 1950s

This photo appeared in the March 1953 issue of *Registered California Pictorial.* It pictures Le Richeux Originals by the La Mirada Potteries after the purchase by Tom Hamilton of the line originally produced at the Harper Pottery. Charles Le Richeux was the first professional name used by Donald Fleischman, better known as Marc Bellaire.

LE RICHEUX ORIGINALS by La Mirada Potteries, Inc. Hand decorated in rich colors accented by sgraffito and gold. No. 905, 10½" vase, $25.00 retail. No. 913, 7" sq. ash tray, $7.50 retail. No. 900, 6" pillow vase, $7.50 retail. Available in native on Siamese, autumn leaves on gray, bird on violet, abstract on yellow, sea fantasy on green. PRYOR & CO., 527 W. 7th St., Los Angeles 14, Calif.

Monterey jardinière, 6¼"H x 7½"D. Another pottery with an enigmatic history is the Monterey Pottery. What has been revealed is that there were two phases of the business. The first phase began about 1948, when a small pottery was established in the idyllic Carmel Valley. Evidently only the early ware was signed "Monterey Pottery." Vases and bowls with a variegated glaze simulating the veining seen in semi-precious jade were produced. It's uncertain whether Monterey Jade was ever used to mark the product at this time. Sometime in the 1950s, Rudi and Nancy Marzi bought the business and the Monterey Jade trademark began to be used (more frequently?) to market the line. Artware, including bowls, vases, figurines, and other novelties were produced and were marketed as souvenirs of Carmel by the Sea and Monterey, longstanding tourist destinations. This example exhibits the typical amalgamation of blue, green, and yellow. Incised "Monterey Jade G4." $80.00.

Monterey vase, 7⅝". This unusual freeform-shaped bud vase probably dates from the late 1950s. It has the commingling of colors typical of the Monterey Jade line and is incised "Monterey Jade" plus it retains a paper label reading "Made for Craft House, Carmel by the Sea." $85.00.

The 1950s

Monterey low bowl, 1½"H x 9⅛"W. This piece is difficult to categorize. Perhaps designed as a base for flower arrangements, it's a striking example regardless of its intended purpose. The attractive glaze is accented with a narrow offset border on two sizes of matte black, and the underside with circular foot is also glazed matte black. Incised "Monterey Pottery." $120.00.

Monterey candleholders, 1¾" x 3½". The Monterey Jade glaze can easily overpower a shape, but it provides just the right touch on these small flared candleholders. It's proof positive that less of a good thing can have more impact. Incised "Monterey Jade L-3." $75.00 set.

Paper label on Freeman-McFarlin vase.

Freeman-McFarlin vase, 4", and bowl, 2½" x 9¼". Freeman-McFarlin of El Monte produced a very respectable facsimile of Monterey Jade in the late 1950s — early 1960s. It seems that anytime a really successful line was produced by a California company it would be copied by another company (or companies) sooner or later. Freeman-McFarlin repeated this deed a few times in their long history. This cone-shaped vase with predominantly bluish hues has an in-mold mark obscured by a large circular paper label. $60.00. The low bowl in turquoise and green has the same circular paper label. $75.00.

209

Heath jardiniére, 8¼"H x 9½"D. Edith Kiertzner Heath was a well-respected studio potter before she and husband Brian Heath founded the Health Pottery in Sausalito in 1947. She is known worldwide today for the simple yet enduringly contemporary stoneware dishes and cookware she produced for decades. This jardiniére would be considered unusual and not an item commonly found. It has an interesting combination of form and glaze, specifically a horizontally striated satin-matte glaze with random bumps on the surface. In-mold: "Heath" with pot logo. $200.00+.

Edith Heath, c. 1970.

Heath vase, 7". Heath vases are a rare find and because this one is marked, its authenticity is not in doubt. Unglazed on the outside, the color of the stoneware clay is highlighted. On the inside is a light gray matte glaze. The only ornamentation is the succession of horizontal grooves on the outer surface. Very simple yet elegant and reminiscent of the dinnerware for which the company is famous. In-mold: "Heath" with pot logo. $150.00+.

Heath bowl, 3" x 6½", and vase, 6". Whether Edith Heath or the Heath factory in Sausalito produced these items remains in doubt. Efforts to determine their true identity have not proved conclusive. They do exhibit certain similarities to known Heath ware, but at the same time they have enough unfamiliar qualities to make attribution uncertain. Both are incised "Heath" in a form also unfamiliar. Anyone knowing the truth is urged to share his or her knowledge. NP.

Howard Pierce porcelain vases, 7¼" (left) and 4¼" (right). After an apprenticeship with William Manker in the late 1930s and wartime duty in the early 1940s, Howard Pierce, with his wife Ellen, established a ceramics business in Claremont in 1945. It was later relocated to the desert community of Joshua Tree. The production was porcelain-based and the glazes were many and varied with testing of new glazes a constant activity. The vase on the left (c. 1950) shows the influence of another well-known Claremont potter, Harrison McIntosh. $125.00. The inside is gloss white with some bleed of the outer matte glaze at the top. In-mold: "Pierce." The glaze on the vase on the right is an homage to Pierce's mentor, William Manker. It dates from the early 1950s and is ink-stamped "Howard Pierce Porcelain." $80.00.

In-mold mark on Cemar buffet server.

Cemar buffet servers, 11"L x 12"W (left) and 11⅛"W x 14"L (right). Cemar Clay Products introduced its Trade Winds Lanai Ware in 1952 and the popular line continued in production for several years. It was an extensive line of buffet serving ware perfect in every way for the patio luau, as it capitalized on the growing interest in all things Polynesian and Hawaiian by Americans following WWII. Combining ceramic dishes shaped like Hawaiian flora with rattan handles, the ware came in a choice of colors. On the left is a two-sided serving dish in salmon pink. In-mold: "Cemar 848, Trade Winds Lanai Ware." $135.00. The single server on the right is glazed dark green, the color most commonly found. $120.00.

Brad Keeler buffet server, 2" x 11½". Brad Keeler produced a wide variety of buffet serving ware in the 1940s and early 1950s until his untimely death in 1952 at age 39. Besides bird figurines, he is best known for his lobster-themed buffet items that capitalized on the brilliant red glaze the company developed in advance of the industry. There proved to be numerous other applications for the glaze as well. One use was for a line of crab servers. The example shown has four separate sections. Ink-stamped "BBK Made in USA 284." $75.00.

In-mold mark on Enchanto buffet server.

Enchanto buffet server, 3¼"H x 12½"W. The Enchanto Co. made this shell-shaped chip and dip server. The business was located in Burbank, at 1827 N. Keystone. Little is known about the business, but this buffet server would be representative of the type of ware produced in the 1950s. $45.00.

Bauer buffet server, 7½". In the 1950s, the J.A. Bauer Pottery of Los Angeles was no longer the industry leader it had been and was doing its best to modernize and keep pace with the competition, both foreign and domestic. The Moonsong line was a buffet line introduced in the late 1950s and was the only Bauer line to utilize the modern ram press. This chip and dip server with brass-plated metal stand has a matte specked glaze called spicy green and is marked in-mold "Bauer." $100.00.

Miramar buffet server, 3½"H x 10½"W x 15"L. Buffet ware was good business for the industry in the late 1940s and 1950s as the casual California lifestyle caught on nation-wide. This Miramar of California divided serving dish in brass-plated stand has ceramic handles that swivel and conform to the contour of the hands. Pink was one of the most popular decorator colors during the 1950s. Miramar was located at 613 Ford Blvd. in Los Angeles. Production of Melamine plastic dinnerware was begun in the late 1950s. $60.00.

Photo of mark on Miramar buffet server. (Why can't all pottery marks be this unambiguous?)

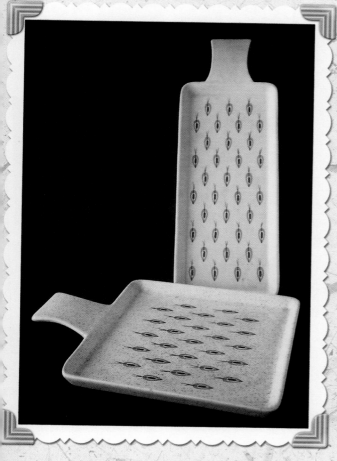

Barbara Willis buffet servers, 14½"L x 5¼"W (top) and 11"L x 8½"W (bottom). These handled servers are from Barbara Willis's Swedish Modern line of the 1950s that also included kitchen canisters and spice jars. By the mid-1950s, her line was evenly geared to both the ultra-modern and provincial trends in home decor. NM, $65.00 each.

Brock lazy susan, 4¼" x 14½" (including base). This Brock lazy susan is an example of an industry trend during the 1950s. Buffet ware was hot but susans were the hottest of the hot. Many California manufacturers added them to their line and some companies produced them exclusively. Most of these handy devices had bases equipped with a ball bearing mechanism that allowed the base and inserts to spin around easily. Brock's lazy susans usually had transfer decorations that matched their popular dinnerware patterns, but this example with daisies is not a known dinnerware design. Ink-stamped "Brock of California." $80.00.

In-mold mark on Valley Vista lazy susan.

Valley Vista lazy susan, 7" x 16" (including base). Valley Vista Potteries was located at 2413 W. Empire Blvd. in Burbank. This company was one of the many that specialized in the manufacture of lazy susans and the one pictured here was a good seller as they turn up rather often today. It has a strawberry motif with a pink speckled glaze. The small covered casserole in the center was a feature of many of the company's susans. $50.00.

Doranne of California (Los Angeles) was a major producer of lazy susans in the 1950s and 1960s. This ads was placed in the Giftwares issue of August 1954.

FOR SUSANS THAT SELL... LOOK TO **DORANNE OF CALIFORNIA** LARGEST SOURCE OF SUPPLY FOR SUSANS

L, 15B Lazy Susan shown— 16", six inserts, two large, four small and a full quart covered casserole—rich colors of Burgundy/Sand, Chartreuse/Green, Pink/Gray—4.50 individually packed.

OUR SPECIALIZATION MEANS ... LOWER COST ... GREATER MARKUP ... MORE PROFITS FOR YOU

64C 1 Qt. Casserole and stand—18.00 dz. Same colors as Lazy Susan. Warmer Stand Available for Casserole—7.80 dz.

USE REPLY CARD #127

DORANNE OF CALIFORNIA

527 N. Hoover   Los Angeles, Calif.
Manufacturers of Distinctive Giftware

Northington casserole with frame, 5¼" x 10". Casserole also became popular in the 1950s as convenient one-dish meals proved to be a timesaver for busy homemakers. Northington was the trendsetter with its casseroles in decorative metal frames. The metal frame came in various plated finishes to match the mood or decor. Northington, Inc. was located at 6610 Melrose Ave. in Los Angeles and was owned and operated by Royce Diener. The company also produced lazy susans and expandable metal trivets, among other things. This all-white casserole has a copper-plated rack with Tigertail design. NM, NP.

Bauer casserole with frame, 5¾"H x 12¾"L. This is Bauer's version of the casserole in metal frame. A feature of the company's kitchenware line of the late 1950s, it was produced in various solid and speckled glaze colors. Bauer casseroles came in one-quart, one and a half-quart and two-quart sizes including a French casserole with ceramic handle. The metal frames were brass plated and some had a built-in candle warmer. In-mold: "Bauer." $55.00.

Brusché casserole, 4¾"H x 9½"L. J.H. Brutsché, a long-time Bauer employee, established Brusché of California in Glendale in 1948 but circumstances made it necessary to consolidate the line with Bauer's in the early 1950s. To his credit, Al Fresco dinnerware was included in the Museum of Modern Art's Good Design exhibit at the Chicago Merchandise Mart in 1950. This two-quart casserole combining lime and olive green was produced at the original factory and dates from about 1950. In-mold: "Brusché California USA." $65.00.

Heath casseroles, 4¼"H x 9¼"D (left) and 3¾"H x 10¼"L (right). Heath's stoneware line has been produced continuously since 1947 in Sausalito (just north of San Francisco). In 1950, the company introduced the casserole style seen on the right with wing-like handles. Four different sizes were produced. The satin-matte glaze on this example is called sand. In-mold: "Heath Sausalito Calif." $85.00. In 1953 the design was modified to a continuous rim. On the left is an example of this style. The glaze on this one is called sea and sand. In-mold "Heath" and pot logo with "®" included in the mark. $65.00.

The 1950s

Jaru pitchers, 10½", and cup, 2½". The eccentric shape as well as the decoration on the pitcher at left is credited to Edmund Ronaky, who was one of the artist-potters who produced items for Jaru Art Products in the 1950s. Incised: "Ronaky 114 Cal." $150.00. The pattern called Starburst that graces the same pitcher and small cup at right was an original concept by co-owner Jack Hirsch. These slightly later examples were produced by Jaru's manufacturing arm, Houser & Red Ceramics. Paper label on pitcher. Cup, $10.00; pitcher, $75.00.

Jaru pitcher, 21", and mugs, 6". Worry Bird is the bestselling decoration on this set consisting of a towering pitcher and four mugs. This set received other decorative treatments as well during the 1950s. Pitcher only is incised "Ronaky." $350.00 set. Pitcher, $200.00; tumblers, $25.00 each. (Larry Gill photo)

Jaru (left to right): cup, 2½"; decanter, 15½"; decanter, 13⅜"; cup, 2⅞". On the left is a decanter and cup designed and produced for Jaru by the Peterson Studios of El Segundo. Greta Peterson's small business supplied Jaru with items such as this, but she also marketed some of the ware independently. Decanter with paper label, $90.00. Unmarked cup, $6.00. The shape of the decanter and cup on the right in black with Starburst pattern is rarely seen. NM, decanter, $120.00; cup, $7.50.

Postcard of the Peterson Studios of El Segundo picturing representative items produced.

Sascha Brastoff ashtray, 3¼"H x 8¼"L. Jaru had its Worry Bird but Sascha had his Chi Chi Bird, and it's the name of the decoration seen on this ashtray. Sascha Brastoff created an incredible collection of ashtrays at his Los Angeles factory and they were in all probability the biggest selling single item produced. Sascha Brastoff backstamp in gold. Signed "Sascha B" on inside. $60.00.

Cleminsons ashtray, 3¾" x 8¼". This tri-footed ashtray with its modern shape and abstract fruit decoration is one of the items produced in the late 1950s after the Cleminsons began adding contemporary items to their line. The decoration was skillfully hand painted before a final low luster glaze was added. Ink-stamped Cleminsons logo plus "Hand Painted" and "©." $40.00.

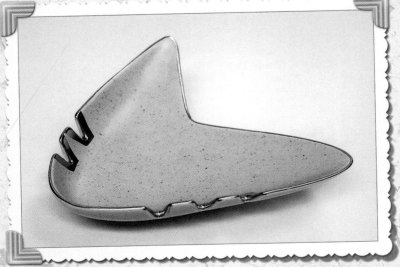

Barbara Willis ashtray, 4¾". Barbara Willis produced a group of items for the contemporary home in the mid-1950s, and this boomerang shaped ashtray in a satin-matte speckled blue glaze with gold trim would be one of them. NM, $45.00.

Jenev bowl, 4¾" x 14¼", and ashtray, 1¼" x 20¼". These two items in satin-matte black are examples of the refined Jenev line of the 1950s. They are not easy to find but worthy of the hunt. The bowl is incised "Jenev 106." The ashtray is incised "Jenev 105W." NP.

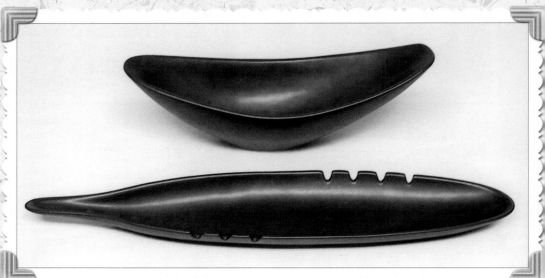

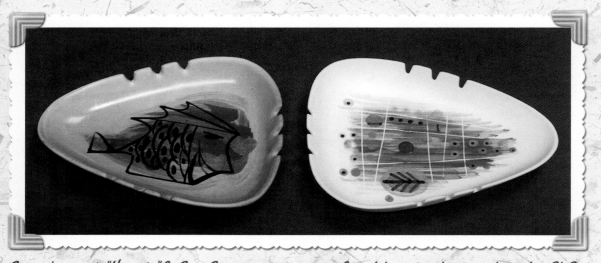

Saar ashtrays, 1½"H x 10½"L. Saar Ceramics got its start in Lawndale in 1950 but was relocated to El Segundo in 1952. Owner Richard Saar studied at the Jepson Art Institute in Los Angeles prior to establishing the business. Mary Rodney, of New York, represented the ultra-contemporary Saar line that included dinnerware and giftware, all of which was hand decorated. William Saar, who was Richard's brother, ran the business from 1960 until it closed in 1962. At most, eight people were employed. Painted mark: "Saar." $50.00 each.

Robaul cigarette box, 2⅛"H x 5½"L x 3¼"W. This Robaul of California cigarette box matches the wallpocket by this company seen earlier. There undoubtedly was a matching ashtray. If any readers have pertinent information about Robaul, please contact the author. In-mold: "Robaul of California." $50.00.

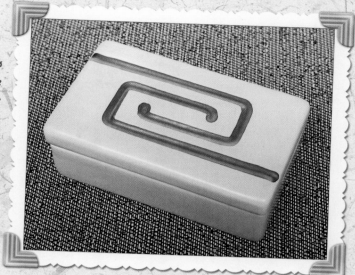

Pixie Potters cigarette box, 3¾"H x 7⅝"L. Millesan Drews is known today as the originator of the pixie craze of the 1940s and 1950s. In 1949, as a change of pace, she introduced her Surf Line of half a dozen pieces inspired by "the rhythm of the pounding surf," to quote from a vintage ad. The item pictured was called the Breaking Surf box. There was a matching ashtray. The wholesale price when the cigarette box debuted was $48.00 a dozen, but it was lowered to $24.00 a dozen just a year later. It's doubtful this interesting line charmed the buyers since very few have surfaced. In-mold: "Surf Line, Trademark Copyright by Pixie Potters, Pats Pend." Also "40-A." NP.

Stamped mark (in gold) on Santa Anita cigarette box.

Santa Anita cigarette box, 4"H x 7⅝"L. Santa Anita Potteries was established at 3025 Fletcher Dr. in Los Angeles in 1942. In a list of Southern California Potteries of the 1940s published in China, Glass & Lamps, G.V. Gilkey was listed as owner. Sometime prior to 1953, the name of the business was changed to Santa Anita Ware and it became a division of the National Silver Co. The address changed also, to 3117 San Fernando Rd. in Los Angeles. This cigarette box was an accessory to the company's Mist dinnerware of the 1950s, which was a copy of Sascha Brastoff's Surf Ballet dinnerware. $40.00.

219

Sascha Brastoff 17" chop plate, 11³/₄" dinner plate, cup, and saucer. Sascha Brastoff began producing his most popular dinnerware called Surf Ballet in the late 1940s, and steady sales continued for about 10 years. It was produced, not unlike coloring Easter eggs, by dipping an item with a solid colored background (several colors were used over the years) into a suspension of either gold or platinum prior to firing. The swirled patterns that resulted were unique and no two pieces were ever the same. The very large chop plate has a pink background with platinum swirl and the Sascha Brastoff backstamp. $100.00. The large dinner plate has a yellow background with gold swirl and is signed "Sascha B" on the backside. $30.00. The cup and saucer have a white background with gold swirl and both have the Sascha Brastoff backstamp. $25.00.

Backstamp on Sascha Brastoff teapot. This printed mark should not to be considered a full signature.

Sascha Brastoff teapot, 8". This large Surf Ballet teapot with black background and gold swirl pattern is marked with the Sascha Brastoff backstamp that includes his trademark chanticleer. $150.00.

Entrance to the Heath factory
showroom in Sausalito.

Heath (clockwise from top) 13" chop plate, 10¾" dinner plate, 4" mug, 6" saucer, 6½" soup bowl, salt and pepper.
Heath dinnerware is an American modern classic and has changed little over the years since its introduction in 1947.
Most of the ware has been produced on a dark-brown stoneware body. Slight modifications have been made to a few
shapes while others have come and gone. Both coupe shaped dishes, like those pictured here, and dishes with narrow
unglazed rims have been produced. And a porcelain-like white stoneware has been added in recent years. But never has
there been any added decoration to these simple yet elegant shapes. Several marks have been used during Heath's long
production span including ink-stamped marks (early) and a variety of impressed and in-mold marks. Items with the in-
mold "Heath" and pot logo are the most commonly found. Certain items and seconds were generally not marked. Chop
plate, $40.00; dinner plate, $25.00; mug, $25.00; saucer, $5.00; soup bowl, $20.00; shakers, $30.00 set.

Heath 10¾" dinner plate. Heath stoneware dinner plate in
the desert ochre color combination made from 1960 to 1966.
Four combinations such as this were produced. The effect
was achieved by dipping the plate in two contrasting colors of
glaze. Stamped mark. $35.00.

Undated N.S. Gustin Co. promotional
brochure for Heath dinnerware showing
the four dipped-glaze colors produced.

221

Heath half-gallon jug, creamer, 16-ounce teapot, and one-quart pitcher. This is a selection of Heath stoneware from recent years. The large jug in sea and sand on the left has the impressed Heath and pot logo. $100.00. The creamer in sea and sand has the same mark. $35.00. The small teapot with cork stopper in the dipped glaze called birch has a factory label on the bottom. $60.00. The ovoid pitcher in sandalwood has the in-mold "Heath" and pot logo along with "®" and "Made in USA." $65.00.

In-mold Heath and pot logo on large party bowl.

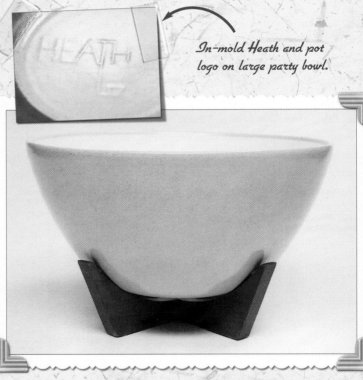

Heath party bowl, 7"H x 13"D with wood stand. This rarely seen bowl is believed to be what the company called a party bowl, which served 24. It has a wood base. This item, in the sand/white porcelain liner glaze, was produced c. 1960. $300.00+.

This undated postcard picturing the Heath Buffet Service includes large party bowls at top.

Metlox 10" dinner plate, cup, and saucer. Metlox's marvelous mid-century modern dinnerware lines included California Mobile. The items pictured here are from this ultra-modern design introduced in 1954. Frank Irwin is credited with the creation of the Freeform shape but it was Bob Allen and Mel Shaw who designed the Calderesque patterns. The dinner plate has the complete printed transfer pattern with colors filled-in by hand. $35.00. The cup has a condensed version of the pattern. $30.00. The saucer is plain. $5.00. Ink-stamped marks.

Metlox serving bowl, 14½" water pitcher, 9½" milk pitcher. The other two closely related patterns on Metlox's Freeform shapes were California Contempora and California Free Form. California Free Form was just like California Mobile except that the colors were different. California Contempora was introduced a year later (1955.) It was matte-glazed and the plates were round not square. On the left is the boomerang-shaped California Contempora serving bowl known as the jawbone. $145.00. The large California Free Form pitcher is for water. $235.00. The small California Mobile pitcher is for milk. $275.00. Ink-stamped marks.

Metlox (clockwise from top) 10½"
dinner plate, creamer, sugar bowl, cup
and saucer, 6" cereal bowl, mug. Pictured here is Metlox's California
Tempo dinnerware in the walnut-blue
combination. Walnut was a constant b
there were four other color choices to
go with it. The walnut glaze was matte
and the optional colors were semi-
gloss. The line was introduced in 196C
and was only randomly marked. Man
large items can be found unmarked bu
everyday pieces usually have a circula
ink-stamped mark reading "Poppytrail by Metlox Made in U.S.A."
Dinner plate, $20.00; creamer,
$20.00; sugar bowl, $25.00; cup
and saucer, $20.00; cereal bowl,
$20.00; mug, $20.00.

Ink-stamped mark or
Hollydale Malibu
Modern dinner plate.

Hollydale (clockwise from top) 10¼" dinner plate, gravy boat, sugar bowl, salt and pepper, creamer, teapot. The Hollydale Pottery
was located at 11708 Center Ave. in Hollydale, a district of South Gate. Otto Hupp and wife were the owners. Malibu Modern
was the company's most successful dinnerware. Although numerous patterns were attempted on the Malibu Modern shapes, the
undecorated shapes remained the most popular with the public. Another dinnerware line produced was called Capistrano. Lazy
susans were also produced in colors that matched the dinnerware. Some Malibu Modern items may be found unmarked or the mark
will be almost illegible. The mark (ink-stamped or in-mold) reads "Malibu Modern by Hollydale, Made in California." Dinner
plate, $25.00; gravy boat, $35.00; sugar bowl, $30.00; shakers, $20.00; creamer, $25.00; teapot, $90.00.

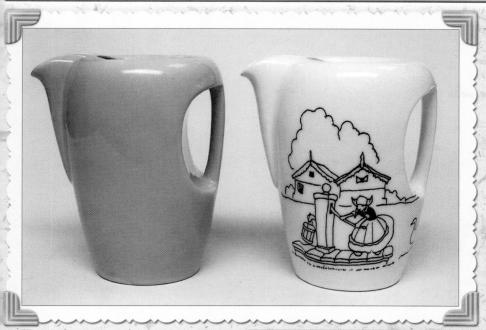

Hollydale 8½" pitchers. On the left is the original Malibu Modern pitcher in gray. It's shape, as well as other shapes in the line, is evocative of dinnerware designed by Eva Zeisel. Hollydale, in fact, manufactured an Eva Zeisel dinnerware design in the late 1950s. On the left is the same pitcher with the Merrie Dutch decoration introduced in 1951. Apparently, this decoration was not successful since it's rarely seen today. Hollydale suffered a serious fire in 1952, which may have contributed to the scarcity. In-mold: "Malibu Modern by Hollydale, Made in California" on both. Gray pitcher, $80.00; Merrie Dutch pitcher, $100.00+.

This Hollydale ad for its new Merrie Dutch pattern appeared in the January 1951 issue of *Giftwares*.

HOLLYDALE POTTERY

Presents

Malibu
"MERRIE DUTCH"

A pattern centuries old—but new to Malibu's Modern Shape — is equally *at home* in Provincial or Modern surroundings.

SEE OUR COMPLETE DISPLAYS
AT LOS ANGELES, CHICAGO
AND ALL OTHER MAJOR SHOWS

REPRESENTATIVES

NEW YORK
Linn Meyers, Inc.
1107 Broadway

LOS ANGELES
Blodgett & Co.
Brack Shops

CHICAGO
Gene Stewart Co.
Merchandise Mart

ATLANTA
J. A. Vaccaro & Co.
125 Ellis St., N.E.

KANSAS CITY
Wennerstrom & Asso.
Merchandise Mart

HONOLULU
S. C. Kling
49 S. Beretania

FACTORY: HOLLYDALE POTTERY, INC.
11708 Center Avenue   Hollydale, Calif.

Hollydale bird pitcher. This small bird-shaped pitcher is believed to be an example of an interesting Eva Zeisel dinnerware design produced in the late 1950s by Hollydale. Due to labor problems at the Western Stoneware Co. of Monmouth, Illinois (the original manufacturer chosen), the Hollydale Pottery took over production of the ware. However, it isn't known at this time how long the dishes were made. Examples are very rarely seen. NM, NP.

Bauer (clockwise from top) 10" dinner plate, cup and saucer, 5" dessert bowl, and 5½" soup/cereal bowl. Contempo was the name of a new line of dinnerware and accessories that J.H. Brutsche introduced in 1960. Actually, it was his previous Al Fresco line dressed-up in new glazes. A few additions were made but Contempo was essentially a revised line. The palette of satin-matte glazes with subtle specks throughout included champagne white, desert beige, Indio brown, pumpkin, and spicy green. Slate, which was speck-free, was added later. Pictured here is a group of items in desert beige. Most items will be found marked in-mold "Brusché California, Made in USA," but some items may be found marked in-mold "Bauer." Dinner plate, $20.00; cup and saucer, $20.00; dessert bowl, $15.00; soup/cereal bowl, $20.00.

Brusché 10¼" snack tray and cup. The original Brusché of California dinnerware called Al Fresco that Bauer eventually absorbed into its own line included these snack trays (called "hostess trays" at the time) and cups. There is a circular depression at one end to hold the cup. Trays are marked in-mold "Brusché California USA." The cups are not marked. $45.00 each set.

In-mold mark commonly found on Denwar Bantu items.

Denwar (left to right) open sugar, 11" dinner plate, 7½" salad plate, 6½" bread and butter plate, cup and saucer, and creamer. Denwar Ceramics was a small business located in Costa Mesa, at 220 E. 16th St. Owners were Jo Dendel and his wife Esther Warner. The name Denwar came from the first three letters of their last names. Bantu dinnerware was the company's most notable achievement. Introduced in the late 1940s, it was popular with avant-gardes of the 1950s. The original shapes were developed by Jo Dendel based on the classic asymmetry of the egg. However, some shapes were modified slightly in later years. The colored glazes were speckled and occasionally two colors would be combined on a single unit. Esther Warner's colors have interesting names including cola brown, gibi green, guinea gold, thatch, benin blue, and bombo smoke. Most items will be found simply marked in-mold "Denwar." Sugar, $20.00; dinner plate, $20.00; salad plate, $15.00; bread and butter plate, $10.00; cup and saucer, $20.00; creamer, $20.00.

Denwar coffee server, 9½". This sleek and modern Denwar Bantu coffee server in thatch has a cover that fits snugly despite its rather precarious angle. Thatch seemingly was the most popular color the company produced, as it's the most commonly found today. NM, $145.00.

Denwar salt and pepper shakers. The Bantu line that included these was partly inspired by the co-owners' experiences in West Africa in the early 1940s, where the couple originally met. The shapes and the names of the colors reflect aspects of the native culture with which they came into contact. The glaze on this set of salt and peppers is known as bombo smoke, a very dark brown. NM, $35.00 set.

Gladding-McBean 9³⁄₄" dinner plate, cup and saucer, shakers, and 5" tumbler. This Franciscan dinnerware line of the 1950s called Tiempo was a revision of an earlier set of dishes designed by Morris B Sanders and produced in the early 1940s as Metropolitan. The satin-matte glazes of the original were replaced with high-gloss colors with creative names: hot chocolate, peppermint, leaf, sprout, mustard, pebble, stone, salt, and copper. The square shape was innovative when first produced and just as up-to-date in its Tiempo incarnation. Most items will be found ink-stamped "Franciscan Made in California." Dinner plate, $25.00; cup and saucer, $25.00; shakers, $15.00; tumbler, $40.00.

Gladding-McBean coffee pot, 7¹⁄₄". This Tiempo coffee server in pebble (reddish tan) has a streamlined profile that is just as progressive today as when first produced as Metropolitan in 1940. Ink-stamped "Franciscan Made in California." $150.00.

Campo (clockwise from top) 9³⁄₈" porcelain dinner plate, after dinner cup and saucer, 1⁵⁄₈" cordial cup, 5½" soup/cereal bowl, 6¼" bread and butter plate, and 5" tumbler. Little is known about the company known as Campo del Mar other than its location was Capitola, a seaside community located on the Monterey Peninsula south of San Francisco. Evidently, Capitola was at one time a popular campsite, hence the name Campo. These porcelain dishes share a common design thread with Franciscan Tiempo but the color choices were quite different. Known colors are black, white, rose, dark green, light green, purple, yellow, and gray. The cordial cup, 6¼" plate, and after dinner cup and saucer were part of a five-piece after dinner set that consisted of these four items plus a small rectangular ashtray. Most items observed have had the ink-stamped mark: "California Campo Porcelain" on their unglazed bottoms. NP.

Campo porcelain cups and saucers. Here are some of the color choices in Campo porcelain dinnerware, which was produced in the 1950s. All items ink-stamped "California Campo Porcelain." NP.

Ink-stamped mark on a Campo coffee cup. The added number is unusual.

Campo porcelain nested set of bowls. This set of perfectly nesting bowls in gray was probably designed for serving such things as condiments or sauces. The largest size measures 3" x 6". Ink-stamped "California Campo Porcelain." NP.

Laurel 10" dinner plate, cup and saucer, shakers. The Laurel Potteries of Stockton had an interesting history but too convoluted to cover in this limited space. The company that preceded Laurel on its site at 3323 S. McKinley was the Joaquin Pottery, manufacturers of California pottery dinnerware in a variety of solid colors. Laurel Potteries was a business partnership that came together in 1947 and resulted in several successful dinnerware lines during the 1950s including the progressive Seaside line pictured here. The line's glazes were the speckled variety in a pleasing array of pastel hues in addition to black. Some pieces from this line will be found unmarked. Those that are have an ink-stamped mark: "Laurel of California U.S.A." in a circle. Dinner plate, $15.00; cup, $10.00; saucer, $5.00; shakers, $25.00.

Laurel 10" coffee pot, covered sugar, and creamer. A departure from the pastel colors usually seen on Laurel's Seaside dinnerware, this coffee pot's color, called desert brown, is not unlike its intended contents. $85.00. The pink sugar bowl and citron creamer are more commonly found colors. NM, sugar, $25.00; creamer, $17.50.

Ink-stamped mark found on both ceramic and wood bases of Vadna dinnerware.

Vadna (clockwise from top) 7" tumbler, cup and saucer, 9³/₄" dinner plate, 7" salad plate, 5¹/₂" soup bowl, and open sugar and creamer. Vadna of California is another enigmatic company. The business was located in Leucadia, a small seaside community north of San Diego. It seems an unlikely place for the production of a set of dinnerware with so many unusual features. For one, these dishes are very thinly cast and lightweight. Secondly, the items combine two highly contrasting colors (in both value and intensity). And the most interesting of all, some pieces have lacquered wood components that are well integrated with the ceramic forms. Too few pieces have emerged to know the full extent of this curious line. Most items are marked with the ink-stamped mark shown. Tumbler, $30.00; cup and saucer, $35.00; dinner plate, $20.00; salad plate, $15.00; soup bowl, $30.00; sugar, $30.00; creamer, $30.00.

De Maray porcelain covered bowl, 3¹/₂"H x 6¹/₂"L x 4¹/₈"W. It should be apparent by now that small companies produced some very interesting modern designs in California dinnerware. Unfortunately, information about them is sadly lacking. The M & L Manufacturing Co. of Azusa, another mystery, produced De Maray porcelain. The ware was represented by Victor McNutt Associates and was featured in the Barker Brothers furniture stores throughout Los Angeles in the early 1950s. As reported in Ceramic Industry, the 1950 line included bowls, vases, and cigarette sets in combinations of charcoal and lime and acorn and lime. It's been confirmed that noted industrial designer Ben Seibel designed a De Maray dinnerware line. This covered bowl with incised linear pattern and wing-like handle is a probable Seibel design although his name does not appear on the item. Incised "De Maray Porcelain 802." NP.

Gladding-McBean pitcher, 10". Franciscan Starburst dinnerware was a well-received line when it was new and its popularity has resurged with the recent back-to-the-1950s trend in home decor. The outrageous pattern is a retro delight and no doubt nostalgic for anyone who remembers the so-called happy days. This large pitcher is transfer printed "Franciscan Earthenware" inside a TV screen-shaped outline with "Gladding, McBean & Co." above and "Made in U.S.A." below. $100.00.

Winfield China divided platter, 14"L x 10"W. This unusual palette-shaped divided platter was probably intended for serving but would function just as well as an individual place setting, especially at a buffet. This fine china pattern is called Dragon Flower and is a cousin to Desert Dawn, which has the same hand-painted design combined with a muted coffee-colored background. This rarely-seen item has the stenciled mark: "Winfield Ware Handcraft China" on its bisque backside. $45.00.

Saar dinner plate, 10½" x 11". Richard Saar produced a seldom seen but striking set of contemporary dinnerware called Etruscan in the mid-1950s. This dinner plate with its hand-painted silhouette of a horse and moon is an example. Saar's New York agent, Mary Rodney, marketed the line mainly on the east coast. Painted mark: "Saar." $50.00.

Brock 10¾" dinner plate, cup, and saucer. B.J. Brock & Co. of Lawndale introduced its offbeat desert-themed Manzanita dinnerware in 1955. The company, owned and operated by Bert J. Brock, was primarily known for its traditional patterns so this was quite a departure. The starkly dramatic scene on the ware was hand painted in over-glaze platinum with touches of pink and white set against a black airbrushed foreground and bright white background. Not easily found today, this fascinating attempt at modernism may have met with limited acceptance. Dinner plate, $30.00; cup and saucer, $30.00.

Printed mark on Brock Manzanita dinner plate.

Ink-stamped mark on Brock Country Modern saucer.

Brock (clockwise from top) 11⅛" dinner plate, cup and saucer, shaker, and 5"H x 9"L butter dish. Brock's transfer-printed provincial lines can be puzzling because only minor differences separate them. Pictured here are examples of the Harvest and Country Modern patterns and the only discernable difference is that one has brown and the other has yellow airbrushed borders, although there are slight variations in the farm scene on the plates. On the Harvest dinner plate (brown border), the yellow areas were hand tinted. $15.00. The cup and saucer belong with Country Modern (yellow border). $20.00. The butter dish shaped like an old fashioned flatiron belongs with Country Modern. $45.00. The milk can-shaped shaker also belongs with this pattern. $7.50. Some items will be found unmarked but most will have an ink-stamped mark.

Brock 11⅛" dinner plate. Brock of California was one of the leading producers of California pottery dinnerware with a provincial theme. Modern and provincial were the two opposites in the interior design field during the 1950s. Although some manufacturers tried to amalgamate them, the two poles remained fundamentally distant. This dinner plate from the California Farmhouse pattern has a yellow border. Also produced was a nearly identical pattern called Country Lane (brown border). Ink-stamped "Brock of California." $15.00.

Brock 10³/₄" dinner plate, cup, and saucer. This Brock provincial pattern called Chanticleer is easy to recognize. The dinner plate is slightly smaller than the other lines and the rooster pattern is distinctive. However, this pattern incorporated many of the same interesting accessory items as the other confusing patterns. Ink-stamped "Brock of California." Dinner plate, $20.00; cup and saucer, $25.00.

Metlox 10" dinner plate, cup, and saucer. Metlox's dinnerware designs of 1950 started the provincial trend in California. Designed to coordinate with the growing popularity of American Colonial furniture and furnishings in the late 1940s, Provincial Blue, Homestead Provincial, and California Provincial — all introduced in 1950 — set the pace. The pictured items are from the California Provincial line. The dinner plate is ink-stamped "California Provincial, Poppytrail by Metlox, Made in Calif. U.S.A." The cup and saucer are ink-stamped "Poppytrail by Metlox, Made in California" in a circle. Dinner plate, $15.00; cup and saucer, $20.00.

Printed mark on Vernon RFD butter dish.

Brock butter dish, 5"H x 9"L, and Vernon Kilns butter dish, 3" x 7½". The butter dish shaped like a mailbox is from the Vernon Kilns dinnerware line called RFD. On the other side of the cover is a rooster-shaped weathervane. $75.00. The Brock flatiron-shaped butter dish with brown edging and no pattern is unusual. NM, $45.00.

Incised mark on
Donna Winston plate.

Donna Winston plate, 13". This plate with
colorful rooster motif is not part of a
dinnerware set, but was made purely for
decoration. Although roosters were almost
synonymous with provincial, there were some
major exceptions as the examples to follow will illustrate.
Donna Winston is an example herself — of the many individual California producers who have been all but lost to history.
Only after a Northern California antiques dealer purchased
her personal effects, including numerous pottery examples, did
her name come to light. In nearly thirty years of buying and
selling pottery, I had not come across a single piece. As it
turns out, she got her start in the mid-1940s as one of Jane
Callender's assistants, eventually leaving to forge a career of
her own. In her case, that career did not bring her fame and
fortune although she did produce some interesting items.
Sometimes failure was just a case of not hooking up with a
competent manufacturer's representative. The alternative was
selling directly to jobbers who often put their own label on the ware, leaving the artist in obscurity. NP.

Undated photo (c. 1953) of Donna
Winston unloading her kiln. She can
also be seen in the Jane Callender
studio view (page 174). She is in the
center of the photo.

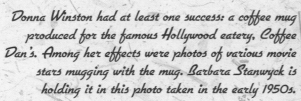

Donna Winston had at least one success: a coffee mug
produced for the famous Hollywood eatery, Coffee
Dan's. Among her effects were photos of various movie
stars mugging with the mug. Barbara Stanwyck is
holding it in this photo taken in the early 1950s.

Hedi Schoop and Cleminsons roosters, 13". Hedi Schoop produced the rooster on the left in her North Hollywood factory in the early 1950s. This colorful object functions as a flower holder because there are openings in the tail and the beak. Ink-stamped "Hedi Schoop Hollywood, Cal." $125.00. After her factory was destroyed by fire in 1958, Schoop helped the Cleminsons create a new line with a contemporary flair. It utilized her innovative technique of decorating the surface of an unfired object with random dribbles followed by a wash of color and a final coat of clear glaze. Hedi Schoop and Barbara Willis molds were added to the shapes specially created for this atypical line the Cleminsons called Happy Talk. The rooster on the right is an example of Happy Talk. Items in this line are usually found unmarked. NM, $75.00.

This undated publicity photo for the Happy Talk line of the Cleminsons includes the Hedi Schoop rooster.

Sascha Brastoff rooster, 16⅛". Sascha Brastoff adopted the rooster as his personal trademark after the legendary factory in West Los Angeles opened to the public in 1953. With the backing of his friend Winthop Rockefeller, Brastoff could afford to lavish his creations, like this large rooster, with a profusion of gold. Signed "Sascha B" in gold. $200.00.

Brayton Laguna rooster, 16³/₄". Ferdinand Horvath created this phenomenal rooster for Brayton Laguna in the mid-1950s. Imposing at nearly 17" in height, it came in a variety of glaze finishes. Many of the abstract animal figures that Brayton produced were designed and modeled by Horvath. In-mold: "Brayton's-Laguna Beach, Cal. H-47." $185.00.

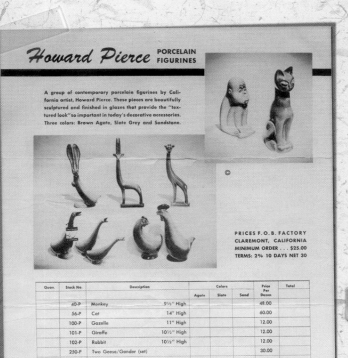

Howard Pierce PORCELAIN FIGURINES

A group of contemporary porcelain figurines by California artist, Howard Pierce. These pieces are beautifully sculptured and finished in glazes that provide the "textured look" so important in today's decorative accessories. Three colors: Brown Agate, Slate Grey and Sandstone.

PRICES F.O.B. FACTORY
CLAREMONT, CALIFORNIA
MINIMUM ORDER . . . $25.00
TERMS: 2% 10 DAYS NET 30

Quan.	Stock No.	Description		Colors			Price Per Dozen	Total
				Agate	Slate	Sand		
	40-P	Monkey	9½" High				48.00	
	56-P	Cat	14" High				60.00	
	100-P	Gazelle	11" High				12.00	
	101-P	Giraffe	10½" High				12.00	
	102-P	Rabbit	10½" High				12.00	
	250-P	Two Geese/Gander (set)					30.00	
	251-P	Rooster/Hen (set)					30.00	

N. S. GUSTIN COMPANY
712 SOUTH OLIVE STREET
LOS ANGELES 14, CALIFORNIA

SAN FRANCISCO
1355 MARKET STREET

CHICAGO
1583 MERCHANDISE MART

NEW YORK
225 FIFTH AVENUE

N.S. Gustin Co. illustrated price list of Howard Pierce figurines that includes the rooster/hen set. The wholesale price for the pair in the mid-1950s was $30.00 per dozen.

Howard Pierce porcelain hen, 7½", and rooster, 9½". Of course, the hen is the other half of the rooster, and here is an excellent, unfussy set produced by Howard Pierce of Claremont in the mid-1950s. The muted sandstone glaze is not commonly found. In-mold: "© Howard Pierce, 251P." $120.00 set.

Cemar swan, 11⁵⁄₈". Cemar seemingly favored these colors in the early 1950s because many figurines were produced utilizing this particular combination. The imposing and graceful swan was modeled by Fred Kaye about 1953. Flocked base. $85.00.

Roselane swans, 7³⁄₄". It is believed that Fred Kaye modeled this swan figurine for Roselane after leaving Cemar to extend his services on a free-lance basis. Kaye was Cemar's principal figure modeler from the mid-1930s to the mid-1940s. The spiky stylized feathers are an unusual feature of this swan. In-mold: "Roselane 261." $70.00 each.

Bill Fields, c. 1956.

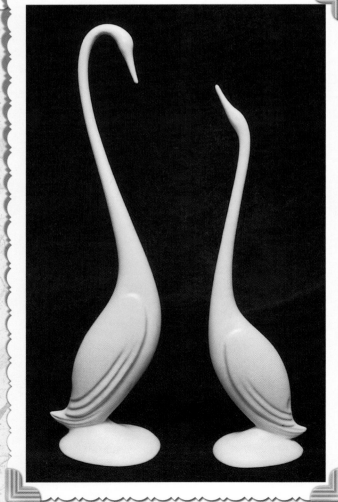

Hallfield swans, 19¹⁄₂" (left) and 17" (right). These towering swans were produced by the Hallfield Pottery, a business established in the early 1950s by Bill Fields and partner James Hall. Fields had founded Roselane in the late 1930s, but decided upon his return from wartime duty to sell his interest in Roselane to his brother Doc. In the late 1940s, Fields designed free-lance for various firms. This set of matte-glazed swans was copied by others, so only marked examples can be considered the genuine article. In-mold: "Hallfield California." $90.00 set.

Fred Wind swan, 10". Fred Wind Ceramics, located in Glendale, was in business between 1950 and 1960. The company was owned and operated by Fred Wind and his father Fred Wind. The elder Fred Wind had previously worked for Pacific Clay Products and McCarty Bros. The bulk of the Fred Wind business was contract work but a few items like this swan were marketed under the company name or Windware. This ware generally was marked in the mold, however this example is not. NM, NP.

A view of the Fred Wind pottery.

Roselane ducks, 4⅛" x 7¼" (left) and 6⅛" x 9¾" (right). These very naturalistic Roselane ducks are not the standard items this company is known for. Dating from the late 1950s or early 1960s, they do have the familiar plastic eyes seen on many of its Sparklers, however all other features of this set including the marks are unusual. The female duck on the left is marked in-mold "Roselane Pottery Calif. U.S.A." The male is marked in-mold "Roselane Pottery Calif." (The word "pottery" is not usually included in Roselane marks.) $100.00 set.

Roselane dove on wood base, 7"H x 7½"L. This Roselane piece is from a superb series of ultramodern animals and birds produced in the 1950s. In terms of sales, the series was less than triumphant. Although this particular example is more naturalistic, most were quite abstract and too advanced for the buyers at the time. All of these objets d'art were attached to lacquered wood bases. The bases were marked (branded) on the bottom "Roselane Pasadena, Calif." $90.00.

Full-page ad in the December 1947 issue of The Gift and Art Buyer advertising the Los Angeles Giftwares Center including the Brack Shops, at 527 W. 7th St.

Shop Conveniently in the Heart of the
Los Angeles Giftwares Market

BROCKMAN BLDG. (HAGGARTY)

BRACK SHOPS

MERCHANDISE MART

GRAND

SEVENTH   OLIVE

When you cover the three important wholesale buildings in the heart of the Los Angeles Gift Market you'll see everything.

Scores of permanent showrooms with hundreds of lines of gifts, artware and decorative accessories.

Select from thousands of original, colorful, authentic items for every department—every occasion—all seasons.

The GIFTWARES CENTER has everything you need to stock your store. Products you preview in the many exhibitors' display rooms are the latest, smartest innovations of new trends, styles, designs and materials.

Your greatest gift resource today is the GIFTWARES CENTER in downtown Los Angeles . . . headquarters for profitable, timely merchandise.

Visit us! You'll find your wishes come true.

The Los Angeles
Giftwares Center
OLIVE • SEVENTH • GRAND

Complete Giftwares Center BUYERS' DIRECTORY available to store buyers —write the Secretary, Room 807, 527 W. 7th Street, Los Angeles 14.

Freeman-McFarlin eagle, 12½" x 8½". Freeman-McFarlin was another California company to contrast large areas of stained bisque with splashes of high-gloss glaze. They typically used a very dark stain, like the one seen on this large and imposing American eagle. Maynard Anthony Freeman was the chief designer and modeler at the time this piece was created, c. late 1950s. In-mold: "Anthony, © Calif. USA, 120." $85.00.

Madeline Originals peahen, 6" x 15" (left), and peacock, 10¾" x 10⅝" (right). This large set of peafowl by Madeline Originals captures the flamboyant elegance of these natives of South Asia and the East Indies without going over the top. Ink-stamped "Madeline Originals California Made in U.S.A." $90.00.

Madeline Originals toucans, 6" (left) and 5⅛" (right). These delightful tropical birds are worth looking out for, but not easy to sight. Ink-stamped "Madeline Originals California Made in U.S.A." $120.00 set.

Josef Originals ostrich, 5½". A male and a female ostrich were produced from the same Josef Originals mold and marketed as a pair. I believe this one is the male. Also produced were offspring: one small hatchling and one in the process of emerging from its egg. They were hand decorated and matte glazed and were just one of many cute animal sets produced in the 1950s. Paper label. $45.00.

Roselane puffin, 5¾". Puffins are exotic birds native to the north seas that bear a slight resemblance to penguins. I don't know of another company that produced a puffin. This one is matte glazed and rather nice. In-mold: "© Roselane U.S.A." $60.00.

Paper label on Bell egrets.

Bell egrets, 9¼". This matte-glazed, highly stylized shore bird is believed to be an egret. Little is known about the Bell Manufacturing and Sales Co., located at 1320 S. Main in Los Angeles. The company name suggests that they were distributors as well as producers of ceramic giftware. $40.00 each.

Brayton Laguna egret, 9⅞". Brayton was one of the first companies to combine and contrast tooled brown-stained bisque (the wood look) with glossy glazes on figures. This Bill Dickenson shore bird is a fine example of how they successfully utilized the technique. A coating of glaze generally strengthens ware, so figurines that have large unglazed (bisque) areas, like this one, are more susceptible to breakage. NM, $85.00.

Alexander Franzka fish, 10½" x 12⅜". This is one exotic fish. Once again, we have the combination of stained bisque and glaze, but the amazing form and mix of colors elevates this example to another level. Unfortunately, nothing is known about the business, but the name of the artist and look of the piece suggests that he was an Eastern European émigré. NP.

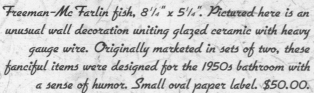

Ink-stamped mark on Alexander Franzka fish.

Freeman-McFarlin fish, 8¼" x 5¼". Pictured here is an unusual wall decoration uniting glazed ceramic with heavy gauge wire. Originally marketed in sets of two, these fanciful items were designed for the 1950s bathroom with a sense of humor. Small oval paper label. $50.00.

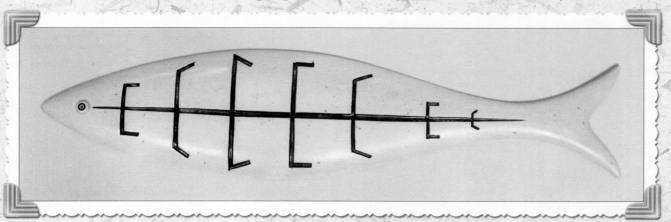

Hallfield fish, 23⅝". Here's another great catch. It's a Hallfield fish for the wall that measures almost two feet in length, and has a pale turquoise matte glaze with subtle specks throughout and a geometric outline in illusionary perspective of the fish's skeletal structure. It's a tour de force that must be seen up close to fully appreciate. NM, $100.00.

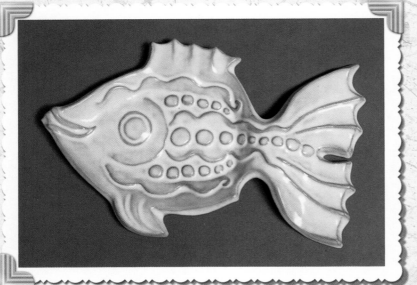

Chalice fish ashtray, 7¼" x 11¼". Either a candy dish or ashtray, this item is striking no matter what its intended use. Charles and Alice Smith, using terra-cotta colored clay and a translucent semi-matte glaze on the topside only, produced it. It's simply incised "Chal." $50.00.

West Coast fish ashtray, 5¾" x 18¾". This elongated fish-shaped ashtray produced by the West Coast Pottery would accommodate a crowd. The airbrushed brown border blended attractively with the turquoise base glaze in the kiln. The slightly raised skeletal structure of the fish is another nice touch. In-mold: "West Coast Calif. 19" Tray." $40.00.

Incised mark on backside of Jaru tray produced by Rónaky.

Jaru platter, 12¾". Edmund Rónaky painted the fish design on this square platter that he produced for Jaru Art Products. Probably intended more for decoration than function, it's an intriguing image. $100.00.

Ceramicraft school of fish with bubbles, largest: 6½" x 9½". These campy wall decorations for the bathroom were a 1950s rage and several California companies made them. Ceramicraft of San Clemente not only produced them, they were the specialty of the house. It's unusual to find a large set like this intact today. The largest of the fish is also a wallpocket. Ink-stamped "Copyright © Ceramicraft, San Clemente, Calif." $125.00 complete set.

Ink-stamped mark on backside of Ceramicraft fish wall pocket.

Ceramicraft wallpocket, 7¼" x 7½". Here is a close-up view of another Ceramicraft fish wallpocket. Many of these wall decorations had vibrant luster glazes. The fish's eye has been hand painted with overglaze gold but most of the colors were applied using an airbrush. The distinctive ink-stamped mark reads "Tropic Treasures by Ceramicraft, San Clemente, Calif." $45.00.

Los Angeles fish wallpocket, 10" x 10". Not marked, but this animated double fish wallpocket is believed to be an item produced by the Los Angeles Potteries of Lynwood. Airbrush decorated except for a dab of green on the eyes. Each orb was inserted into its respective eye socket prior to firing. NM, $65.00.

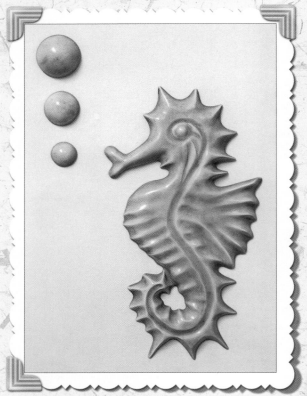

Unidentified seahorse with bubbles, 11½". The maker of this imaginative seahorse decoration is presently unknown. The satin-matte glaze on both seahorse and bubbles delicately blends pink and turquoise. The overall tonal effect has a slight iridescence. On the backside are the incised initials "LMH." NP.

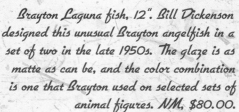

Brayton Laguna fish, 12". Bill Dickenson designed this unusual Brayton angelfish in a set of two in the late 1950s. The glaze is as matte as can be, and the color combination is one that Brayton used on selected sets of animal figures. NM, $80.00.

Freeman-McFarlin fish casserole, 5¾" x 11½". It is believed that the designer of this Freeman-McFarlin fish-shaped casserole of 1959 was Fred Kaye, who had left his position at Cemar and was a free-lance designer at the time. It has obvious similarities to the cookie jar Bauer produced after its acquisition of Cemar molds in the mid-1950s. In-mold: "© FMcF 1959 USA." $60.00.

Freeman-McFarlin llama, 6½" x 6½". This is one-half of a set of llamas Maynard Anthony Freeman modeled for Freeman-McFarlin. The upright companion is missing. Besides being Gerald McFarlin's partner in the business, he was also the chief designer for the business. The dark brown (almost black) stain has hints of light brown. The glazed eyes are pale olive green with black centers, a common Freeman-McFarlin eye treatment on the many animals it produced in the 1950s. $45.00.

Chalice

Incised mark on Chalice hippopotamus.

Chalice hippopotamus, 3⅞" x 8⅛". This hippo has the typical coarse matte finish and incised decoration that Chalice of California favored. Very few animal figures by this company have been sighted. $85.00.

Howard Pierce porcelain giraffe, 9¾" x 6¾". It is believed that this dashing animal by Howard Pierce is a giraffe. Not a commonly found Pierce model, it is nevertheless one of his most striking. The granite-like glaze known as slate gray adds to the appeal of this exceptional example from the mid-1950s. In-mold: "Howard Pierce Claremont, Calif © 25P." $250.00+.

Brayton Laguna gazelle, 12"H. Ferdinand Horvath designed this abstract animal that has been interpreted as both an antelope and a unicorn. An interesting attribute of abstraction is that it allows the viewer's imagination to reinterpret what is represented. A vintage Brayton price list confirms it as a gazelle and part of its Collection Afrique, introduced in 1953. Most items in this large and fascinating assortment were glazed satin-matte black. Incised "H29." $100.00.

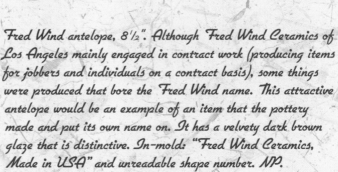

Cemar antelope, 6¼". This antelope on the rocks in a combination of colors favored by Cemar dates from the early 1950s. Fred Kaye is the probable designer. In-mold: "Cemar." $55.00.
(Larry Gill photo)

Fred Wind antelope, 8½". Although Fred Wind Ceramics of Los Angeles mainly engaged in contract work (producing items for jobbers and individuals on a contract basis), some things were produced that bore the Fred Wind name. This attractive antelope would be an example of an item that the pottery made and put its own name on. It has a velvety dark brown glaze that is distinctive. In-mold: "Fred Wind Ceramics, Made in USA" and unreadable shape number. NP.

Florence porcelain squirrel, 8". Distinguished California sculptor Betty Davenport Ford modeled this squirrel for Florence Ceramics of Pasadena. A series of 15 porcelain bisque bird and animal figures were produced in all by the company in the mid-1950s. They were available in a single color or a subtle blend of colors. The color of this particular model is dusk gray. The printed mark reads "Florence Ceramics © Porcelain Bisque." $165.00.

Howard Pierce porcelain monkey totem, 15¼". Another amazing Howard Pierce sculpture, this "hear no evil, see no evil, speak no evil" monkey totem dates from the late 1950s. Pierce received his art training in the 1930s at the University of Illinois and Chicago Art Institute, where he was exposed to the latest developments in modern art. He learned his lessons well, as this piece clearly demonstrates. Although a modernist at heart, he had the ability to create convincing naturalistic models. This piece was produced in both satin-matte brown and black. Ink-stamped "Howard Pierce." $200.00+.

Walter Wilson panther, 3¾" x 13". The black panther became something of an icon in the late 1940s — early 1950s, with the widespread interest in exotic faraway places. This exceptional example is believed to be one produced by Walter Wilson of Pasadena. It is more sleek and sculptural than the average panther or panther lamp of the period. NM, $75.00.

Brad Keeler monkeys (left to right): 3", 3½", 4". These three monkeys pretending to be people are part of a series presumably modeled by Don Winton but not produced until after Brad Keeler's untimely death in 1952. His widow, Catherine M. Keeler, tried to carry on but was unsuccessful. She had her own name put on items produced after her husband's passing. Ink-stamped "Catherine M Keeler, Made in USA." $75.00 each.

Brayton Laguna horse head, 21¼" x 16¾". Unlike Brad Keeler's widow, Durlin Brayton's third wife, Georgia, kept his successful business going for another 16 years after the founder's passing in 1951. This horse head is another impressive piece by Hungarian-born sculptor Ferdinand Horvath that Brayton Laguna produced in the mid-1950s. It had a matte black counterpart that was designed to hang on the wall. Both are rarely seen today. In-mold: "Brayton's Laguna Beach, Calif." $200.00+.

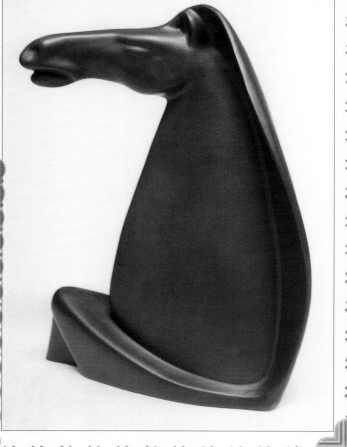

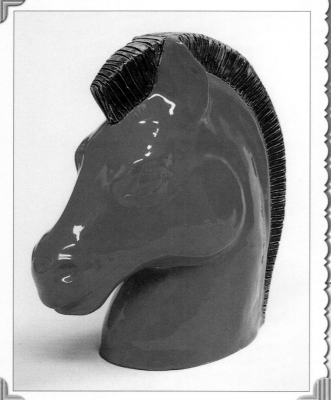

Gene Lodi horse head, 12". Little is known about the Gene Lodi business. This imposing, brilliant red crackle-glazed head of a horse with stained and textured mane probably dates from about 1950 or slightly later. Obviously a talented modeler, he was yet another follower of the Barbara Willis method of ceramic expression. Incised "Gene Lodi 731." NP.

Sasha Studios horse, 7" x 9⅛". Sometimes confused with the work of Sascha Brastoff, Sasha Katchamakoff, a Ukrainian ceramist who studied in England before coming to America in the late 1920s, produced this horse figure. It dates from about 1950. The Sascha Studios was located at 614 N. Robertson Blvd. in Los Angeles. Pictured in a catalog of her work issued during WWII are numerous traditional European items including various reproductions of English Staffordshire dogs. This horse with small pot on its back reveals her flair for modernist design. It has an unusual purple luster decoration. All Sasha Studios pieces can be considered rare. Sasha's logo — a yin-yang symbol formed with a backwards "S" — is in-mold in addition to the painted mark:w "Sasha." $65.00.

Lester horse, 7¼" x 7⅝". Andrew M. Lester was the owner of Lester of California. The business was located in Pasadena, at 2527 E. California. This stylized Clydesdale has overglaze gold with an unusual crackle effect that presumably was characteristic of the ware. Paper label shaped like California reads "Lester of California, Hand Decorated Originals, California Crakel." $65.00.

Winfield China horse, 10¼". Here is a real rarity. Winfield China, produced by the American Ceramic Products Co. of Santa Monica, was not known as a producer of figurines. Yet, this stylized horse (characteristic of models by Fred Kaye) includes a gold paper label with the printed words "Winfield China." $85.00.

Hallfield cats, 6⅞" x 12½" (left) and 5¼" x 14" (right). These fabulous black cats designed by Bill Fields should prove easier to track down than his dinosaurs pictured below. Both felines are glazed matte black. The reclining cat is marked in-mold "© Hallfield." $150.00 set.

Hallfield dinosaurs, 11¾" x 10 (left) and 12" x 13⅞" (right). These extraordinary Hallfield dinosaurs from 1952 could prove to be as hard to find as the remains of an actual dinosaur. Both are glazed matte black with a beige "backbone" and marked in-mold "Hallfield California." $200.00+ set.

Brayton Laguna cats, 7" x 17½" (left) and 16½" (right). Lisa Whitmore was the designer of these large abstract cats that Brayton Laguna produced in the late 1950s — early 1960s. They were also made in woodtone with white crackle faces. In-mold on the upright cat: "Brayton's Laguna Calif." Reclining cat is not marked. $180.00 set.

Brayton Laguna cat, 17⅛". This almost life-sized abstract cat done in white crackle accented with matte black dates from the early 1950s. The designer is unknown. In-mold: "Brayton's Laguna Calif. 40-93." $100.00.

Roselane cat, 2¾" x 17½". Clementine the Cat is what Roselane called this remarkable snake-like feline. This example is glazed blue-gray but various muted colors were used on this creeper. Even the bottom of this piece is interesting. $85.00.

Bottom of Roselane cat showing molded paws and in-mold mark including the © symbol.

Freeman-McFarlin cat, 5½" x 5½", and mouse, 2¾". Not Tom and Jerry, but this cat and mouse have the look of cartoon characters. The cat with bowtie in gunmetal is not marked. $70.00. The mouse in painted bisque spattered with gold retains a small oval paper label. $40.00. Pink with gold spattering has also been noted on these 1950s period items.

253

DeLee hors d'oeuvre server, 7". Horse Durves is what this witty item introduced in 1953 by deLee Art was called. It originally came with an oval under-plate divided into eight sections for serving appetizers. The holes around the base of the racehorse were for toothpicks as shown. This item also came with a hangtag reading "On the racetrack I'm a Flop. I couldn't make the curves. But you will cheer me anyhow. When you try my Horse-Durves." Ink-stamped "deLee Art ©." $60.00 ($85.00 with under-plate).

Paper label on Bevan Kilns hors d'oeuvre server. Note the resemblance to Metlox's paper labels of the same period.

Bevan Kilns hors d'oeuvre server, 3⁵⁄₈" x 7¹⁄₂". This pig-shaped server has 28 toothpick holes to hold as many bite-sized appetizers. Bevan Kilns was established at the Pasadena home of Charles Bevan about 1943 and was later relocated to a larger facility at 97 E. Montecito in Sierra Madre (just northeast of Pasadena). A variety of giftware was produced. $40.00.

Treasure Craft TV lamp, 9". In the early days of television, it was thought that a light source in close proximity to the tube would prevent eyestrain. Numerous pottery makers rose to the challenge and the TV lamp was born. This dynamic Treasure Craft model with two horse's heads dates from about 1955, when the business was still in its original South Gate location. It has the time-honored brown stain/white crackle combination. Paper label. $75.00. (George Higby photo)

Lane TV lamp, 11½". Lane & Co. is believed to have produced this unmarked TV lamp from the 1950s. Many similar items were made by the Van Nuys business. The eyes are the most interesting characteristic of this lamp and are in fact cat's-eye marbles that light up when the lamp in on. NM, $80.00.

Maddux planter lamp, 12" x 9". This Maddux of California swan planter lamp must have been a popular item when it was produced (in the late 1950s and early 1960s) because they are easy to find today, generally an indicator of original sales appeal. This looks like the modeling work of Fred Kaye, who was a free-lance designer at the time. A very nice, if common item. Paper label. $35.00.

Hedi Schoop TV lamp, 11¼" x 12¼". This TV lamp is one of the four designs that Hedi Schoop modeled and produced in her North Hollywood factory in the mid-1950s. Because a disastrous fire in 1958 curtailed production, these lamps are difficult to find today. This model may be the hardest of all to find and, in my estimation, is the most interesting with its Fritz Lang-like city of akimbo skyscrapers in glimmering gold. In-mold: "Hedi Schoop." $600.00+.

Lane lamp, 5³/₄" x 11³/₄". Here is a cool Lane & Co. lamp for the auto enthusiast. The base is a bright red sports car, vintage early-60s, the red being a glaze, not cold paint. However, the tires and seats are finished in flat black paint. One thing that is puzzling is the metal antenna-like protuberance on the trunk of the vehicle. I would understand its purpose if the lamp were also a radio, but it isn't. In-mold: "Lane & Co. Van Nuys, Calif. LS420." $120.00.

Lane planter, 10¹/₂" x 9³/₄". Lane & Co. produced numerous planters and planter lamp combinations in the 1950s and 1960s. This is simply a planter and the rectangular container section is cleverly concealed behind the airbrush painted foliage and blue birds. The only hand-painted parts are the eyes of the two birds. In-mold: "© Lane & Co. Van Nuys, Calif.," plus paper label. $60.00.

Paper label on back-side of Lane planter with bluebirds.

Lane figure with planter, 14" x 13". Interest in exotic far away places and cultures continued into the 1950s and this Nubian figure holding up a leaf-shaped planter is evidence of it. It's totally airbrush decorated and rather gaudily accented with gold. In-mold: "Lane & Co., Van Nuys U.S.A. © 1958 P88B." $75.00.

Yona figures (left to right): 13⅛", 12¼", 10", 11¾". Between the years 1952 and 1957, Yona Ceramics produced a group of figures inspired by the hit Broadway play (and later, movie) The King and I. It is believed that Will Climes (of The Claysmiths) modeled the figures in the Siamese line for owner Yona Lippin. The company, located at 2005 San Fernando Rd. in Los Angeles, utilized a combination of finishes to produce this fascinating series. A base color was dappled onto the figures followed by an abundance of over-glaze gold, silver, or copper applied in the same manner, effecting the look of shimmering metallic luster. The finishing touch was the cold painting of the faces, hands, and bare feet. Matching bowls and ashtrays were also produced. $75.00 – 85.00 each.

Painted and stenciled marks on bottoms of two Yona figures.

Yona figure, 12". It is believed that this figure of a drummer was part of the Siamese series produced by Yona. It definitely is a Yona piece and seems to be related, but there is no hard evidence that it was included in the series. Painted mark: "Yona ©." $85.00.

The 1950s

Yona figures, 6⅞" x 12⅞" (left) and 5⅜" x 8⅝" (right). The success of Yona's Siamese series eventually led to other figures like this ballet set. Again, it is believed that Will Climes was the designer. The Will-George business closed in 1956, providing ample time to produce these additional models. Stamped mark: "Yona Ceramics California, 354." $150.00 set.

Hedi Schoop wall decor, 10½" (left) and 11½" (right). These Hedi Schoop wall-mounted figures of masked harlequins are unusual. They complement a more commonly found set of flower-holder figures that she also produced in the mid-1950s. The striking mix of red and black glazes with overglaze gold adds to their visual appeal. NM, $250.00+ set.

Brayton Laguna figures, 14¾" x 18¼" (left) and 14" (right). Sculptor Carol Safholm made the models for these imposing voodoo dancers. A seated voodoo drummer completes the set produced by the Brayton Laguna Pottery in the early 1950s. The exaggerated gestures and attention to anatomical detail is very impressive. A combination of dark-brown stain, black and white crackle glaze, and overglaze red paint was used on the male figure. On the female, the predominant white crackle glaze is accented with a small amount of yellow and red glaze. It was around this time that red glazes were just becoming commercially available to the industry. A finisher's or decorator's initial can usually found on Brayton items. NM, $800.00+ set.

Treasure Craft figures, 12⅝" (left) and 11½" (right). These Spanish dancers were produced by Treasure Craft of Compton in the late 1950s. Figures like these are often confused with similar ones produced by Brayton, because both companies utilized the brown stain with white crackle glaze combination. Most of the Treasure Craft sets observed have been rather stiff in comparison to their Brayton counterparts, but this set stands as an exception and is one of the finer examples of the technique. NM, $165.00 set.

Treasure Craft figure, 11⅝". This tough looking cowboy is another example of Treasure Craft's use of brown stain contrasted with white crackle glaze. A large stallion was sometimes paired with this figure. Treasure Craft added a satellite factory in Maui, Hawaii, in the 1950s where similar items were produced, but mostly Hawaiian themed for the tourist trade. NM, $80.00.

Brayton Laguna figure, 9", and Miramar figure, 10½". What these bullfighters lack is a bull. On the left is a Carol Safholm matador produced by Brayton. Paper label. $100.00. On the right is an attractive matador produced by Miramar of California. Ink-stamped "© Miramar of Calif." in a circle. $70.00. The bull that goes with the Brayton matador is well documented and the two are usually found together. The Miramar bull is currently a mystery. Cold-painted red on both figures.

Brayton Laguna figures, 8¾" (left) and 8" (right). Carol Safholm modeled several figures for Brayton based on a featured article about the Republic of Peru that she read in *National Geographic*. Most of these figures were produced in sets of two, like this one of Peruvian beggar children. NM, $300.00+ set.

Marc Bellaire figures (left to right): 9", 14", 8½". Marc Bellaire received the major portion of his art training at the Chicago Art Institute and after moving to California, at the Los Angeles County Art Institute (now Otis Art Institute). When Bellaire established his ceramics business in Culver City in the early 1950s, he created entire ensembles consisting of both useful and decorative items with titles like Mardi Gras and Beachcomber. To some of his more successful lines, he added sets of figures like these musicians from the Jamaica line. A seated guitar player completes this ensemble. All signed "Bellaire." $450.00 each.

ILLUSTRATED . . . New Balinese Design, female dancer, 22½" tall, 40.00. Candle Sticks, 8", 9", 10" tall, 3.00, 3.25, 3.50. Cigarette Box, 8" long, 7.00. Ash Tray, 7" long, 2.50.

Look to spring for inspiration . . . look to Marc Bellaire for original creations in ceramic artware for '55. Fifty shapes, five designs, high gloss and matt finish, highly decorative. Phone our *local* representative or write direct.

MARC
BELLAIRE INC.

5895 Blackwelder Street/Culver City, California. • Dept. GB-3

BELLAIRE NATIONAL REPRESENTATIVES . . . LINN MYERS, INC./225 Fifth Avenue, New York, N.Y. • CARL J. METZGER & ASSOCIATES/Merchandise Mart/Chicago, Illinois • CERAMICS, INC./101 Merchandise Mart/Dallas, Texas • BILTMORE GALLERIES, INC./176 N. E. 40th Street/Miami, Florida • ROBERT S. BARKELL CO./Los Angeles and San Francisco. • FACTORY SHOWROOM . . . MARC BELLAIRE, INC./5895 Blackwelder Street/Culver City, California.

This Marc Bellaire ad from the March 1955 issue of Giftwares illustrates items from his Balinese line including a large figure.

Marc Bellaire plate, 15¼". This large plate with its atypical rendering of the usual Beachcomber figure with fishing nets may be an early example. It has a matte glaze, which is also out of the ordinary. It's signed "Marc Bellaire" on the front and has a personalized signature on the backside reading "For Gladys with Love, Marc Bellaire." $400.00+.

Brayton Laguna figure, 11½". William Moore modeled this poignant figure of an African woman and child that was part of Brayton's Collection Afrique of the early 1950s. Moore was also a design instructor at Chouinard Art Institute in Los Angeles. Most items in this series were glazed matte black. In-mold: "Brayton's Laguna Beach, Calif." $300.00+.

Dorothy Kindell figures, 6¼" (left) and 6⅛" (right). These unusual Dorothy Kindell African tribal figures consist of black stained bisque accented with various glaze colors. No other Kindell sets of African figures have been documented. In-mold: "Dorothy Kindell ©" on both. $225.00 set.

Unidentified figure, 5"H x 8"L. Here is a marvelous piece composed of two separate black figures that have been attached. Possibly inspired by the hit Broadway play *Porgy and Bess*, this hand-painted piece is signed but, unfortunately, the mark is faint. It appears to read "Milli Hointe 51." Aid in identification would be most appreciated. NP.

Howard Pierce bust, 10½". Production of this superb Howard Pierce piece was strictly limited, and the artist was surprised to see it when it was brought to his studio in 1983. Glazed brown agate, it exemplifies Pierce's modernist tendencies that more often than not proved to be marketing successes. In-mold: "Howard Pierce Claremont Calif." and (raised) "50P." $500.00+.

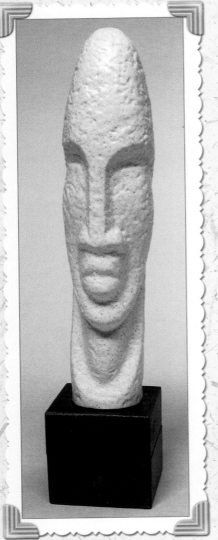

Jaru head with wood base, 16¼". This primitive Polynesian head (ceramic part, 13") mounted on a laminated wood base was produced by Jaru Art Products in the late 1950s. This same sculpture was produced in Jarustone (a synthetic composition product) in two larger sizes during the 1960s. Jaru succeeded while so many other businesses were failing because the company stressed diversification. Besides ceramics, they offered an assortment of useful and decorative objects for the home in a wide variety of materials. Triangular paper label. $150.00.

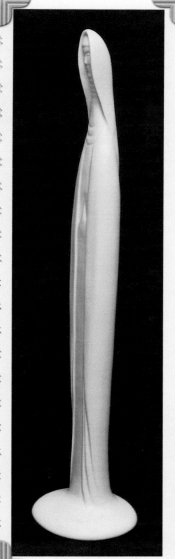

Hallfield figure, 20". Bill Fields created this Brancusi-like Madonna. Constantin Brancusi was a noted Romanian sculptor who reduced forms to their ultimate simplicity and is sometimes cited as the father of Minimalism. There is no doubt that the modernism observable in 1950s ceramics was the direct result of developments in the fine arts. This extraordinary piece from about 1953 is glazed matte white and marked in-mold "Hallfield Calif. U.S.A." $125.00.

Sascha Brastoff plaque, 19³/₄" x 9¹/₂". Sascha Brastoff's Guatemalan vacation was the inspiration behind his Mosaic line. A primitive sun god figure in high relief is depicted on this wall plaque along with the abstract image of a snake. Masks and other wall decor were included in this unusual collection produced in 1958. Signed "Sascha B" and "M38" on the backside in addition to the printed Sascha Brastoff logo. Also on the back is an original price tag with $25.00 printed on it. $250.00.

Hedi Schoop figures, 11" (left) and 12" (right). This is the other side of Hedi Schoop's work that people seldom see. She was a very imaginative artist who was forced to curb her more inventive impulses in order to satisfy the demands of commerce. Here however, she has let her imagination run wild and the result is a pair of tree people. Probably made for jobber-turned-manufacturer, Lou Honeg, after her own production ended in 1958. In-mold "Hedi." $135.00 set.

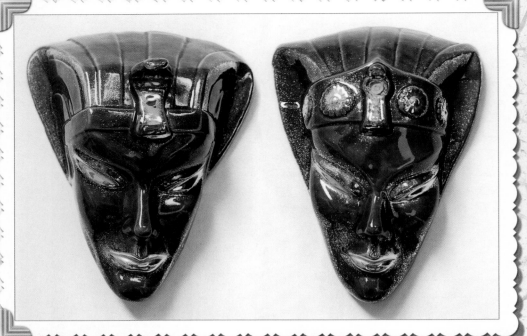

Yona masks, 11". These Egyptian masks produced by Yona Ceramics in the mid-1950s were designed by Will Climes. This set was also obtainable in white with gold and perhaps other colors. The molds were sold to Maddux of California when Yona closed in 1958. Painted mark: "Yona." $135.00 set.

Paper label on Maddux mask.

Sascha Brastoff mask, 11½". This is the female half of a set of Egyptian masks by Sascha Brastoff that date from late 1950s — early 1960s. This example is about as austere as his production got. A simple matte white glaze with a hint of gray is the only decoration on the sculptural form. NM, $120.00.

Maddux mask, 11". This is one of the Egyptian masks that Maddux of California produced from molds purchased from Yona Lippin in 1958. I believe this painted bisque finish was the only one offered. It's quite a contrast from the original version produced by Yona. $50.00.

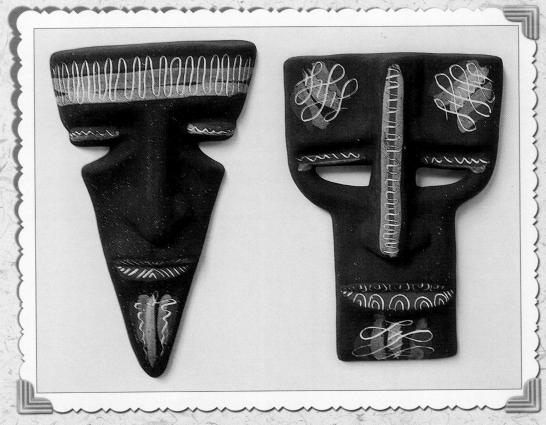

Chalice masks, 11½" (left) and 10" (right). These two Chalice of California masks are part of a set that Charles and Alice Smith produced in the early 1950s. They have all the features of typical Chalice ware including a slightly rough-textured matte glaze and incised loopy squiggles. Incised "Chalice." $85.00 each.

Metlox plaques, 8" x 6" each. Carl Romanelli made the models for these Egyptian head wall plaques. They were included in an artware line produced in the 1950s by the Metlox Potteries called Art Treasures of the World. All of the items were designed to be evocative of artifacts of antiquity. The simulated mosaic tile background of these plaques was a feature of the collection and complemented the company's Mosaic Originals line. Signed "Romanelli" on the face. No mark on the back. $300.00+ set.

Millesan Drews figurine, 2⅛" x 4¼". Millesan Drews, whose proper name was Millicent Andrews, was responsible for starting the pixie craze of the late 1940s and early 1950s in California. She began hand-making these little creatures in Portland, Oregon, in 1939. Her inability to keep up with demand, despite their high price, forced Drews to relocate to Los Angeles and establish a business called Pixie Potters in the late 1940s. She hired a mold maker to make molds of her elfin good-luck charms in various positions and the resulting models were mass produced and marketed at a budget-friendly price. In 1955, Millesan Drews assigned production of her pixies to Hagen-Renaker. The pictured pixie is one of her originals and has a triangular paper label on the back reading "Drews Pixie." $85.00.

This early publicity photo is of a handmade pixie by Millesan Drews.

Pixie Potters figurine, 2¾", and Cali-Crown mug, 4⅜". Millesan Drews's decision to mass produce her pixies was trumpeted in the trade in 1949. Ruth Sloan represented the budget-priced Pixie Potters models and featured them in her showrooms in Los Angeles and New York. The slip-cast pixies had unglazed hands and faces and red-painted lips. Ultimately, red-glazed pixies and even a pixie house planter were produced in California. The pixie handle on the Cali-Crown child's mug was completely glazed because of the hard use it was expected to receive. Cali-Crown Importers of Los Angeles arranged to have Millesan Drews's pixies produced even more cheaply in Japan in the early 1950s. In-mold: "Cali Crown ©." Pixie Potters pixie, $35.00; Cali-Crown mug, $40.00.

Cleminsons figurines, 3" (average height), inside Brayton Laguna low bowl, 1½" x 13". These elusive Gremlins by Betty Cleminson were produced in the early 1940s when the business was known as Cleminsons Clay. Each figurine's name began with the letter "G." The names were usually printed on the bottoms of the figures. No other marks. $100.00 each. The Brayton flower bowl dates from about 1960. $50.00.

Detail of a Cleminsons Clay sales brochure of the early 1940s includes Betty Cleminson's renderings of the five Gremlins.

The Good "GREMLINS" Gustave, Gilroy, Godfrey, Granville, Guthrie, bring luck to the Owner. Tags included. $9.00 Dozen.

Walker planters, 3¾" x 4¼". The Walker Potteries of Monrovia added pixies to its line in the late 1940s. In the Walker catalog of 1950, ten different pixies including four that were also planters were pictured. However, by 1952 they had mysteriously vanished from the pages of the company catalog. Walker pixies and pixie planters are heavier than most other brands. NM, $45.00 each.

Drummond figurines (left to right): 3³/₄" x 4¹/₄", 4⁷/₈", 6", 5¹/₄" x 5". The Drummond Pottery produced this pixieland band. The company may have specialized in these little fellows and when the pixie craze faded, so did the business, because no mention of it has ever been found in the trade journals. These pixies have great expressions and to some extent resemble Gilner's pixies. They all have an opening for flowers or whatever. Ink-stamped "Drummond Pottery ©." $65.00 each.

Gilner planter, 7¹/₈". This may be the largest pixie in captivity. Most pixies were less than four inches in height, so this one from the early 1950s is a giant. The unglazed hands and faces of Gilner's Happy People, as they were called, are usually pink with hand-painted features. Female pixies were known as Merry Maids. In-mold: "Gilner © 1951." $65.00.

Gilner figurines, 4¹/₂" and 3³/₄", and planter, 4⁵/₈" x 6¹/₂". Gilner Potteries was owned by Beryl Gilner and his son Burt, and was located at 11821 Teale St. in Culver City. They were one of the largest artware manufacturers in California in the early 1950s. In 1953, they unleashed their Happy Cannibals on an unsuspecting public. Billed as the "cousin folk of the happy people," they were mischievous natives with tiny brass earrings. Some were stand-alone figurines, like the two on the left. NM, $40.00 each. Some were attached to planters, like the one on the right. In-mold: "Gilner California ©." $50.00.

This Gilner Potteries ad from the March 1952 issue of Giftwares, announces the Happy Cannibals collection.

Paper label on backsides of Kipp figurines.

Kipp figurines, 6". Before there were hippies, there were Kippies. Kippies were made by Kipp Ceramics of Pasadena and were the company's contribution to the pixie parade. However, most of the ones noted have been the usual happy-faced variety, not these sourpuss types. Perhaps these were the anti-pixies. $65.00 each.

Freeman-McFarlin figurines (left to right): 2⅞", 3⅛", 3", 3⅛". Don Winton may have modeled this group of impish babies playing sports for Freeman-McFarlin. All of these adorable kiddies have brass diaper pins fastened on and most have overglaze gold trim. Some have retained their small oval paper labels. The tennis player is marked in-mold "© Freeman McFarlin Originals, El Monte Calif." $40.00 each.

Josef figurines, 4½". These kids masquerading as clowns are characteristic of the small figurines of children that Muriel Joseph George modeled and produced in Pasadena in the early 1950s. In the late 1950s, she opted to have her line manufactured in Japan. Overglaze gold and red cold paint were used on this pair. Paper labels. $65.00 each.

Robyn figurines (left to right): 5⅜", 3½", 5". Robyn Ceramics of Fallbrook produced these charming ballerina angels in the early 1950s. Robyn Sikking's line included many figurines of angels, both singles and sets. Although similar in design to the Josef Originals figurines, Robyn's attention to detail was much greater. The angel on the left has a painted mark reading "Moonbeam, Original by Robyn." The angel in the center is similarly marked "Dawn, Original by Robyn." The one on the right has "Starlight, Original by Robyn." $75.00 each.

Robyn figurine, 5⅝". Robyn's Fallbrook business included a gift shop that featured ceramics by many California producers in addition to her own. When Robyn moved the business to Idyllwild, a separate and larger gift shop called The Grey Squirrel was opened in nearly Fern Valley. This Robyn figure of two dancing children is titled The Square Dance Angel. Abundant overglaze gold was used on this model. It has a painted mark reading "Give Her a Little Twirl, Original by Robyn 1952." $100.00.

The 1960s and Beyond

The once-booming pottery business in California had diminished considerably by the 1960s. For some reason, the years 1958 and 1962 saw the greatest number of company closings. Those busineses that managed to survive did so by catering to the changing times, and the 1960s and 1970s were decades personified by change, some of it wrenching. By the 1980s, only a few of the core companies were still hanging on. Very few producers of any size remain today. The rise of the individual artist potter has completely eclipsed factory production in the state.

Desert Sands vases, 7" (left) and 6¾" (right). The history of Desert Sands is actually the history of five generations of the Evans clan of potters who began producing handmade pottery in the Ozark Hills of Missouri prior to the Civil War. It is not known when the production of pots that blended together various colored clays began. Similar in concept to the Mission ware of the Niloak Pottery of Arkansas, Desert Sands swirled pieces differed because a final transparent glaze was added to preserve and enhance the colors. Prior to relocating to Barstow in the 1960s, the Desert Sands Pottery was located in Boulder City, NV. The last of the Evans family of potters was Terrell Evans, who threw all the ware on the potter's wheel. Besides vases and related artware, a line of dinnerware was made. The vase on the left is ink-stamped on its unglazed bottom "Hand Made Desert Sands Pottery, 1555 West Main, Barstow, Calif." The cone-shaped vase on the right is marked the same way. (This mark is the best guarantee that a Desert Sands item was made in California.) $65.00 each.

This small photo card showing a member of the Evans family throwing on the wheel and a brief history of the business on the reverse side was sometimes included with the ware.

The 1960s and Beyond

Jaru vase, 7³/₄". The ownership of Jaru Art Products changed in 1968. Original owners, Jack and Ruth Hirsch sold the company that had been founded in 1950 to the 42 Products Corp. The business was relocated to Culver City and changed hands again before finally closing in the 1990s. This muted orange vase with an Asian look was produced in 1979. In-mold: "© Jaru 1979." $50.00.

Covina planter, 3" x 14½". This serpentine dish garden by the Covina Pottery with speckled yellow glaze dates from the late 1960s — early 1970s and is a typical example of their florist line. The company specialized in planters and outlasted most of its competitors. In-mold: "Covina 903 USA." $40.00.

904
11 x 4 x 3

912
7 x 7 x 3

903
14 x 4 x 3

955
7 x 3

951
14 x 4 x 3

202
5 x 4

914
10 x 5 x 3

901
10 x 6 x 3

917
3 x 5 x 3

913
8 x 6 x 3

Ceramic Planters

COVINA POTTERY, INC.
528 No. Second Street
Covina, California 91723

"Luron-Color" by Weller Co., a Division of
Colorpress, Inc., North Hollywood, Calif.

Covina Pottery promotional sheet with a selection of planters that were primarily used by florists.

Paper label on Treasure Craft vase.

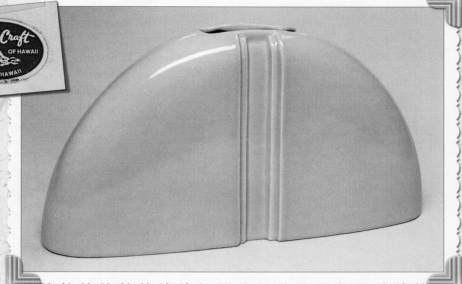

Treasure Craft vase, 7½" x 14½". This Treasure Craft vase is an interesting example of the Deco Revival that has resulted from the widespread collector interest in the original objects produced during the Art Deco period. This renaissance of interest is still going strong today. This vase was produced at Treasure Craft's plant in Maui, Hawaii, in the 1980s. $60.00.

Paper label on Vohann vase.

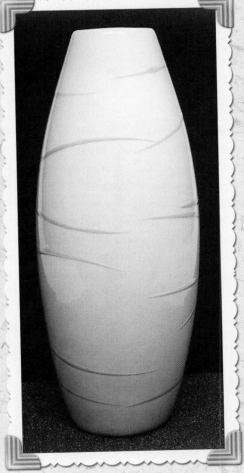

Vohann vase, 11". This Vohann of California vase is from a group of similarly styled objects dating from the 1970s. Thin, randomly spaced stripes of pastel-colored slip are the minimal decoration. $45.00.

Vohann vases, 6³⁄₈" x 3⅛". These black and white vases that look like giant salt and pepper shakers were not intended for cut flowers. The small holes on the tops were designed to hold a few dried flowers or the straw flowers that were very popular in the 1960s and 1970s. Again, the minimalist shapes are mimicking events in the art world. $35.00 each.

Treasure Craft vase, 5³/₈". Treasure Craft seemed to have a finger on the pulse of the growing collectibles world. The antique pottery of the Native Americans and its passionate following was undoubtedly the motivation behind this vase design. Although cast, it's an homage to the dynamic geometric patterns seen on the hand-coiled tribal pots of the Southwest. In-mold: "© Treasure Craft, Made in USA." $45.00.

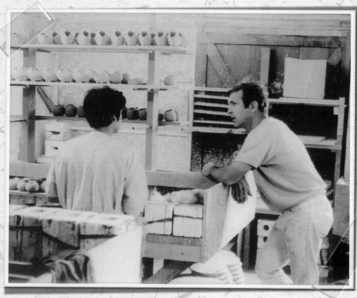

Robert Maxwell and assistant in his Venice studio, c. 1964.

Robert Maxwell vase, 3³/₄". Robert Maxwell began his career as a production potter in Venice in 1960, after graduating from UCLA where he studied with Laura Andreson. He was a highly skilled potter who threw polished and distinctive stoneware pieces on the wheel in addition to the more economical cast ware. This spherical production vase with overlapped glazes that resemble teardrops dates from the mid-1960s. Maxwell relocated to Fallbrook in the early 1970s and focused almost entirely on hand-thrown pottery. Paper label. $80.00.

Paper label on Robert Maxwell vase. There were large and small sizes of these labels.

Robert Maxwell vase, 5¹/₄". Robert Maxwell produced this handsome stoneware vase with narrow neck and rutile glaze in the mid-1960s. Maxwell's Venice-based business was located across the street from the studio of celebrated furniture designers Charles and Ray Eames. Paper label reading "Robert Maxwell Stoneware, Handcrafted Designs, California." (See photo of label.) $80.00.

Street entrance to Robert Maxwell's
Venice studio of the 1960s.

Robert Maxwell vases (left to right): 9½", 5¼", 3⅜". Three more examples of the
rutile-glazed stoneware produced by Robert Maxwell in the 1960s are seen here.
The base glaze was a high-gloss black, with the semi-matte rutile glaze poured over
it in typical Maxwell fashion. All examples retain their oval paper labels. Tall vase,
$100.00; medium vase, $60.00; squat vase, $60.00.

Robert Maxwell planter, 4½"H x 5¼"D. This small
hand-thrown planter with Maxwell's distinctive
hand-carved sunburst design on the outer surface
dates from the early 1970s. It's glazed only on the
inside. Incised "Robert Maxwell." $120.00.

Robert Maxwell vases, 10½" (left) and 13" (right). Pictured here are two hand-thrown vases that Robert Maxwell produced at his Fallbrook studio in the mid-1970s. His characteristic method of pouring overlapped glazes was used to good effect on the vase at left. Incised "Robert Maxwell." $200.00. The tall slender vase on the right was glazed on the inside and only as far down as the concave neck on the outside. The rest was carved to draw attention to the natural color and texture of the stoneware clay. Incised "Robert Maxwell." $250.00.

Paper label on Pottery Craft vase.

Pottery Craft vase, 6½". Pottery Craft, a division of Treasure Craft of Compton, was begun in the late 1960s as a business arrangement between Robert Maxwell and owner Alfred Levin. The outcome of the merger was not an entirely favorable one for Maxwell, since his molds and method were used as the foundation of the line without appropriate compensation. The Pottery Craft division of Treasure Craft manufactured cast stoneware vases, bowls, planters, teapots, and related articles, and was productive for a number of years. $35.00.

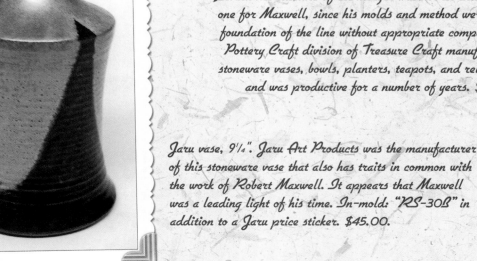

Jaru vase, 9¼". Jaru Art Products was the manufacturer of this stoneware vase that also has traits in common with the work of Robert Maxwell. It appears that Maxwell was a leading light of his time. In-mold: "RS-30B" in addition to a Jaru price sticker. $45.00.

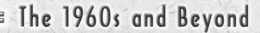

Interior view of the San Marcos factory of Freeman-McFarlin.

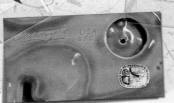

In-mold mark and paper label on Freeman-McFarlin wall decor.

Freeman-McFarlin mushrooms, 2³/₄". The Freeman-McFarlin Potteries produced these mushrooms after adding a second plant in San Marcos (San Diego County) in 1968. They are the smallest of the three sizes produced. In the mid-1970s, all production was consolidated at the San Marcos location. About 150 people were employed at the time. When Freeman-McFarlin ceased operations in 1980, Hagen-Renaker occupied the facility in order to enlarge its Designer's Workshop division. Paper label. $45.00 each.

Freeman-McFarlin wall decor, 20". Maynard Anthony Freeman modeled this large and lifelike wall decoration. Freeman-McFarlin produced this double sunflower and a smaller, single replica in pink, turquoise, and possibly natural colors in the 1960s. $75.00.

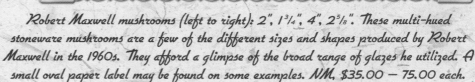

Robert Maxwell mushrooms (left to right): 2", 1³/₄", 4", 2⁵/₈". These multi-hued stoneware mushrooms are a few of the different sizes and shapes produced by Robert Maxwell in the 1960s. They afford a glimpse of the broad range of glazes he utilized. A small oval paper label may be found on some examples. NM, $35.00 – 75.00 each.

277

Freeman-McFarlin birds, 3⅛" (left) and 3" (right). When Kay Finch closed her shop in 1963 she sold some of her animal and bird molds to Freeman-McFarlin who continued to produce them, albeit in their own glazes and finishes. This charming pair of birds in a green tone on tone glaze is not marked. $80.00 set.

Howard Pierce owls, 12¾". This tree stump with two owls perched on it was created in the 1980s, after Howard Pierce and wife Ellen had moved to Joshua Tree and a life of semi-retirement in the desert. It shows the naturalistic side of his modeling skills, although he could get even more true-to-life than this. Animals and birds were a joy to him and he treated them with utmost respect even in the most abstract representations. Ink-stamped "Howard Pierce." $150.00.

Brayton Laguna owls, 17¾". These stylized Brayton owls perched on a modernistic base date from about 1967, the end days for the business. Glaze was used very sparingly on this piece; the balance of the textured bisque remaining in the raw state. Times had changed for the company and the rest of the country by then and demand for the type of ware it had been so proficient at had diminished. In-mold: "Brayton's Laguna Beach, Calif." $100.00.

Robert Maxwell owl, 7³/₄" x 9³/₄". Robert Maxwell produced this marvelous stoneware owl on branch about the same time as the Brayton owls on the previous page. While Brayton was reducing its glaze usage in order to economize, Maxwell liberally applied glaze to this superbly sculpted model. Production of Robert Maxwell's bird series was limited so they are sighted rather infrequently. NM, $150.00.

Robert Maxwell roadrunner, 6³/₄" x 11³/₄". Some of the Robert Maxwell birds, like this roadrunner, were mounted on natural wood bases. A single steel rod anchors the forward momentum of the roadrunner. A simple olive green and brown glaze gives it added vitality. NM, $125.00.

Jaru fish, 10¹/₂" x 12¹/₂". The shapes of these Jaru fish have been reduced to their essence and no glaze was used in their production. The fish on the left has been painted a dark teal and the one on the right is the natural clay color. The oval cutouts for eyes are lined with gold leaf. Although very reductive, a sensation of animation is communicated. These items were produced in the early 1980s after Jaru became affiliated with the Harris Marcus Group, Inc. Clear plastic label on both plus the handwritten model number (#59). $60.00 each.

Vohann seahorse rack, 7 ³/₄". This salmon colored seahorse's tail fin curves outward forming a hook for hanging a towel or bathrobe. Coordinated ceramic ensembles for the bath were a specialty of Vohann during the 1980s and these accessories were produced in various monochrome glazes. Some were figural like the seahorse and others were simply utilitarian. Most of these articles were marked with a sticker that was easily removed. NM, $35.00.

Metlox canister, 9" x 11", and shakers, 3¹/₂". These kitchen items were part of Metlox's line of the 1960s called Sea Servers. The collection included serving dishes with bright red lobster handles not unlike Brad Keeler's popular servers of the 1940s. This fish-shaped canister in red with a hint of black also makes a great cookie jar. Paper label. $250.00. The shakers have a bit more black shading. NM, $30.00 set.

Los Angeles casserole, 8" x 11 ³/₄". This Los Angeles Potteries oval-shaped casserole has an over-the-top cover with a variety of colorful marine life in relief and a giant pink lobster holding court. The olive green base has a basketweave pattern in low relief. A joy for any seafood fancier, it dates from the 1970s and has an in-mold mark reading "Los Angeles Potteries, California USA, Ovenware 305, © '61." $75.00.

Freeman-McFarlin fish, 11¾"L. This rare and outrageous sleepy-eyed fish appears to be lounging on the waves. It was listed as *Playful Fish* in a Freeman-McFarlin catalog of the mid-1970s and was available in either gold leaf or white glaze. Paper label. $150.00+.

Exterior view of the Freeman-McFarlin factory in San Marcos.

In-mold mark on Jaru turtle includes the date of manufacture. Note felt pads on bottom of feet.

Jaru turtle, 4⅜" x 11¼". A fantastic cubist design adds distinction to this Jaru Art Products turtle from 1978. Jaru began dating its ware in the 1970s, which certainly makes life easier for the historian. A sandy beige colored glaze covers the outside and inside cavity. Many potteries started adding little felt pads on the bottoms of ware in the 1960s, and this can be helpful in dating items. $90.00.

Marc Bellaire plate, 14¾". After his Culver City factory closed, Marc Bellaire spent much of his time teaching, lecturing, and writing about art and ceramics. His published instructive books include *Brush Decoration* and *Underglaze Decoration*. In the 1980s, he moved to Cathedral City (near Palm Springs) and established a studio dedicated to painting, sculpture, and ceramics. This large plate by Bellaire with hand-painted Southwest lizard motif was undoubtedly inspired by his desert locale. It has a rather rough texture and matte finish and is incised "Bellaire 1990." $200.00.

Maddux Tang horse, 11½" x 12". This impressive Tang horse in gunmetal glaze appears to be the work of Maynard Anthony Freeman, although his name does not appear on it. It closely resembles his model of the same subject that was produced by Freeman-McFarlin. In-mold: "Maddux of Cal © 60, 949." $100.00.

Bauer wild boar, 5¼" x 10¼". This highly stylized wild boar is truly rare, the first in a series of exotic animals that was planned for Bauer by designer Tracy Irwin. The collection would have included several of Irwin's designs but production was cut short by a strike that shut down the factory and ultimately the business in 1962. Glazed in a white speckled glaze, it has no mark. Irwin showed me his original model for it shortly before his death. $500.00+.

Vohann otter, 7½" x 14". This large Vohann otter is one of several animals that one ordinarily sees only at the zoo that were produced by the company in the 1970s. Relatively naturalistic, it has a straightforward monochrome glaze. Oval paper label reading "An Original Design by Vohann of Calif. Inc, Capistrano Beach, Calif." and "Design © by Vohann of Calif. Inc." $65.00.

Vohann hippopotamus planter, 4" x 11". Not a pink elephant but a pink hippo. Some of the zoo animals that Vohann of California manufactured in the 1970s were designed to be useful as well as attractive. Paper label. $50.00.

Pottery Craft bighorn sheep ashtray, 3" x 6¼". From a series called Clay Menagerie, this Pottery Craft ashtray is marked in-mold "Pottery Craft © Made in USA." $65.00. (George Higby photo)

Lane cat, 17½". This cat shaped dual-purpose item dates from the 1960s and is believed to be a product of Lane & Co. of Van Nuys. It can be used as a serving tray (or ashtray) but it also has a hole for hanging, and when it's on the wall, its sole purpose is decorative. In-mold: "Made in Calif. USA." $85.00.

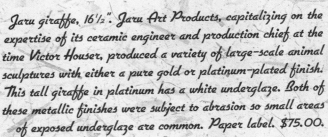

Jaru giraffe, 16½". Jaru Art Products, capitalizing on the expertise of its ceramic engineer and production chief at the time Victor Houser, produced a variety of large-scale animal sculptures with either a pure gold or platinum-plated finish. This tall giraffe in platinum has a white underglaze. Both of these metallic finishes were subject to abrasion so small areas of exposed underglaze are common. Paper label. $75.00.

Unidentified monkeys, 6⅛" (left) and 4¼" (right). A great deal of speculation has surrounded these and similar monkey figures, that also came in white. Jaru has been a top prospect but no real evidence that they produced them has come to light. These characters with cigarettes in their mouths are indicating how to make a monkey of yourself. NM, NP.

Freeman-McFarlin dragon, 10¼" x 19½". This may be the most stunning Freeman-McFarlin figure ever produced. Obviously a dragon, it has amazing detail and a very threatening appearance. Completely gold leafed except for the tiny menacing eyes, it's undoubtedly a Maynard Anthony Freeman creation. In-mold: "913 USA" plus paper label. $250.00+.

Robert Maxwell rhinoceros, 4" x 6½", and hippopotamus, 2¾" x 6". In the late 1960s, Robert Maxwell produced a series of zany zoo animals in stoneware. According to Maxwell, the heat of the kiln is what ultimately determines the color of fired stoneware, which can vary from beige to a dark red-brown. The tonal variation is very slight on these particular examples. The rhino is impressed "Stoneware of California, Copyright U.S.A." and retains an oval paper label. The sad-eyed hippo has the same impressed mark but has lost his label. $100.00 each.

Robert Maxwell lion, 4⅞". Both sides of another witty zoo animal by Robert Maxwell are shown here. This example is nicely glazed. NM, $125.00.

The 1960s and Beyond

Robert Maxwell animals (left to right): 3⅛" x 5½", 2½" x 4¾", 3¾" x 7". Robert Maxwell is probably best known for the small animal sculptures he produced in the 1960s that are commonly called beasties or critters. Maxwell has referred to them as the "missing links between prehistoric animals and those around today." On the left is a light-colored stoneware beast with added glaze and the in-mold mark: "© Robert Maxwell, Fig 6." $65.00. The one in the middle looking like a grenade that grew a snout is marked in-mold "© Robert Maxwell, Fig 12." $45.00. The big beast on the right has a sandpaper-like texture. It's marked in the same way as the others, with "Fig 3." $75.00.

Robert Maxwell ashtray, 3½" x 7", and bank, 8" x 8½". Here we have two beasts of burden. They perform a function as well as lighten the mood. On the left is an ashtray with white glazed interior. In-mold: "© Robert Maxwell 1966." $45.00. The big guy on the right, called the Penny Eater, is the largest slip-cast beastie known to exist. Only a limited number were produced so they may be nearing extinction. A bonus would be finding one with an original cork plugging the opening on the bottom for retrieval of coins. In-mold: "Robert Maxwell." $200.00+.

Interior view of the
Robert Maxwell pottery.
Note ashtray beasties.

Robert Maxwell covered bowls, 4½" x 5½". All was not levity with Robert Maxwell. He had his serious side and these elegant covered stoneware bowls are proof. The one on the left is unglazed on the outside with a white-glazed interior. The attractively glazed bowl on the right is marked exactly like the other one. $85.00 each.

In-mold mark on the Robert Maxwell covered bowls.

Vohann soap dish, 1½"H x 8"L. This is another example of a Vohann figural bath accessory. This gator is glazed chocolate brown and has a gold foil label on its bottom. $35.00.

In-mold mark on California Originals ashtray.

California Originals ashtray, 2½" x 10¼". California Originals of Torrance produced this alligator-shaped ashtray. Formerly Heirlooms of Tomorrow, the reorganized and relocated company produced a wide variety of giftware and housewares. This gator has a hand-painted simulated wood finish that is quite convincing. $35.00.

California Originals ashtray, 3" x 8¼". Another California Originals figural ashtray, this one in the shape of a lion. It has an good-looking blended glaze accented with sponged gold. In-mold: "Cal Orig." $45.00.

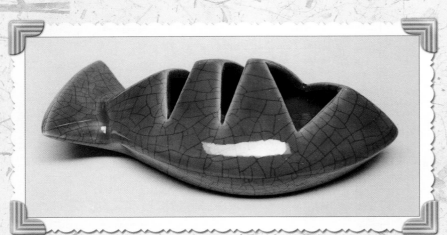

Vohann ashtray, 2½" x 7½". This abstract fish ashtray with turquoise crackle glaze is from a Vohann line called Hoodwink. The line was designed by Charles Chaney and included ash-trays (including wall-mounted designs) and other household accessories. In-mold: "Hoodwink, Vohann U.S.A.." $45.00.

Vohann advertising its latest smoking accessories in the August 1954 issue of Giftwares.

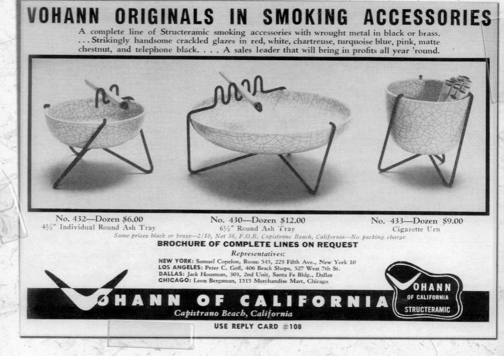

Metlox flower holder figure, 8¾". California ceramist Helen Slater designed an extensive line of figures and figures with attached containers that Metlox produced in the 1960s and 1970s. Called Poppets by Poppytrail, these earthenware items were produced using a single firing cycle and successfully simulated the look of handmade stoneware. The various Poppet models came with a hanging nametag. This one is named Conchita. NM, $60.00.

Brayton Laguna figure, 7¾". Ferdinand Horvath modeled a curious group of eight bearded gnomes for Brayton Laguna in the mid-1970s. This model is holding an umbrella and his shoes and hat are the only parts glazed. In-mold: "Brayton's Laguna Beach, Cal, H-63." $70.00.

Helen Slater figure with wood base, 8½". For the official program of the 94th Annual Tournament of Roses held in Pasadena in 1983, California ceramist Helen Slater, creator of the Metlox Poppets, was commissioned to make a set of marching band figures for the cover. Although this particular figure did not make the cover, it is believed to be one of the models produced for the commission or at about the same time. NM, NP.

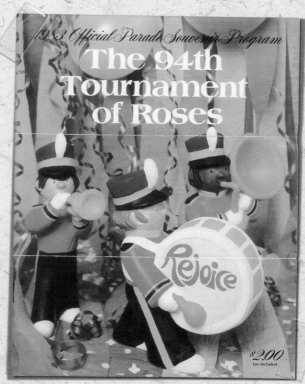

Cover of the 1983 Official Parade Souvenir Program for the 94th Tournament of Roses with Helen Slater's figures that resemble her Poppets by Poppytrail.

289

Howard Pierce figure group, 11¼". This Howard Pierce Family Group is a smaller version of the monumental sculpture that he made for and donated to a medical center in Joshua Tree, the desert community where he spent his semi-retirement years. It's his abstract representation of the modern family and was produced in a variety of glazes, but this particular one is outstanding. Ink-stamped "Howard Pierce." $175.00.

Treasure Craft figures, 11½" (left) and 8" (right). Treasure Craft produced these Tiki gods with simulated wood finish and Ray Murray is believed to have been the modeler. The large one on the left was made in the Compton factory and is marked in-mold "Treasure Craft 19©59, No. 550." The smaller Tiki was made in the Maui plant and is marked in-mold "Treasure Craft 19©59, Hawaii No. 173." Tall Tiki, $185.00; short Tiki, $135.00. (George Higby photo)

You Are Now The Proud Owner Of A California Originals "Collectable Tankard." These Hand-some Items Are Finely Hand Detailed By Our California Artists. This Series Will Be Added To Frequently In The Years To Come. The Result Will Be A Beautiful Collection Of Which You Can Be Proud!

Hangtag from the Darth Vader tankard designed by Jim Rumph for California Originals.

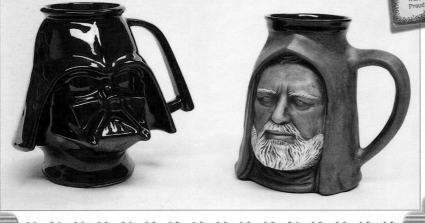

Rumph tankards, 7" (left) and 6¾" (right). Although Jim Rumph created some amazing and unconventional items in a couple of Southern California locations, he is probably best known for the tankards he modeled of characters from the original Star Wars movie. California Originals of Torrance was the manufacturer under license from 20th Century Fox Film Corp. On the left is the Darth Vader tankard in high gloss black and it's just as intimidating as the original film characterization. In-mold: "Star Wars © 1977 20th Century Fox Film Corp, Rumph, Calif. Originals." $80.00. The mellow Ben (Obi-Wan) Kenobi tankard on the right is matte finished with gloss black interior. It is marked the same way. $80.00

Label on bottom of wood base for the Robert Maxwell figure.

DISTRIBUTOR N. S. GUSTIN CO.
ROBERT MAXWELL
STONEWARE CERAMICS
DESIGNER
NOEL OSHEROFF
712 S. OLIVE, LOS ANGELES, CALIF.

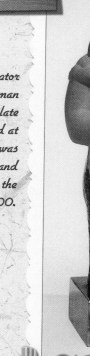

Robert Maxwell figure with wood base, 12¹⁄₈". Sculptor Noel Osheroff made the original model for this woman with child figure that Robert Maxwell produced in the late 1960s. Several other models were created and produced at the Maxwell studio in Venice. The N.S. Gustin Co. was Maxwell's representative, and the Guston name and address is included on the label on the underside of the wood base that this example is mounted on. $85.00.

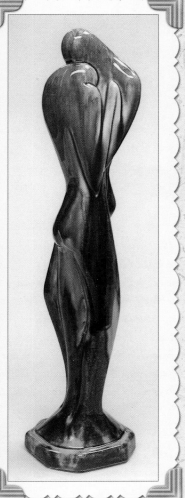

Marcia figure, 19⁷⁄₈". Marcia of California was located in Los Angeles at 1755 N. Eastern Ave. Owned by George Siegal and sons, the specialties of the business during the 1950s were cookie jars and lazy susans. This extra-ordinary modernist sculpture of two figures locked in an embrace dates from the 1960s. It has a blended polychrome glaze with traces of iridescence. In-mold: "Marcia, Calif, USA" plus oval paper label reading "Handmade by Marcia of California." $120.00.

Pottery Craft bust, 17". The exceptional design of this Pottery Craft stoneware bust is reminiscent of an earlier Deco era piece. The identity of the company that produced the original is uncertain. This adaptation probably dates from the late 1960s or early 1970s. Paper label on backside reads "Pottery Craft, Compton Cal. 90222, Handcrafted Stoneware." $200.00.

Brayton Laguna cookie jar, 12¾". Brayton Laguna was one of the first pottery companies to produce figural cookie jars. They produced their first model in the mid-1930s. This Mammy design by Frances Robinson was one of their most popular jars. It was introduced in the early 1940s and remained in production until the mid-1950s. This particular one is an early example because the red is cold paint. It is included here because of the numerous copies and adaptations that have appeared on the market in recent years. Although this jar is not marked, most of them were. $700.00+.

Treasure Craft cookie jar, 11½". This is an adaptation of the Brayton Mammy cookie jar produced by Treasure Craft. Figural cookie jars have had a resurgence in popularity in recent years due largely to the interest in the older ones by collectors. Treasure Craft produced many interesting new jars in the 1980s and 1990s, some of which were made at their Nogales, Mexico, factory. Alfred Levin founded the company in 1946 in South Gate but it later relocated to Compton. Pfaltzgraff of PA acquired the business in 1988. Printed mark: "Treasure Craft, Mexico." $100.00.

King's cookie jar, 11⅞". Another recent adaptation of the Brayton Laguna Mammy jar, this one has excellent hand painting and a painted mark reading "King's Pottery 991-2909." NP.

Twin Winton cookie jar, 13". In 1952, twins Don and Ross Winton sold their interest in Twin Winton to their older brother Bruce Winton, who relocated the business to El Monte. It was later moved to the well-equipped factory in San Juan Capistrano that Brad Keeler was contructing at the time of his death. This woodtone cookie jar by Don Winton, who modeled numerous designs for Twin Winton on a free-lance basis, was called Tommy Turtle. It was in production between 1963 and 1975. NM, $150.00.

Los Angeles cookie jar, 11½". This colorful Los Angeles Potteries cookie jar is covered with fruit and vegetables. Is this a gentle reminder that these foods are better choices for snacking? Cookie jars were one of the numerous hand decorated products produced by the company until its liquidation in 1970. It had been a holdout, continuing the hand decoration of its ware when most businesses had abandoned the less-than-cost-effective practice. Some molds were sold to the N.S. Gustin Co. and were reproduced by Designcraft, a West Los Angeles pottery it had acquired. Indecipherable in-mold mark. $120.00.

Metlox cookie jar, 12½". Vincent Martinez was the designer of a marvelous dinosaur cookie jar trio produced by Metlox in the 1980s in four solid colors: yellow, rose, aqua, and French blue. Lavender was produced as well but in very limited quantities. This French blue glazed Rex (Tyrannosaurus Rex) model is marked in-mold "Metlox Calif. U.S.A. © 87 By Vincent." $100.00.

Treasrue Craft/Mc Me cookie jar, 10½". This Dale Evans cookie jar naturally has a companion Roy Rogers jar. Treasure Craft was the original manufacturer but Mc Me Productions of Simi Valley took over production in the mid-1990s. Treasure Craft produced only about 500 of the jars before the Whittier earthquake destroyed all 34 of its kilns in 1987. The following year, the business was sold to Pfaltzgraff who shifted all production overseas. At the time of its sale, Treasure Craft had expanded to 225,000 square feet and was the last full-scale pottery manufacturer in Southern California. The pictured jar was produced by Mc Me and is marked in-mold "Mc Me Productions Simi Valley, Ca, Made in So. Ca. © Roy Rogers Enterprises" along with "#275/2000" (limited edition of 2000) in gold paint. $150.00. (George Higby photo)

Mc Me Productions promotional sheet for their limited edition Roy Rogers and Dale Evans cookie jars. Note facsimile signatures on backsides.

Cookie Jars

Dale Evans   *Roy Rogers*

10½" High   11½" High

Gold Signature Editions

Mc Me Productions are proud to introduce the first authorized Roy Rogers & Dale Evans Cookie Jars. Upon approval for production Roy & Dale signed the original clay models thus enabling us to reproduce their autographs for you in each jar. The signatures have been highlighted in gold. Roy & Dale are hand painted and finished with the finest ceramic paints and glazes available. The cookie jars are produced in Southern California. Editions limited to 2500 each.
Produced by and available from Mc Me Productions under license of Roy Rogers Enterprises

MC ME PRODUCTIONS • 3428 LEORA ST. • SIMI VALLEY, CA 93063 • (805) 583-2850

Recent Developments

This section, small though it may be, is a sampling of current work by the few remaining California companies and individuals.

Jerome Ackerman serpent bowl, 4⅝" x 6½". This bowl from 2002, with twin serpents encircling its rim, is an example of the hand-thrown and reduction fired stoneware that Jerome Ackerman currently produces in his Culver City studio. A complex matte glaze edged with black accentuates its carved and appliqued surface texture. Incised "Ackerman." (Evelyn Ackerman photo)

Bill Fields sculpture, 6" x 9". Bill Fields, the founder of the Roselane and Hallfield potteries, turned to folk art in 1991 and has made about 150 different models since. This imaginative critter was produced in 1999 and is composed of wood, plaster of Paris, and wire. NM.

Hagen-Renaker pixies, 2⅜". These pixies are representative of the recent line of miniatures produced by Hagen-Renaker of San Dimas. Both models were retired in 2001. Because it has always specialized in miniatures, has kept pace with new trends, and not compromised the quality of it product, it is one of the few remaining companies. Ink-stamped "H R."

Heath teapot, 6½" x 8½". This is a recent example of the classic Heath eight-cup teapot introduced in 1947 and still in production (and essentially unchanged). It has a sturdy copper handle interlaced with fine plastic webbing. Heath Cramics has resently been sold. The new owners are Cathy Bailey and Robin Petrovic. In-mold: "Heath ® Made in USA, Sausalito, California."

Recent Developments

Robert Maxwell animal sculptures, 5¼" x 6¾" (left) and 6¾" x 11¼" (right). These recent stoneware animals come from the fertile imagination of Robert Maxwell. The basic forms are thrown on the potter's wheel with added body parts, facial features, and texture added when the clay is leather hard. Most of Maxwell's critters are not glazed. Animal on the left is incised "Robert Maxwell 1999." Animal on right is incised "Robert Maxwell 1998." Hand-thrown vases, bowls, and lamp bases round out the current work of this accomplised potter.

Barbara Willis vase, 10¼". Barbara Willis has been producing robust handmade pottery like this vase in her Malibu studio in recent years. Her new work is pressed by hand into fabricated or found molds, removed from the mold, alowed to dry, glazed, and baked in a one-fire process. Incised "Barbara Willis 2000."

Detail of Don Winton cookie jar.

Don Winton cookie jar, 10"L. In recent years, Don Winton has been producing commissioned portrait busts in bronze in his Corona del Mar studio. He also makes one-of-a kind cookie jars for the annual National Cookie Jar Convention in Nashville, Tennessee. This amazing jar, of a 1929 Model A Ford with separate figures of himself and his twin brother Ross as teens (in 1936, at the time they established their business) and various Twin Winton cartoon animals, sold at auction at the 1999 convention for a record $9,000.00. Signed "Don Winton."

Postscript of California

If anyone doubts that the word "California" added cachet to a company name during the heyday of the industry, this list of businesses might change your outlook. Bear in mind, this is only a partial accounting of vintage identities.

Alex of California	Jaska of California	Priscilla of California
Alvi of California	Judy of California	Roday of California
Allen of California	Karen of California	Saar of California
Alma of California	Kert of California	Savage of California
Bell of California	Kirk of California	Saxony of California
Bow of California	Lodi of California	Sharon of California
Chalice of California	MacConnells of California	Simone of California
DeForrest of California	Marcia of California	Stewart of California
Doranne of California	Maurice of California	Sunset of California
Elinor of California	Miramar of California	Vadna of California
Erma of California	Muriel of California	Vohann of California
Hutchins of California	Nan of California	Weil of California
Jae of California	Nattini of California	Zaida of California

About the Author

Jack Chipman has been collecting, selling, researching, and writing about California Pottery for nearly 30 years.

He has had two books on Bauer Pottery published. The first, co-authored with Judy Stangler, was published in 1982. Collector Books published the second, Collector's Encyclopedia of Bauer Pottery, in 1997. In 1982, his reference guide to the Southern California ceramic industry, Collector's Encyclopedia of California Pottery, also from Collector Books, was released. In 1999, it was updated and expanded into a second edition. In 2003, he self-published Barbara Willis: Classic California Modernism.

Chipman's "other life" as a fine artist is not so well known. He is a graduate of the Chouinard Art Institute (now California Institute of the Arts) in Los Angeles, and has exhibited his contemporary paintings, collages, and assemblages throughout California and abroad. He himself has recently begun making pottery, and has worked with legendary California ceramists Barbara Willis and Robert Maxwell. Because of his background as a painter, he has found glazing the most appealing aspect of this challenging medium.

The author is eager to hear from readers who have information pertaining to any of the companies and individuals included in this book, especially information about unidentified pieces. He regrets that he cannot offer free appraisals.

Jack Chipman, PO Box 1079, Venice, CA 90294-1079

E-mail: jack@jackchipman.com   Website: www.jackchipman.com

Bibliography

Bray, Hazel V. The Potter's Art in California: 1885 – 1955. The Oakland Museum, 1980.

Chipman, Jack. Barbara Willis: Classic California Modernism. Venice, CA: Jaba Books, 2003.

_____. Collector's Encyclopedia of Bauer Pottery. Paducah, KY: Collector Books, 1997.

_____. Collector's Encyclopedia of California Pottery, Second Edition. Paducah, KY: Collector Books, 2002.

Coates, Carole. Catalina Island Pottery and Tile: Island Treasures. Atglen, PA: Schiffer Publishing, 2001.

Conti, Steve; DeWayne Bethany; Bill Seay. Collector's Encyclopedia of Sascha Brastoff. Paducah, KY: Collector Books, 1995.

Conway, J. Gregory. Flowers: Their Arrangement. (New York: Afred A Knopf, 1940.

Derwich, Jenny; Mary Latos. Dictionary Guide to United States Pottery & Porcelain. Franklin, MI: Jenstan, 1984.

Dommel, Darlene Hurst. Collector's Encyclopedia of Howard Pierce Porcelain. Paducah, KY: Collector Books, 1998.

Duke, Harvey. The Official Price Guide to Pottery and Porcelain. New York: House of Collectibles, 1995.

Gibbs, Jr., Carl. Collector's Encyclopedia of Metlox Potteries, Second Edition. Paducah, KY: Collector Books, 2001.

Elliot-Bishop, James. Franciscan, Catalina, and Other Gladding, McBean Wares. Atglen, PA: Schiffer Publishing, 2001.

Ellis, Michael L. Collector's Guide to Don Winton Designs. Paducah, KY: Collector Books, 1998.

Gordon, Maddy. Head Vases Etc: The Artistry of Betty Lou Nichols. Atglen, PA: Schiffer Publishing, 2002.

Harris, Dee; Jim & Kaye Whitaker. Josef Originals: Charming Figurines with Price Guide. Atglen, PA: Schiffer Publishing, 1994.

Held, Wilbur. Collectable Caliente Pottery. Claremont, CA: privately printed, 1997.

Nelson, Maxine Feek. Collectible Vernon Kilns. Paducah, KY: Collector Books, 1994.

Nickel, Mike; Cindy Horvath. Kay Finch Ceramics: Her Enchanted World. Atglen, PA: Schiffer Publishing, 1996.

Pasquali, Jim. Sanfords Guide to Garden City Pottery. Campbell, CA: Adelmore Press, 1999.

Piña, Leslie. Designed & Signed. Atglen, PA: Schiffer Publishing, 1996.

Pratt, Michael. Mid-Century Modern Dinnerware. Atglen, PA: Schiffer Publishing, 2002.

Roerig, Fred; Joyce Herndon. Roerig, Collector's Encyclopedia of Cookie Jars Book II. Paducah, KY: Collector Books, 1994.

Roller, Gayle. The Charlton Standard Catalogue of Hagen-Renaker, 2nd Edition. Birmingham, MI: The Charleton Press, 1999.

Schaefer, Joanne Fulton. deLee Art: The Pictorial Story of a California Artist and Her Company. Butte Valley, CA, privately printed, 1997.

Snyder, Jeffrey B. Pacific Pottery. Atglen, PA: Schiffer Publishing, 2001.

Stamper, Bernice. Vallona Starr Ceramics With Prices. Atglen, PA: Schiffer Publishing, 1995.

Stern, Bill. California Pottery: From Missions to Modernism. San Francisco: Chronicle Books, 2001.

Stewart, J.A. Ceramics For All. New York: Barnes & Noble, 1950.

Producers

Index

Trade Names

Lines

Names and Titles

Index

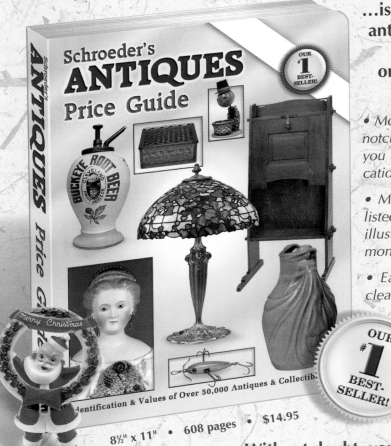